THE

PHILOSOPHERS

OF GREECE

THE

PHILOSOPHERS

OF

GREECE

Robert S. Brumbaugh

State University of New York Press
ALBANY

Published by State University of New York Press, Albany, 1981

For information, address State University of New York Press,
State University Plaza, Albany, N.Y., 12246

Library of Congress Cataloging in Publication Data

Brumbaugh, Robert Sherrick, 1918–
The philosophers of Greece.
Originally published: New York : Crowell, 1964.
Bibliography: p. 259
Includes index.
1. Philosophy, Ancient. I. Title.
[B171.B78 1982]   180   81-9120
ISBN 0-87395-550-1   AACR2
ISBN 0-87395-551-X (pbk.)

To My Parents

PREFACE

THE STORY of the discovery and development of philosophy
in ancient Greece is one of the greatest epics of intellectual adventure there has ever been. In my Introduction, I will discuss the
bearing of these Greek ideas on our world of today, and my
reasons for telling the story in the way I have done. There remains, by way of preface, my thanks for help which has made
the book in its present form possible, by contributing to the
means, motive, and opportunity involved in its writing.

The opportunity for leisure to write was provided by fellow-
ships from Yale University and the American School of Classical
Studies in Athens. The writing was one of the enterprises I was
able to carry out during a year in Athens and on the Aegean
islands in 1963-64.

My conviction that this material was relevant, interesting, and
important, and that I understood it well enough to write about
it, reflects my indebtedness over many years to teachers, students,
and colleagues, an indebtedness to so many persons, over such
a long time, that it cannot be acknowledged in detail.

For permission to reproduce illustrative material and to discuss interpretation, some detailed thanks are in order. The American School of Classical Studies has given me permission to
reproduce the photographs of Athenian jury ballots, the lottery-
machine, the ostracism tiles, the cooking bell with its caption,
and the reconstruction of the ivory copy of Apollo of the Lyceum, from publications writing up their Athenian Agora Excavations. The two photographs of pages of thirteenth-century
Greek manuscript are reproduced by courtesy of the Trustees of
the Yale Libraries and the Beinecke Rare Book Library; the
coastlines in my reconstruction of Anaximander's map follow
W. H. Heidel's in his *Frame of Ancient Greek Maps*, by permission

of the American Geographical Society. The nineteenth-century map of ancient Athens is reproduced by courtesy of the Map Collection of the Yale University Library, from a map in their collection; the map showing the movements of ideas in Greek philosophy is reproduced from N. P. Stallknecht and R. S. Brumbaugh, *The Spirit of Western Philosophy*, by permission of David McKay Company. My thanks are due, also, to the Institute of Mathematics and Science of the University of Athens, for their invitation to present and discuss my interpretation of Zeno's paradoxes of motion.

I have particularly appreciated the help, both in general planning and in detailed presentation and style, of my editor, Martin Mann; and the continuing interest and encouragement of my publisher, Robert L. Crowell.

Finally, I want to thank my wife and my son Robert for their critical reading and suggested improvements of the early drafts of the book; and my daughters, Susan and Joanna, for their patience with the intrusions of composition, typing, and discussion during their Grecian holiday.

CONTENTS

INTRODUCTION   1

IONIA AND ITALY   5

I. THALES   *Inventor of Physics and Philosophy*   11

II. ANAXIMANDER   *The Idea of Neutral Matter*   18

III. ANAXIMENES   *Change Without Personality*   26

IV. PYTHAGORAS AND HIS SCHOOL   *The Music of the Spheres*   30

V. HERACLITUS   *Time Versus Eternity*   43

VI. PARMENIDES   *Logic and Mysticism*   50

VII. ZENO OF ELEA   *The Paradox of Motion*   59

VIII. EMPEDOCLES   *Too Much Imagination*   68

IX. DEMOCRITUS AND THE ATOMIC THEORY   *Materialism*   78

ATHENS: THE SCHOOL OF GREECE   93

X. ANAXAGORAS   *Mind Orders All Things*   100

XI. ARCHELAUS   *The First Athenian Scientist*   108

XII. THE SOPHISTS   *How to Succeed in Athens*   112

XIII. SOCRATES   *The Search for the Self*   123

XIV. PLATO   *Order, Fact, and Value*   133

XV. ARISTOTLE   *The Organization of All Reality*   172

[ix]

CONTENTS

CONCLUSION   206

NOTES   210

SUGGESTIONS FOR FURTHER READING   256

BIBLIOGRAPHY   259

INDEX   269

ILLUSTRATIONS

Centers of Greek Philosophy: Ionia, Italy, Attica   6

Land, Sea, and Sky: An Aegean Island (Samos)   9

Anaximander—The First Map   22

Polyclitus: Diadoumenos   38

The Charioteer of Delphi   53

Sirens: A By-Product of Empedoclean Natural Selection?   74

An Ancient Secret Ballot: Athenian Jury Ballots   90

An Athenian Lottery Machine (*Kleroterion*)   91

Classical Athens   94

The Theater of Dionysus   98

Ostracism Ballots (*Ostraka*)   99

The Pnyx: Meeting Place of the Athenian Assembly   114

Cooking Bells   127

Thirteenth-Century Greek Manuscript   176

Praxiteles: Apollo of the Lyceum   181

INTRODUCTION

THE DEVELOPMENT of philosophy in ancient Greece from Thales through Aristotle is an exciting intellectual odyssey.

This story of Greek thought traces the building up of a "capital of ideas" that we have been living on ever since. Though it may seem surprising, it is true that the ideas of *matter, mechanical causality, mathematics, form,* and *the self,* all had to be discovered and were by the early Greek philosophers. These ideas, and others like them, have become so much a part of our way of looking at the world today that we can hardly think without them. If "common sense" means the habits of talking and acting that a culture takes for granted and does not question, our own American common sense can be described as an inheritance from Greek discoveries. For this reason, this is our own story, which helps us to understand our world and ourselves.

And further, the study of the Greek philosophers is a perfect introduction to the field of philosophy itself. "Philosophy," as the term is used here, is the attempt to answer three fundamental questions. The first question is "What is real?" or "What is being?" This question supposes that there is a difference between appearance and reality, between the way things seem and the way they are. It also supposes that all the different things there are in the world have something in common: that which gives them existence. At first, philosophers sought to define this common something as matter—all things are spread out in space and last through time. But with the discovery of pure mathematics and its suggestion that numbers, too, are "real things," though not physical objects, philosophers turned their attention to form in defining what all things are.

The second question is about the inner self, rather than about the outer world. It is simply the question, "What am I?" This question comes later in our story than "What is being?" The reason for this is that it was not until both natural science and social theory had been discovered and developed that philosophers realized how different human beings are from the other things in nature. Neither science nor social studies could explain what the self is satisfactorily, and Socrates' recognition of this fact introduced this second major question into Western philosophy.

The third question is harder to formulate briefly; perhaps, "One world or many?" is a way to phrase it. With the development of civilization, specialization must increase. With the increase of specialization, society begins to find that each specialist has his own professional way of looking at the world and at other people. But each of these ways is different: a chemist and a lawyer, for example, look for very different things when they talk about, say, "the worth of an individual." Is there any way to chart out the provinces of our experts, to integrate their findings and make it possible for them to talk together? We have not yet answered this question for our own society. The philosophies of Plato and Aristotle, however, suggest that this sort of integration can be brought about by philosophy. For their own culture, they succeeded in assembling the many special perspectives into a single world view; and their work is a model from which our own speculative philosophy can profit.

Our contemporary philosophers would all agree that there is a value to the study of ancient Greek thought. As we follow the journey of these ideas, we seem to see our familiar world emerging from a mist of myth which hides all the familiar outlines and distinctions. But philosophers today hold divergent views concerning the value of the study. Some hold that the study is good primarily because it makes us share the outlook of a time when intelligence had not yet separated reality into bits by introducing sharp distinctions. Others hold that it is good because it makes us realize how very well grounded in past experience and testing our modern common sense is. Others hold that many of the central doctrines of Greek philosophy are still true today and can be applied to solve our own problems—some, if not all, of them. But we all agree that we are still seeing the world in an ancient Greek way, and that there is a gain in seeing clearly the ideas which are by now so built into our thinking that we are unaware of them.

Even if it did not help us to understand our own world and ideas, Greek philosophy would command our appreciation. The pre-Platonic philosophers light the way to Plato's and Aristotle's master systems of philosophy, systems which are as great as the Parthenon or the finest Hellenic sculpture. To appreciate these gives us a new vision, a heightened realization of the power of the human soul to create and understand.

Although a study of Greek philosophy is both interesting and valuable, writing an introduction to Greek thought which is neither a textbook filled with specific fact nor an appreciation in general terms without specific content proves to be very hard. We have far too little information about early Greek thought, from its beginnings through Socrates, while for the second, systematic phase represented by Plato and Aristotle, we have far too much. The reconstruction of the earliest philosophers is a delicate, painstaking job; none of their works survive, and one must reconstruct their ideas and contributions from scattered direct quotations, anecdotes, and criticisms of later periods. It is comparable in some ways to trying to re-create John Dewey's philosophy two thousand years from now, with none of his writings, but only a set of direct quotes, criticisms, and stories to go on. Nor is this problem solved when we have collected all of the relevant materials, and formed some judgment of the reliability of each. It is necessary to determine not only what someone said but what he meant when he said it. And, in its early stages, philosophy was expressed in many literary forms, from epic to epigram, each of which had its own rules of meaning. Even if there were not this diversity, we still would be dealing with meanings in the context of a stage of language and thought very different from our own. Our temptation to read back modern ideas must be watched critically if it is not to mislead us.

But with Plato and Aristotle, there is the opposite problem. Their works have been preserved almost entirely, and the whole range of Platonic dialogues and Aristotelian lecture-outlines focuses on many subjects from many standpoints. It is a monumental task to work all the way through and finally be able to see the outline of the important features of each system as an organic whole.

Just at present, there is a revival of interest in Greek thought occurring in our contemporary philosophy. Different philosophers, however, find Greek philosophy interesting for different reasons. In France and Germany, existentialists believe that it is valuable and exciting because it helps us to recapture a sense of confrontation with the world as a whole, not yet cut up and marked off by sharp either-or logic and classifying intelligence. In England and America, scholars concentrate more on precision, their work lacking metaphysical excitement.

But we naturally begin to learn with what Alfred North Whitehead called a "stage of romance," a sense of fascination with a subject which we see as a whole but have not studied piece by piece. This leads us to go on to a "stage of precision," in which we pay attention to analysis, classification of detail, mastery of the necessary technique. Finally, we arrive at a "stage of generalization," or "of mastery." At this stage we again see the subject as a whole, with all of the details articulated and held in place by a few basic principles. This is a good description of education, and an account that exactly fits the historical emergence of Greek philosophy.

In this book I have tried to introduce the subject in a way that does not eliminate all romance in favor of precision, but that does go beyond the first excitement of encounter to fill in what seems to me the most significant precise detail. The final stage of generalization, with judgments of importance and appraisal of truth, is something that the reader himself must supply.

There remains one very important remark. My account is told directly, without the many qualifications and mentions of alternative views that would be the more normal academic style. There is some disagreement over practically every fact or interpretation bearing on Greek thought. This is to be expected when interested scholars are actively exploring new approaches and dimensions, trying different research techniques. But, unfortunately, if one stops at every point to say, "Though the alternative possibility of so-and-so must be taken into account, still, on balance, it is my opinion that . . . ," the main line of the story is lost in a fog of uncertainty and verbosity. And the qualifications are interesting and important only because of the interest and importance of the main story they qualify. To some extent, evidence and alternatives relevant to my text are taken account of in the Notes and Bibliography.

IONIA AND ITALY

THE STORY of Greek philosophy, from its earliest stages to the Athenian culmination in the fourth century B.C. begins in the early sixth century and has its setting on the Greek frontier. In the east in Ionia, the part of the Greek world that included the islands of the Aegean Sea and the Greek cities on the coast of Asia Minor, and in the west in Southern Italy and in Sicily, new ideas arose. These new ideas were to change the Western view of the world from one that we feel is alien and primitive to an outlook that is recognizably similar to our own.

In the early Greek world, mythology was still the only method available either to record history or explain nature. Mythology assumes a world in which all happenings are due to the decisions and more or less capricious interventions of personal beings, like ourselves. This is an anthropomorphic world in which many compartmentalized gods are causes, with no natural law and little predictable order. In such a world one must be satisfied with a mythical "explanation" that takes the form of an aesthetically plausible story. So when Greek philosophy began, it took its origin from a world in which there was no accurate history, no science, no pure mathematics, no notion of the distinctions we automatically accept today between mind and matter, subject and object, animate and inanimate things, miracles and natural causes. Instead of history there was a body of legends, some accurately reporting a real past, others going back to old creation myths. Instead of science, there was nothing at all, unless we count technology and calculation, which were the necessary precursors of science. It is true that, in the Near East, the Babylonians had done remarkable work in astronomical record keeping and calculation; but astrology was the direction they took when they looked beyond their tables for any further "explanation." Pure mathematics, as distinct from applied, was not yet discovered.

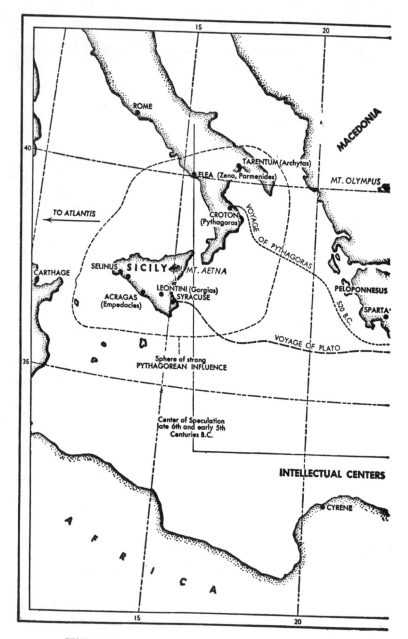

CENTERS OF GREEK PHILOSOPHY: IONIA, ITALY, ATTICA

Greek philosophy began on the coast of Asia Minor, in Ionia, made later gains in southern Italy, and finally reached its highest point in Athens during

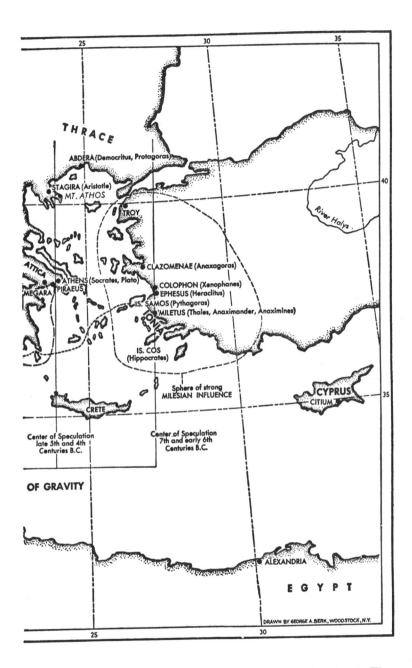

THRACE

ABDERA (Democritus, Protagoras)

STAGIRA (Aristotle)
MT. ATHOS

TROY

River Halys

CLAZOMENAE (Anaxagoras)

ATTICA

ATHENS (Socrates, Plato)
MEGARA PIRAEUS

COLOPHON (Xenophanes)
EPHESUS (Heraclitus)
IS. SAMOS (Pythagoras)
MILETUS (Thales, Anaximander, Anaximines)

IONIA

IS. COS
(Hippocrates)

CYPRUS
CITIUM

Sphere of strong
MILESIAN INFLUENCE

CRETE

Center of Speculation
late 5th and 4th
Centuries B.C.

Center of Speculation
7th and early 6th
Centuries B.C.

OF GRAVITY

ALEXANDRIA

E G Y P T

DRAWN BY GEORGE A. BERK, WOODSTOCK, N.Y.

the fifth and fourth centuries B.C. (From Stallknecht and Brumbaugh, The
Spirit of Western Philosophy, *by permission of David McKay Company.)*

Though some Babylonian tablets do preserve interesting patterns of solution for some types of equations, they do not represent pure mathematics. The Egyptians, despite some modern admirers of the occult who relate the history of the world to the measurements of the pyramid of Cheops, had no science of a pure sort at all. Ancient Egypt seems a case of a civilization with high standards of technology, art, and culture, but with none of the scientific components that became so important to the West.

It is no accident that formal logic was not invented in Egypt or Babylon, for formal logic presupposes the existence of mathematical and scientific schemes of rational explanation from which it can generalize. It would be a nightmare for the modern logician if he were to try to formulate a generalization from the patterns of thought that occur in magic, myth, and folklore.

The religion associated with the myths of the early Greeks was a complex of diverse strands. The Olympian gods were worshiped, and by degrees, the Olympian religion incorporated local cults and deities. (Often we find records of this in stories of Zeus's love affairs.) The Olympians, in popular opinion, seem to have been exactly like a human family, though immortal and much more powerful. They were thought of as human in form, so that the statues in the temples were intended to be exact likenesses. These gods disagreed, played favorites, could be persuaded by gifts, and were easily angered if mortals neglected them. Side by side with the worship of the Olympians, which was in part a civic affair, there existed the mystery religions attributed to Orpheus. These were groups that offered the initiated a special insight into the afterlife and an enhanced chance for individual salvation. And Greek epic and tragedy reflect a sense that there is, somewhere beyond the gods themselves, a Fate which issues irrevocable decrees that neither gods nor men can evade. But the exact character of Fate is vague, and little else in the multiplicity of gods, cults, and revealed mysteries would lead a pious Greek to look for any of the intelligent order or general law in nature that we sometimes, as a result of a long tradition, think of as naturally suggested by our own religion.

In this world of the Greek frontier there was a constant sense of adventure. Its most important features were the mountains,

LAND, SEA, AND SKY: AN AEGEAN ISLAND (SAMOS)

The rugged landscape of Samos is typical of the east coast and islands of the Aegean Sea. In this setting, one can see how imagination could have supplied concrete pictures for the new concept of "basic stuff" that were proposed and explored by Thales, Anaximander, and Anaximenes. (Photograph courtesy of Greek National Tourist Office.)

the sea, and the sky. Geography affected every step of daily life. The tides, the stars, and the hills were objects of importance that required close attention.

Alien neighbors, too, made the Greeks of the frontier aware of civilizations other than their own. In the east, the empires of Persia and Egypt carried on trade, occasional war, and cultural exchange; in the west, Carthage stood as an unknown hostile power, occupying the western end of Sicily and preventing Greek ships from venturing too far west in the Mediterranean.

The political organization was one of city-states, a decentralized pattern that developed naturally and was well suited to the geography of the Greek mainland. On the coast of Asia Minor and its nearby islands, and in the Sicilian plains, this proved a relatively unstable form of organization. The cities of Asia Minor could not cooperate effectively enough to avoid conquest, one by one, by Persia; and the political histories of Samos and Sicily show that at times there would be a strong central dictatorship, at others a rather loosely organized democracy.

Although the cultural background was the same in many respects, there were also differences between the two regions. In Ionia, the center of importance was always the sea. Persia might be hostile, but at least there were many lines of communication and the eastern Greeks recognized it as a civilized society. A cosmopolitan commerce and a tradition of technology tended to invite the settlers to break with their traditions and question the old ideas. In the west, farming and horse-raising were important as well as sailing. Carthage seems to have been far more aloof and to have seemed more alien and savage than Persia. And, in the west, for a time at least, the great temples remind us that the colonists felt themselves poised on the edge of nowhere, and tried to hold and intensify the religion they had brought with them.

Probably the sense of adventure on the frontier was a necessary component in the emergence of Greek science and philosophy. However, it is not so clear why philosophy, as it developed, should tend in the east toward a combination of materialistic explanation with an early recognition of the haunting fact of constant unstable change, while in the west it tended toward a formalism, with an early expression of the intuition that there is some permanence, unchanging, that lies beyond the world of sensible reality.

I. THALES

Inventor of Physics
and Philosophy

Thales of Miletus taught that "all things are water."
ARISTOTLE, *Metaphysics*

The Greeks thought of Thales as a great inventor, because of his achievements as an engineer. How much they underrated him can be seen from the fact that Thales could, with some right, have claimed the ideas of matter, of physics, of science, and of philosophy as his inventions. However strange this may seem, all of these ideas had to be discovered. And to be discovered, mythology had to be abandoned. To state—as Thales did—that "All things are water" may seem an unpromising beginning for science and philosophy as we know them today; but, against the background of mythology from which it rose, it was revolutionary. The break was not complete; it could not have been. Thales still had no abstract idea of matter, as opposed to an imaginative picture of a fluid sea; the two were mixed together. And his idea of change was still based on a feeling that "All things are full of soul." But he had asked a new kind of question. His question has given distinctive shape to Western thought.

A N   O L D Chinese book reads: "Everything that is, is in space; and everything that is in space has a sound." Today we are unlikely to agree with the second of these notions, but the first

[11]

has more plausibility. Current concerns of our scientific-research workers include questions about the nature of space and matter, ways of changing mass into energy, new cyclotron designs, and so on. We think of these as "science," and sometimes we—or, at least, the science editors of our newspapers—describe today's science as being concerned with finding the ultimate nature of reality. Whether or not this is actually so depends on the truth of the statement that everything that is, is in space and made of matter; and that is a broad philosophic, rather than a narrow scientific, question.

It is to Thales of Miletus that we owe the first appearance of both science and philosophy in the West.[1] Miletus, in Asia Minor, was noted for its engineers, and in Thales' time—in the first quarter of the sixth century B.C.—it was a flourishing cosmopolitan seaport, a center of trade with Egypt, Greece, and the Persian Empire. Athens and Sparta, at this date, were small provincial towns.[2]

As with most new things, the first appearance of philosophy was a rather modest one; and, as with many old things, its history is hard to sift out and recover.[3] In fact, our most important source of evidence about Thales consists of the brief quotation from Aristotle that begins this chapter: "Thales of Miletus taught that 'all things are water.' "[4]

The fragment is striking because it is new both in the question underlying Thales' statement and in the kind of answer it proposes. In early Greece and in the Near East, no one had attempted before to answer "What all things are"; such explanations as there were for the natural world took the form of animism and mythology.[5] Sir James Frazer, the great anthropologist of the nineteenth century, has suggested that prescientific people mistook the "association of ideas in their minds" for "causal relations between things."[6] And though we are now much more knowledgeable about primitive culture and mythology than Frazer was, his is still an illuminating remark. The practice, in sympathetic magic, of trying to injure an enemy by destroying his image, is an excellent example; because the idea of a given man is associated with his image, the practitioner assumes there is a real causal connection between them. And on the less primitive level of early Greek culture, the natural world was thought of as peopled with agents like ourselves, though more remote and larger, who "make things happen." The wind blew, they believed, because someone like themselves was puffing out his cheeks in the same way that they did when they blew. These agents tended to be willful and unpredictable in their behavior; and there was nothing in this sort of explanation to suggest that there are unchanging regularities and laws in nature. The planets, for example, which seemed to wander about the sky were simply "travelers."[7]

Thales, on the other hand, was looking for explanations in terms of causal relations between bodies in space and time, rather than in terms of subjective associations of ideas.

Let us look more closely at the fundamental question that Thales answered. To seek to provide an answer to the question, What are all things?, required tremendous insight and imagination. For the question assumes that everything forms a part of some single world of being, and that all things have some common property. It raises the question of what being is, as opposed to less general questions about what these or those particular beings are. And prior to answering the question, Thales had assumed that there is enough system among the infinite variety of things in the world to permit some sort of single answer.[8] This assumption marks the beginning of philosophy.

Philosophy, as we shall use the term, is among other things the attempt to find a single intuition of being, a single system of reality, that will synthesize and hold together the many facets of our specialized knowledge and specialized social structure. There is no indication that anyone before Thales was concerned with this question, or would have expected, had they been interested, that observation and generalization from the physical world could provide an answer. The Near Eastern legends that describe the earth arising from water after a cosmic flood answer a different question, How did the world originate? They are not concerned with, What is it? They give a different kind of answer, Somebody made it—not, Things of this kind always behave in this way.

In the Greek language of Thales' period *hydor* ("water") was a word that was not confined to H_2O but was used for "any sort of matter in a fluid state." (Much as *aqua* was used by the alchemists for any liquid chemical in the Middle Ages, where we find *aqua fortis*, *aqua regia*, *aqua vitae* as names of their chemicals.) Thales, of course, had none of the precise words or ideas that we supply when we talk about "matter in a fluid state." The idea of matter was his own invention; there was no chemical catalogue, as yet, of kinds of water.

What led Thales to his idea? Although we do not know, we can suggest four factors that relate to his theory. First, he was an engineer. Miletus was a training center for the engineers of the Persian Army, and stories about Thales identify him with this profession. Second, he was a Milesian. In Miletus, where Greek, Persian, Egyptian, and Lydian merchants and travelers mingled, the conventional ideas of Greece were easier to set aside than they would have been elsewhere. Third, he was a traveler and sailor: we learn of his trips and his new navigation rules from later stories. Like the other Ionian Greeks, his world was centered on the Aegean Sea. Fourth, water in that part of the world—fresh water—was not taken for granted. Its value for living things, its flavor were appreciated: the poet Pindar, a century later, could write, "best of all things is water."

Whatever the combination of these suggestive experiences was, a new idea arose from them, the idea that the differences of things trace back in some way to transformations of water, from fluid to fiery or gaseous or solid state; that there is an underlying uniformity because all natural things are matter at rest or in motion.

In short, Thales singled out the essential properties of physical reality as those that answered his new philosophic question; so he is entitled to acclaim for being the first to discover science, as well as philosophy.[9]

A second fragment of Thales' thought is again a brief direct quotation preserved by Aristotle: "the magnet has a *psyche* because it moves iron."[10] Just as *hydor* in the Greek of Thales' time did not always mean just one kind of fluid, so *psyche* ("soul") did not mean the kind of conscious self that the translation at once suggests to us. To Thales, a *psyche* may have meant nothing more than a source of motion, an inner power. (Thales had observed another such psychic power in the electrostatic attraction of amber.) But the report does show that

Thales' "fluid matter" was still, in some degree, alive; and change and action in nature were partially explained by this aliveness.[11] The concept of the impersonality of nature in which neutral matter automatically transfers momentum—and there is no exception to the causal chain—did not occur to Thales. We are, therefore, not entirely correct when, in talking about his ideas, we use such terms as "nature" or "matter" or "mechanical causality." The complete separation between the views of nature as mechanical and of nature as alive was first thought of about eighty years later.

It is no accident that "fluid" and "soul" are such ambiguous words in the Greek language of Thales' time. No one before him had even started out on the track of a clear idea of matter; and without that idea, neither the notion of physics (the study of matter in motion) nor of materialism (the philosophic view of all reality as material) could occur to anyone. The Greeks still had no clear idea of the self, or spirit, or conscience; they tended to identify a person's self with his body. It was almost two centuries after Thales that the idea of a person's soul as an inner self, different from his body, appeared on the philosophic scene.

Some philosophers would argue that vision and precise distinction don't go together. They hold that philosophy inevitably loses the vision as science, life, and learning create the distinctions. We should, as we look at the history of thought, ask if the evidence shows that such an opposition is necessarily, or always, so.[12]

Supplementing Thales' doctrines of water as the basic substance and of the *psyche* as the cause of motion, there is only a tangle of anecdote and legend.

Thales, thanks to his many talents, was not only a hero to later historians of philosophy; the ancient Greeks made him a hero as well. His versatility and ingenuity appealed to them, and any number of wise sayings and adventures were attributed to him. Probably the first absent-minded professor story in the West is the one told about Thales.[13] (This ancestor of all later jokes about the absent-minded professor goes: "One night, Thales was looking at the stars, and fell into an irrigation ditch. A young Thracian maid servant pulled him out, and scolded him: 'How do you expect to understand what's going on up in the sky, if you can't even see your own feet?' ")

Among these stories and anecdotes, a number seem to go back to some basis in fact, giving interesting—if tantalizing—glimpses into the career of this early Greek thinker. It is certain, for example, that Thales predicted an eclipse of the sun, which stopped a battle when it occurred on May 23, 585 B.C.[14] He is said to have measured the heights of the Egyptian pyramids by their shadows and devised a method for measuring the distance from the shore to ships at sea. To silence his friends who teased him because, for all of his intelligence, he was not wealthy, he is said to have cornered control of all the local olive-oil presses and made a fortune—which he spent on a votive statue at Delphi. (Aristotle told this story of Thales' "corner" and suggested that someone should bring together accounts of ways in which people made money.[15] I myself like this story and think that it certainly should have happened, though I reject the later embroidery which makes Thales predict a bumper crop by astrology.)

Thales is also said to have redirected the course of the river Halys for Croesus, king of Lydia; written an almanac; advised the small Greek cities of Asia Minor that, if they did not unite, they would fall severally to the Persian Empire;[16] measured the ratio of the diameter of the sun to the total arc of the heavens; offered some new practical rules of navigation (but what these were seems to have been hopelessly muddled in the transmission of the story).[17] Much of this legend probably has a factual basis, and the picture it gives of an intense, curious, versatile mind is an attractive one.

Sometimes Thales is supposed simply to have been repeating Near Eastern flood and creation myths; sometimes he is supposed to have been only an engineer, given credit for philosophic insight by later admirers. But neither interpretation does justice to the facts. It is quite true that there is something sensible, engaged, and normal about Thales which runs counter to the popular notion of a philosopher as ascetic, mystical, enigmatically poetic. But this notion itself involves a rather one-sided view of what philosophy is.

The reader who likes historical detective work will find the sources and scholarly studies that reconstruct and interpret Thales' sayings and doings fascinating. (Some standard sources and special studies have been listed in the Bibliography. In particular, the *Lives and Opinions of Eminent Philosophers*, a scrapbook compiled by Diogenes Laërtius probably in the second century after Christ, is full of anecdotes and stories. It is fun to read, even though Diogenes is not critical of his sources and often unreliable.)

II. ANAXIMANDER

The Idea of Neutral Matter

All things arise out of the Boundless . . .
ANAXIMANDER

To the Greeks, Thales' concept of a systematic development of natural science made him the great pioneer of thought. But modern scholars are likely to choose for their hero his successor, the more poetic and flamboyant Anaximander. He can truly be called the first real philosopher.

Leaping beyond the brilliant yet simple notion that all things are made of the same stuff, Anaximander showed how deep an objective analysis of the real world must penetrate. He made four distinct and significant contributions to human understanding:

1. He realized that neither water nor, indeed, any such ordinary material could be the fundamental form of matter. He saw the basic stuff as a more sophisticated though somewhat obscure boundless something (apeiron). This theory was to serve science well for twenty-five centuries.

2. He extended the concept of law from human society to the physical world—a clean break with the older view of a capricious, anarchic nature.

3. He invented the use of models to make complex natural phenomena easier to understand.

4. He deduced, in a rudimentary way, that the earth had changed over the ages and that higher forms of life might have evolved from lower ones.

EACH OF Anaximander's contributions is a discovery of the first magnitude; we can get some idea of their importance if we imagine taking away from our modern ways of thought all vestiges of the ideas of neutral matter, natural law, scale-model apparatus, and evolution. Not very much of science, or even of our popular common sense, would be left.[1]

Anaximander was a Milesian who was born about forty years after Thales (hence his mature activity would date from about 540 B.C.). He has been described as Thales' pupil and his successor in the Milesian school of philosophy. But both the date and the description rest on later accounts that are not accurate in their chronology and that transfer the idea of organized schools into the early period of Greek thought, when, in fact, no such formal associations of philosophers and scientists yet existed. We can be certain, however, that Anaximander was a younger fellow townsman of Thales, who knew and appreciated the novelty of Thales' ideas and gave them the extensions we have mentioned. Anaximander was a philosopher in the sense that he was concerned, among his other interests, with philosophical questions, but at this early age philosophy and science had not yet separated into specialized professions. We do better to think of him as an amateur than to follow the suggestions of later historians who project back their images of professional philosopher.

To these facts about his native city, date, and acquaintance with Thales, we can add a few more. Anaximander was a versatile and practical man. The Milesians chose him as leader for a new colony, which argues his political importance.[2] He is supposed to have traveled widely, and this is perhaps supported by three specific items in his biography. He was the first Greek geographer to make a map; one trip from Ionia to the Peloponnesus is attested by the account of his setting up a new instrument in the form of a sundial to measure off the seasons in Sparta; his observations of fossilized fish high in the hills indicate that he must have climbed, and observed sharply, in the mountains of Asia Minor.[3] Putting together the tradition of Miletus as a home city of engineers and the uses Anaximander made of technology in his designs of instruments, maps, and models, we can also guess that he, like Thales, was at least a competent and perhaps a professional engineer.

Anaximander's first major contribution was his new analysis and concept of matter. He agreed with Thales in thinking that all things are made of some common stuff, but he thought this could not be a familiar substance, such as water, but rather a "boundless something" (*apeiron*) that originally contained every sort of shape and quality but had no definite, specific characteristics of its own.[4]

Anaximander's reasoning here is interesting. If everything real is matter with definite qualities, it must be possible for this matter to be hot in some cases, cold in others, sometimes wet and sometimes dry. Anaximander thought of qualities as always being contrary pairs. If one identifies matter with one quality of such a pair, as in Thales' "all things are water," how can one explain the existence of the contrary quality? If "to be is to be material," and "matter is water," then it would seem to follow that "to be is to be *moist*." All right; what happens when things become *dry*? If the matter they are made of is always wet (and this is Anaximander's definition of *hydor*), drying would destroy the matter of things; they would become immaterial and cease to be. In the same way, matter cannot be identified with any one quality to the exclusion of its opposite. From this, the concept of matter as the boundless, a neutral indeterminate something, follows. From this reservoir, the opposite qualities "separate out"; from the boundless all specific things arise, and to it they return when they cease to be.[5]

This step from water to the boundless is an advance from a primitive description of matter to one that is almost our own. In fact, until the present century, the description of matter in modern science and philosophy was often "a neutral stuff," very like Anaximander's *apeiron*.[6] But in one way there is a drastic difference between the modern idea and its ancient ancestor. Anaximander had not yet recognized the difference between an imaginative image and an abstract construct. A genuinely abstract concept of matter does not appear until two centuries later, with the advent of the atomic theory. The boundless may very well have suggested to Anaximander a picture of grey mist or dark haze at sunset or a fog from which outlines of hills emerged only to be swallowed up by it again. Nevertheless, the direction taken by this attempt to define the common stuff of physical reality led straight toward the later refinements that we find when materialism emerges as a fully developed system of philosophy.

Anaximander's introduction of models into the study of astronomy and geography was a no less crucial step in the development of science.[7] Very few people realize the importance of models, though we all use them and could not do without them. Anaximander tried to build objects that would reproduce the same operations or relations as the things he was studying but on a different scale of size. One result was a pair of maps: one of the earth, the other of the stars. The map reduces to small scale the distances and directions of places; if we had to depend on travelers' diaries and our own impressions for information about where other states and cities are, travel, commerce, and geography would be in poor shape. Anaximander also built a model of the motions of stars and planets, with circling wheels moving at different speeds. Like our modern planetarium projections, this made it possible to speed up the observed patterns of planetary motion and find in them a regularity and definite ratios of speed. How indebted we are to the use of models can be briefly indicated by pointing out that the Bohr atomic model played a crucial role in physics, and that even a test-tube experiment in chemistry or a rat experiment in psychology is an application of model technique.

The first astronomical model was rather simple and homely; but, primitive as it was, this is the ancestor of the modern planetarium, the mechanical clock, and a host of other related inventions.[8] Anaximander supposed the earth to be a disk in the center of his world, surrounded by rings of hollow pipe (a modern stovepipe gives the right idea) of different sizes and different speeds of rotation. Each pipe is full of fire; but the pipe is made of a hard shell or bark (*phloion*) which keeps the fire inside, except at certain openings (breathing-holes, from which the fire escapes as though blown by a blacksmith's bellows); these openings are what we see as the sun, moon, and planets moving across the sky as the circles turn. There are also dark clouds between the wheels and the earth; these are the cause of eclipses, which occur when they hide the openings of the pipes from our view. The whole system has a daily revolution, but in addition each wheel has a proper motion of its own.[9]

Whether the model also treated the fixed stars in this way is not entirely clear. Anaximander seems to have designed a celestial sphere mapping out the heavens, but we don't know how this extension of map-and-model technique was related to the moving mechanism of wheels and fire.

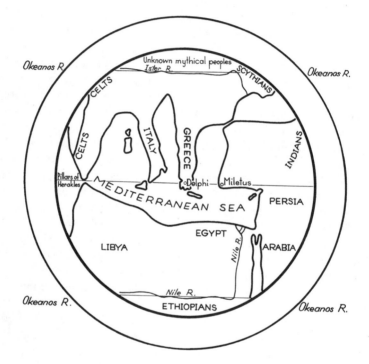

ANAXIMANDER—THE FIRST MAP

This map of the world is a reconstruction of what is thought to be the first geographical map ever drawn. Its center is Delphi, where a stone—the omphalos, or "navel"—marked the exact center of the earth. The cartographer was Anaximander, a Greek philosopher and practical scientist who lived in Miletus from about 611 to 547 B.C. Early maps were all circular. Half a century later, Herodotus commented: "I laugh to see how many before now have drawn maps of the earth, not one of them showing the matter reasonably; for they draw the earth round, as if fashioned by compasses, encircled by the river of Ocean . . ." (Drafted by Nina Thiel; coastlines are based on W. H. Heidel, The Frame of Ancient Greek Maps, *Plate I, by permission of the American Geographical Society.)*

Anaximander's great contribution was the general concept of models, which he immediately applied in all the ways we do now. The construction of the first map of the known world shows the same combination of mechanical ingenuity and scientific insight. Just as a moving model could show the long-term relations of astronomical periods on a smaller, easily controlled and observed scale, a map is a model that projects relative distances and directions on a smaller scale, where one can grasp them in a single glance, without having to travel for months, or to try to make sense of scattered jottings giving traveler's itineraries of places, distance, and direction.

The map itself shows a fondness for neatness and symmetry which was characteristic of Greek science and of later classical maps and models. The world comes out a circle, with its center at Delphi (where a sacred stone, the *omphalos*, was believed to mark the exact center of the universe), enclosed by a surrounding ocean. Like the "stovepipe" wheels, it is a primitive ancestor of the enormous progeny of maps and charts that made possible modern navigation, exploration, geography, and geology. Perhaps the "star-map" was an even more striking illustration of an early original, scientific mentality at work: instead of seeing the constellations as omens or ornaments, the project of mapping the skies supposes a unity of celestial and terrestrial phenomena and an attempt to understand which is neither aesthetic fantasy nor irresponsible superstition.

But this use of models to duplicate and study the regularities of nature, important as it has since proven, is only a footnote to the more general idea that nature is regular and predictable, which Anaximander expressed in his notion of natural law:[10] "All things arise out of the boundless . . . and they make reparations and pay penalties to one another for the injustices they commit, according to the measure of time."[11]

Although Anaximander seems to be echoing ideas from great tragedy, where *hybris* (an excess of pride) inevitably leads to nemesis (a fall), his language is taken directly from a court of law, where an injury which one person commits against another is compensated for by a penalty. His model for natural periodicity here is not the cycle but the pendulum. The "all things" that alternate in trespass and penalty are the contrary qualities that "separate out" from the boundless. Events in nature do often swing from one extreme to another; we have the ebb and flow of the tide, summer and winter as evident examples. This is the pattern of Anaximander's "laws of nature": one contrary tends to develop to excess, crowding out its opposite; so "justice" sets it back, penalizing it for its encroachment. But then, as time passes, the opposite that had been losing out grows stronger and oversteps in its turn, and must "according to the measure of time" be set back within its own proper bounds.

The advance over Thales' world in which the individual *psyches* of things are responsible for change and motion is remarkable, though the tendency toward personification and mythology has not entirely lost its hold. It is interesting historically to find that the concept of a law of nature actually arose by extending the idea of law already established in society; we would rather have expected the opposite, since to us nature seems so much more orderly than a human community. To Anaximander, however, the model of a legal code seemed the best illustration he could find of his new insight into an exact periodicity and regularity in the natural order.

Anaximander was led to the idea of evolution by observations of babies and fossils.[12] High in the mountains of Asia Minor, he had seen fossilized sea animals in the stone. He concluded from this that these mountains had once been covered by the sea and that the ocean level had gradually become lower. This was, we can see, a special case of his law of alternation of opposites: flooding and drying up. He correctly reasoned that, if all the earth had once been covered by sea, life must have had its beginning in this ancient ocean. He is quoted as saying the first and most primitive animals were "sharks." We are not told why, but probably this was because (1) the sharks seemed to him like the fossil fishes he had seen, and (2) the very tough sharkskin seemed to him a sign of primitive organization. From looking at human children—he had at least one son of his own—he concluded that no animal so helpless could have survived in nature without a protective environment. Life on land had come from sea life, animals adapting by forming prickly skin as the water dried up. Human beings, because of their long helplessness in infancy, however, needed some additional process.

And here Anaximander was baffled: he could only suggest that perhaps human beings developed within sharks, escaping at a more self-sufficient age when the sharks died.

In his thoughts about biology and botany, Anaximander expressed another original idea: that throughout nature, all growing things develop on the same pattern. They grow in concentric rings, the outermost of which hardens into a "bark" —the bark of trees, sharkskin, the dark shells around the wheels of fire in the sky. This is a way of bringing together the phenomena of development found separately in astronomy, zoology, and botany; but this "shell" theory, unlike the other ideas we have been discussing, was never taken very seriously. Later philosophers of science have, from ancient Greece to modern America, taken either physics or zoology—the extreme cases of simplicity and complexity, respectively, of subject matter—as their models of what science should be; Anaximander's notion is more like a philosophic generalization from botany.[13]

Anaximander, with his combination of scientific curiosity, poetic imagery, and genius for provocative insight, can certainly share with Thales the credit for the dawn of Greek philosophy. With him, Greek thinkers could begin to see that the new questions raised by Thales had implications that went far beyond the answers that either Thales or Anaximander himself proposed; and we can also see science and philosophy poised with the whole new world of abstract thought opening before them, awaiting exploration.

III. ANAXIMENES

Change Without Personality

All changes are condensation and rarefaction.
ANAXIMENES

Thales and Anaximander were the first to discover a new world of natural science and philosophy. But they were still bound by ancient mythological ways of thought. Personalized agencies— the psyches of Thales and the goddess Dike of Anaximander— were responsible for changes in the world. It was Anaximenes, the third philosopher from Miletus, who broke through this last trace of myth. He discovered that change in nature can be explained mechanically.

ANAXIMENES thought that all changes were the result of changes in density brought about by the condensation and rarefaction of one underlying form of matter, which he called *aer*. The great virtue of this new idea was that it gave the scientist experiments, models, and clear-cut physical explanations of changes and their causes.[1] This is still our own way of thinking. Today, when we wonder why water turns to steam, we no longer think of a "soul" or "sin of pride," but of the fire as exerting a pressure or force that "spreads apart" the molecules of water. And Anaximenes argued that the different qualities and states observed in matter are simply the result of shifting pressure, creating different degrees of density. His explanation still leaves something to be desired in the direction of precision, for the idea of matter as made up of particles that could be packed more closely together or spread apart did not appear until a century later. Rather, Anaximenes' matter had continuity, and stretched or shrank in some way that was not too well specified.

An application of this new idea of change to astronomy suggested an improvement in Anaximander's first model of the universe. Given a "rotating vortex," a *dine*, Anaximenes could picture the denser, hence heavier chunks of compressed matter drifting into the center, just as a stick is drawn to the center of an eddy in water, while the lighter matter is pushed to the outside. At the same time, there would be changes and collisions that would keep the system shifting, as heating and cooling changed the densities of regions on the outside and at the center. Apart from the need to explain its initial motion, this vortex model gives a system of nature that is complete and self-explanatory: it needs no souls or deities but only matter in motion. And, with improvements in detail, the spinning world remained the key model for astronomy and natural philosophy through the following ten centuries.

For example, Aristophanes in his Athenian comedy *The Clouds* refers to "a ceramic vortex" model. Aristophanes disliked the kind of irreligious science it represents, and he has an old man, who at first is impressed by it to the point of declaring, "Zeus rules no more; the Whirlwind rules instead . . ." end by returning to the religious way of thinking:

"Forgive me, Zeus! I have mistaken a whirligig of clay for an ever-living god. . . ." This shows that the *dine* model remained the standard scientific one as late as 423 B.C., when *The Clouds* was written.

To recognize the magnitude and importance of the Milesian achievement, with its three progressive insights into the materiality, uniformity, and mechanical causality of nature, the modern reader must realize that here we have the ancestors of contemporary physics and astronomy. For example, in a fascinating book treating *The Birth and Death of the Sun*, Professor George Gamow shows how modern astrophysics can trace the life histories of stars in terms of *alternate increases and decreases in their density.*[2] Of course, there is an immense distance between the ancient and modern scientist in experimental accuracy and sophistication. Some of the concepts in Professor Gamow's book, such as "gravitational forces," "nuclear reactions," "orbits of electrons," are technical ideas that required two millenniums of experiment and thought before they could be precisely stated or measured. Yet the view of the world that modern physics and astronomy offers, of which the account of the evolution of the sun is an application, is still, in the main, Milesian. Consequently, when we come at a later date to Socrates' criticism of the Milesian view, we may find it interesting to ask how far his critique would apply to our science of today.[3]

In addition to his idea of natural change as mechanical, Anaximenes put forward another idea: that the basic stuff of the world is neither water nor the boundless, but rather *aer*.[4] It seems a puzzling backward step that someone with Anaximenes' demonstrated genius could think this idea of matter was an advance. We must remember, however, that our idea of matter is very distant from the Milesian notion of a basic principle of things. If, in fact, Anaximander's "boundless" suggested grey mist or fog, we can see why *aer* might occur to Anaximenes as a more concrete specification of what this indeterminate stuff was. In this period, air was not recognized as "corporeal." Not until half a century later did Greek scientists prove that air does take up space and offer resistance to other bodies when it is compressed. And in fact air does seem indeterminate and insubstantial as compared to water or earth: it transmits sound and light freely, and unless it is in rapid motion, seems to offer no resistance to our passage through it.

Anaximenes may also have chosen air because at that time it conveyed the idea of "breath," the "soul" that "animated" men and animals. This identification suggested a connection between life and matter.

The word *aer* itself was used by Homer and later writers to refer to a dark mist or fog: a hero could be made invisible by a veil of *aer*. The related word *aither* referred to bright air and the shining sky. *Pneuma* was used for "breath," the "vital spirit" in men and animals. There was no sharp distinction between these words, and *aer* could be used with all three meanings combined.

The "dark mist" *aer* was exactly the imaginative picture associated with the boundless. To express "the neutrality" of his basic stuff, Anaximenes shifted this slightly, and chose *aer* in its clearer, more common form—in the sense of our word "air" today. Since he had made nature purely mechanical, he now needed some account of life and soul; and the traditional association of *aer-pneuma-psyche* suggested a way of including life within the natural order.

Nevertheless, though we can understand it, the shift to air from the boundless was a temporary backward step. "The boundless" is a term that challenges us to go beyond concrete imagination in our science; "air" loses that challenge entirely.

In discussing Anaximenes' first new idea, we pointed out how essentially similar the Milesian view of the spinning world is to that of our modern physics and astronomy. But the notion of *aer* shows the important qualitative difference between insights at that early stage and the same ideas today.

In his writings on comparative culture and a scientific method, Professor F. S. C. Northrop makes exactly the distinction that is relevant here between two types of thought. He calls it the difference between "concepts by intuition" and "concepts by postulation."[5] Most persons and cultures give "meanings" to their ideas by associating or identifying them with concrete pictures in imagination: when we think of matter as a sea, like the restless Aegean, perhaps full of waves and blue in color, this is an intuitional concept. "Concepts by postulation," on the other hand, are purely intellectual, arrived at by an act of generalization that leaves imagination behind; they are abstract ideas that cannot be pictured. Such concepts by postulation are not known to us by direct experience: our eyes cannot see the square root of two or the law of gravity. Rather, the connection is by "indirect verification," through the study of particular instances and cases which *are* observable. According to Northrop, the distinctive features of the scientific and legal mentality of the West are the result of the Greek discovery of generalizations. In the three Milesians who initiated Western science and philosophy there is an attempt—still rather primitive—to use concepts by postulation to explain things. But these men had neither the experience nor logic to go beyond the mixture of idea and image that is a "concept by intuition."

IV. PYTHAGORAS
AND HIS SCHOOL
The Music of the Spheres

The Pythagoreans . . . having been brought up in the study of mathematics, thought that things are numbers . . . and that the whole heaven is a scale and a number. . .

ARISTOTLE

Answering Thales' original question, Pythagoras and his followers held that all things are numbers. His study of the mathematical ratios of musical scales and planets led Pythagoras to believe that quantitative laws of nature could be found in all subject matters. He further expected such laws to have the simplicity of those governing music.

Western thought owes to the Pythagoreans: first, the discovery of pure mathematics; second, a sharpening of the notion of mathematical proof; third, an awareness that form and structure give things their individual identities.[1] Their work initiated the scientific search for quantitative laws and the philosophical tradition of formalism, which finally culminated in Plato.[2]

Among the Pythagoreans, philosophy became a central part of a religious way of life. For Pythagoras was a moral teacher and religious leader as well as a mathematician, and "the Pythagorean Order," was a social and religious community as well as a scientific study group.

THE CONCEPT of form and the Greek word *eidos*, which finally came to express that concept, have a rather complicated history. At first, *eidos* meant "the look of a thing" or "the face" —as it does in Homer, when Achilles furious at Agamemnon calls him *"kyneidos!"* ("dog-faced one!"). *Eidos* in medicine had the sense of "the look of a patient"—his physical type, relevant to diagnosis and treatment. In mathematics, *eidos* was a near synonym for *schema* ("shape") and referred to the mathematical structure. The medical use, relating "the look" of the patient to health and disease, merged with the idea of "good form," important in athletics and dancing, to suggest that form is a standard of value. Plato and Aristotle tried in different ways to bring these two senses of form, the mathematical and the ideal, together.

This formalist philosophy began in 530 B.C. when Pythagoras, an outstanding intellectual figure, moved from his native Samos to the city of Crotona in southern Italy. Crotona was the site of an important medical school, and this may have been an important factor in Pythagoras' choice of a new home. Very soon there was formed "the Pythagorean Order," whereby a number of Greek communities in southern Italy followed a social and ethical plan taught by Pythagoras, and we find new ideas in mathematics and philosophy credited to Pythagoras and his followers. Pythagoras combined the roles of a religious and social leader, of a philosopher and scientist, and also of a practical artist. He may have been the designer of a new type of Italian coinage issued shortly after his arrival.[3]

Later historians, from the time of Aristotle on, have found it difficult to see how the two sides of Pythagoreanism, the scientific and the religious or ethical, could have existed together, for by Aristotle's time a sharp distinction between science and religion had come to be taken for granted. Depending on their own preferences, later writers have treated the Pythagorean groups as either purely scientific-research organizations or as strictly religious communities.[4] The following discussion will consider first the intellectual achievements, then the religious practices of the order.

The philosophical ideas characteristic of the Pythagoreans can be summed up in the two phrases: "Numbers are things" and "Things are numbers."[5] The first precept extends the notion of reality well beyond the Milesian idea that, "To be is to be material"; it reflects the discovery of pure mathematics made by the school. The second expresses a notion that grew from another discovery of the Pythagoreans, namely, that mathematical formulas can be applied to explain the physical world. From this discovery, they generalized to the philosophic thesis that the ultimate nature of reality is mathematical. Just as the Milesians, impressed by their discovery of physics, thought that perhaps matter was the complete key to the nature of things, the Pythagoreans, impressed by their discovery of mathematics, thought that this was the whole of philosophy. These two suggestions challenged subsequent Greek philosophers to reconcile the claims of both form and matter as constituents of reality.

The development of pure mathematics seems to have been Pythagoras' own doing. Recent studies of the history of science show that in Egypt there was a civilization and technology where science and pure mathematics played no part. The Babylonians had developed some techniques of computation, but were not curious about the nature of number and figure as such. But it is just such a curiosity that is needed to lead to the discovery that numbers, figures, and relations have a kind of reality of their own and to the philosophical doctrine that numbers are things.

Pure mathematics requires a remarkable step of generalization. Instead of thinking and counting sets of things, so that a different form of the number two results from adding together pairs of pigs or pebbles, one must pay attention to the number two itself, as just "two," and not as two this or two that. In most, if not all, primitive languages, we find these "numerary adjuncts"—words indicating the kind of thing being counted. English still has some: we speak of "two *pieces* of bread," "two *head* of cattle," and so on. Japanese has many more: "two *round-shaped* pencils," "two *flat-shaped* sheets," and so on. These are relics of a mental state where numbers were used only as numbers *of* something, so that if one said, "Two," his hearers would ask him, "Two what?" It is only possible to recognize that "numbers are things" when two or any other quantity has been separated from this dependence on numerary adjuncts.

The Pythagoreans found they could think about shapes in the same way. Instead of thinking of particular pieces of land that were triangular in shape, they could think about *triangularity*, about *any* triangle, or *any* right triangle.[6] It is hard for us today, familiar as we are with pure mathematical abstractions and with the mental act of generalization, to appreciate the originality of this Pythagorean contribution. And, in fact, some aspects of Pythagorean mathematics strike us as rather odd. In the first place, much of this new mathematics was impure: it still depended strongly on pictures and imagination. Numbers had shapes and even personalities. Like the concept of matter in the Milesian school, the concept of number had to develop from intuition to postulation. (Historians of mathematics have often hidden this fact by reporting only the specific theorems and ideas that were pure and neglecting all the rest.) More striking, perhaps, to us is the tremendous excitement, almost religious enthusiasm, the Pythagoreans felt for mathematics. The new vision of form came to its earliest discoverers with the force of a mystical revelation.

We get some idea of the extent to which mathematics developed in the period between Pythagoras and Plato by studying the geometry of Books I-V of Euclid's *Elements*, which are a re-editing of earlier, Pythagorean treatises on geometry.[7] In addition, there are stories and specific theorems that give us clues. The "Theorem of Pythagoras," supposedly discovered by Pythagoras himself, is the source of many legends. Aristotle reports a Pythagorean proof from an early date in the school, that "the diagonal of a unit square is incommensurable with its side." This particular demonstration—we still use it today— shows that the Pythagoreans' techniques of proof and ability to think abstractly could on occasion reach very advanced levels.[8] Reports that the Pythagoreans identified the regular solids of solid geometry with the molecular parts of the material world show their interest in extending mathematical methods to the study of solids and in extending mathematics to natural science. We also find an account of a "sieve" that will pick out all of the primes from the number series, and the beginnings, in a peculiar form, of number theory.

The clues are sufficient to show that there was really a new insight into form. We need to consider the philosophical implications of the statement that "Numbers are things," which is a generalization of this insight. Perhaps it will be clearer if we rephrase the Pythagorean notion and say that "Numbers are real," since the word "things" in English carries a connotation of material objects and this distorts the meaning. Now, in what sense are numbers or shapes real? In the first place, they are independent of the observer; no matter what we might wish, the sum of two and two will always be four, and two an even prime number. They have precise identities, unlike Anaximander's formless or boundless void; each one is exactly itself. They are public: they are the same for every observer, unlike private subjective fantasies or passing impressions. They are systematically related to each other. All of these properties seem to justify recognizing shape, number, ratio, as real. But, unlike the reality of material objects, numbers have no history and no location; they exist in a world where there is not motion or change. And numbers are visible only to the mind; we can't touch them or look at them as we can at stones or streams. There is thus a whole new world for philosophy to explore, in addition to the sphere of physical reality which the Milesians had recognized.[9] And it is a world with real relevance to human interests and problems, since these abstract ratios and figures give science the tools it needs for understanding nature.[10]

Yet, in spite of the occasional refinement of their proofs and definitions, the Pythagorean numbers maintained a much closer connection with the imagination than our abstract numbers do today.[11] The Pythagoreans thought of numbers as "sets of units" (*monads*), and believed that the "natural" notation for writing them was as groups of dots, so that each number had its own distinctive natural pattern. This is the way we still represent numbers on dominoes and dice, and the association of numbers with spatial arrangement is preserved in our modern terms "square" and "cube" numbers. In fact, throughout the Middle Ages, "figured numbers" were a standard major section of arithmetic. Scholars studied such theorems as that the successive sums of the integers are "triangular," that is, that their component units can be written in exact triangular form (as in the "tetractys of the decad," of the table which follows). This mixture of imagination and abstraction made it easy to associate numbers with shapes and objects. For example, the writing of numbers as sets of units immediately suggested some correlation between the units of arithmetic and the points of Pythagorean geometry; and some members of the school tried to build the physical world out of spatial points.

Not only did numbers still carry with them the notion of physical shape and pattern for the Pythagorean mathematician, but they had other qualities as well. Each number had its own personality—masculine or feminine, perfect or incomplete, beautiful or ugly. This feeling modern mathematics has deliberately eliminated, but we still find overtones of it in fiction and poetry. Ten was the very best number: it contained in itself the first four integers—one, two, three, and four—and these written in dot notation formed a perfect triangle. Pythagorean lists were usually arranged either in groups of four or ten. In the later history of numbers in the West, mathematics went its own way, while the idea of personality and value properties of numbers inspired the whole magical tradition reflected in numerology and geomancy.[12]

Because their mathematics still had not reached a perfect degree of purity, the Pythagoreans found it easy to believe that, "Things are numbers." The philosophic insight expressed in this view is that the definite quantitative form of each thing gives each thing its identity. The number and shape of parts, for example, is what distinguishes the different species of the animal kingdom.[13] Take away the form, and only a puddle of amorphous stuff is left.

PYTHAGOREAN MATHEMATICS AND COSMOLOGY

I. Figured Numbers

To show how each number is a "collection of monads," the groups of monads were represented by small *alphas* in the Pythagorean "natural" notation. Thus one gets:

				a		a	a
a		a	a	a	a	a	a
1		2		3		4		etc.

The study of "figured numbers" develops by considering what the general forms are of numbers that can be written in a given pattern, for example, those that are products of equal factors are all "square." The sums of the successive integers, 1, 1+2, 1+2+3, 1+2+3+4, and so on, are "triangular."

II. The Tetractys of the Decad

The figure with the most marvelous properties, combining the first four integers, the triangular shape, and the "perfect number" ten, is the "tetractys of the decad," the triangle of ten monads built up from the integers 1, 2, 3, 4:

```
      a
     a a
    a a a
   a a a a
```

III. Table of Contraries

"Some Pythagoreans," according to Aristotle, explained the generation of numbers and of the rest of the world by a Table of Contraries:[14]

LIMIT	UNLIMITED
ONE	MANY
ODD	EVEN
LIGHT	DARK
GOOD	BAD
RIGHT	LEFT
STRAIGHT	CURVED
MALE	FEMALE
SQUARE	OBLONG
REST	MOTION

We find this interpretation in the early Pythagorean Table of Contraries (reproduced at III in the preceding table). In one column are the "formal" qualities, which are like or caused by number; in the other are their contraries lacking in form, which become definite only when they are given "determination."

Other members of the Pythagorean school gave the "things are numbers" thesis a more literal interpretation. Since the laws of nature proved to be quantitative, it was tempting to regard the objects governed by those laws as quantitative, too. And, if one could set aside as an exception to be accounted for later the existence of "irrationals," the imaginative association of the arithmetical unit with the geometrical point seemed to provide a simple model for actually building things out of sets of points. Each set of points matched the pattern of some set of units constituting an arithmetical "number."

The beauty of the thesis that things are numbers lay not only in its philosophical suggestiveness but in the practical results that appeared when Pythagorean scientists began measuring and counting. According to tradition, Pythagoras himself made the discovery that led to the idea of "the music of the spheres," an idea that has inspired much later Western science and poetry. Measuring the lengths of a vibrating string that gave concordant sounds, Pythagoras discovered that the ratios of these lengths for the octave, fifth, and fourth were exactly $2:1$, $3:2$, and $4:3$ —the simplest possible set of integral ratios. And observation, within tolerable limits of error, showed that *these same ratios* related the periods of planetary motion. Thus, the celestial system was a scale, a harmony which, like music, had an order of extreme mathematical simplicity.[15] (Although this analogy was taken literally by some enthusiasts who held that each planet in its motion gave off a sound with pitch proportional to its speed, the sounding of all seven notes of the musical scale at once is scarcely what one would term a celestial noise!)

This resemblance of scales and stars suggested that throughout nature all of the laws would show this same sort of mathematical simplicity. And the Pythagoreans set out, in various places and various ways, to discover what the fundamental quantitative relations are. That the study of quantity is the way to penetrate to the basic natures of things is a lesson that modern science has taken to heart and takes for granted today. But when the notion was new, we can imagine the excitement as the method succeeded sometimes and failed on other occasions as it was tested.

The Pythagorean ideas were, from the outset, successful in music and astronomy. As members of the school explored further, other fields seemed to show the power of their new technique as well. Medicine in Sicily had already formulated a

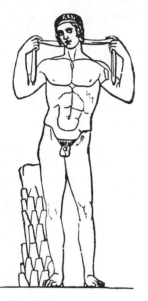

POLYCLITUS: DIADOUMENOS

The young athlete in this statue illustrates Polyclitus' belief that there are ideal proportions of the human figure which can be determined by mathematics. In this theory he was strongly influenced by the Pythagoreans. (From the Farnese Diadoumenos of Polyclitus in the British Museum.)

definition of health as *isonomia*, an equilibrium or balance of contrary qualities—hot and cold, moist and dry—in the body.[16] This is a notion very congenial to the Pythagorean way of thinking. And, although I have not seen any specific study on this point, it seems clear that medicine would immediately profit from the attempt to measure body temperature. Thus, Pythagorean ideas combined with older notions to create the Italian-Sicilian medical theory, which was the main Greek rival to the more empirical Hippocratic medicine. In sculpture, the famous Polyclitus, among others, believed that the same relation held between beauty and right ratio that obtained in music. He thought there was a set of "many numbers" that delimited the perfect proportions of the human figure, and he both wrote an account of them and created a statue to embody what became known as the canon. In chemistry, provocative ideas were advanced about the geometrical simplicity of the smallest parts of matter. The importance of right proportion had, of course, been a central theme in Greek architecture. There seemed no limit to the power of number and ratio to penetrate the innermost natures of things; and it was this power that gave the thesis that things are numbers its continuing interest and plausibility.

The Pythagorean Order, in addition to its intellectual work, had three aspects: political, religious, and ethical. These other activities of the order include their rethinking of the political ideas of Utopian communities, the religious notions of purification, metempsychosis, and some sort of immortal soul, and the ethical idea of a good life as one in harmony with the order of the universe.

The Order always had a political dimension. Pythagoras had the ideal in mind of small communities, in which property was held in common, women given equal opportunities and education, and interest in music and mathematics shared as part of the regular social life. The community was to recognize its civic responsibility in shaping the policy of the larger city-state of which it was a part. It was committed, therefore, to taking a role in practical decisions outside its own immediate boundaries. Admission was selective, we are told, on the basis of intelligence and character; but about this we have very little information. It was, of course, the notion of responsibility for the larger community that proved fatal to this early social experiment. In an age characterized by violent factional strife, Pythagorean policies inevitably ran counter to other powerful parties. Their opponents seem to have been able to convince enough people that they were dangerous radicals or strange witches to instigate attacks that, over a period of twenty years, wiped out the Pythagorean communities.[17]

The religious dimension of the Pythagorean Order reflected a general revival of religion throughout Greece in the sixth century B.C. Its immediate inspiration was not the civic Olympian religion, but the Orphic strand, which revealed its mysteries to the initiate as an aid to individual salvation.[18] Intense emotional excitement accompanied this revelation. Many priests claimed to be specially inspired and to have supernatural powers. Stories about Pythagoras make him such an inspired leader. He is said "to have been, on the same day at the same hour, in Metapontum and in Crotona." He tamed the savage Caulonian bear by talking with it, and the bear became a vegetarian. Once, at the Olympic Games, he showed that his thigh was made of gold. Abaris, a priest of Apollo from the far north, sought out Pythagoras and, "gave him the magic dart with which Abaris found his way in forests." There are enough stories of this kind to fill a large book.

Though the legend grew continually for ten centuries, while later scientists tried to reject it entirely, a few fragments of a book about Pythagoras by Aristotle show that the legend of supernatural powers was already current in Aristotle's time. And, in his character of prophet, Pythagoras gave rules for a way of life to his followers. Among these rules are many practices that a modern anthropologist would recognize as ritual taboos of a primitive character. Among them are, "Smooth out your bedclothes on arising," "Never stir a fire with iron," "Do not eat beans or red mullet."

He also taught *metempsychosis*, the transmigration of the soul. At death, the soul leaves one body, and moves to another: in some cases, though they are rare, a person can remember his previous lives; Pythagoras, for example, remembered that he had been the Trojan hero Euphorbus. Depending on its purity, a soul might move from a human body to an animal one in its next incarnation. This inspired the poet Xenophanes to invent the story that Pythagoras, asking someone to stop beating a dog, said, "It is my late friend: I recognize him by his voice!"

Pythagorean religious teaching also included a large group of myths; these picture a last judgment in the underworld, followed by a period of reward or punishment, and a return to live another life. I am not surprised that many of these ideas seemed strange to the general public and were poked fun at in Greek comedy. But they are all in the religious tradition of the time, and it is not possible to explain them away, even though they are "unscientific."

Where Pythagoras broke with the traditional religion was in the new interpretation that he gave to purification. In Orphic religion, a soul was purified by magic ritual; sacrifices and enchantments, duly purchased, were the means to increased chances of salvation. Pythagoras, on the other hand, thought that the study of mathematics and music was the best way of achieving harmony of soul and purification. This reinterpretation of purification as self-realization and intellectual development is an important advance in the history of religion, and is one place where we see the scientific and religious aspects of the order becoming relevant to each other.

The ethics that Pythagoras taught centered around the idea of harmony in the soul. A good soul has a proper order among its impulses and standards of value; and the aim of education is to instill a love of harmony. We become harmonious persons through appreciation of and contact with the beauties of music, the orderly abstractions of mathematics, the concrete sublime system of the stars.

One interesting application of this theory to medicine was the use of music to treat mentally disturbed patients; the idea of re-establishing a right *cosmos* in the person by presenting him with harmony was used in this way in practical therapy.

In their ethical practices, the Pythagoreans were famous for their mutual friendship, unselfishness, and honesty. The story of Damon and Pythias illustrates the role of friendship in the order. Dionysius, the dictator of Syracuse, having heard how highly friendship was regarded in the Pythagorean Order, decided to test this. He imprisoned a young Pythagorean, Damon, and declared his intention of executing him. Damon asked for time to arrange his affairs. Dionysius said he would grant this, if Damon could find a friend who would take his place as a hostage. Damon's friend, Pythias, agreed immediately and stayed imprisoned until Damon returned. Dionysius then gave both of them gifts and, according to some stories, asked them to include *him* in their friendship. They refused; and when we encounter Dionysius again, in connection with Plato, we shall see why.

What drew together the scientific interests of the Pythagorean school and its character as a religion, prescribing a way of life, is the common presence of harmony and order as criteria for truth and beauty in both the natural and the human sphere. The Pythagoreans were among the first Greek thinkers to call the universe a *cosmos*, a term that means a system or order. And they respected order as a condition of value, whether it was the cold order of systems of mathematical abstractions, or the engaged order of a human life in a community, or the all-encompassing order of nature reflected in the procession of the stars.[19] To this extent, the way of life Pythagoras taught was not completely opposed to or independent of the interest in mathematics and philosophy of his school. Beyond this point, it is almost impossible for a twentieth-century reader to see quite how the combination of scientific explanation and religious ritual was accepted with no feeling of inconsistency.

The Pythagorean contribution to philosophy and science is hard to overestimate.[20] Their conquest of pure mathematics gave the West its most valuable tool of explanation; their search for quantitative laws in nature proved the most fruitful direction science has yet taken.[21] To philosophy, their new sensitivity to order and form offered a corrective to the rather naïve Milesian materialism, and opened a new range of important speculative questions. Their ethics and religion, at least, suggested a notion of the human soul and its destiny and of the possibility of a planned social order. These ideas persisted until they became explicit again in Athens, in the second, systematic phase of Greek philosophy.

V. HERACLITUS

Time Versus Eternity

You cannot step into the same river twice,
for other waters are ever flowing on.

HERACLITUS

Heraclitus of Ephesus belongs neither to the tradition of materialism, which the Milesians began, nor to that of mathematical and logical formalism, which the Pythagoreans started. A poet, rather than an engineer or mathematician, Heraclitus expressed in oracular epigrams the tension between the changeless, general ideas of philosophy and the transient concrete facts of life and death, of flow, of restless change. This dynamic aspect of reality cannot be described or explained by static abstract concepts—a point our existentialist philosophers have reminded us of in the present century. In discussing Heraclitus, therefore, we must try to share an insight that he did not express in clear concepts or precise theorems, but which he correctly believed added a new dimension to philosophy.

P E R H A P S Heraclitus, like his predecessors, began by looking for the one stuff underlying the changing world we observe all around us. Yet he falls neither in the Milesian nor Pythagorean group. Reality for him consists of motion, process, power, strife, and flow. The world is more like a restless fire than a machine made out of some material stuff. These ideas of Heraclitus are ones that added an important new dimension to Greek philosophy.

When we have asked the question, What is being? and under-

[43]

stood that we are asking for some common property in which all existent things share, the return to the world of finite particular beings carries with it a sense of paradox. For the kind of answer that is most obvious to the question about reality—that it is some permanent stuff, or some unchanging realm of form—makes us think of all real things as part of some single continuous whole that is neither created nor destroyed. Yet our experience confronts us everywhere with restless change, unique individuality, and the sense of isolation of particular finite beings.

Reason tempts us to be satisfied with an outline view of the permanent properties of things; but our own experience everywhere finds us immersed in a world of individuals, not types, of flow, not of frozen form. Naturally enough, for a thinker aware of this paradox, there is a tendency to reconsider the relation of philosophy to abstract thought. In the first place, the cosmic paradox is more important than the tidy theorem; in the second place, the abstractions of physics and mathematics are *not* adequate to communicate truths about concrete existence, decision, and flowing life.[1]

The revolt against essence in the interests of existence is a dominant theme in the philosophy of our own century; the paradoxical tension between time and eternity is a dominant theme in Japanese Zen Buddhist thought; and, in the light of these later attempts to explore the concrete existence of finite things, Heraclitus of Ephesus might qualify as "the first Western existentialist," because of his new direction of approach to philosophy.[2]

Heraclitus was known in antiquity as "the Obscure" or "the Dark"; those of his individual sayings that have been preserved are like the riddling words of the Delphic oracle: cryptic, vivid, sometimes reinforcing sense by sound. (For example, *"autoisi potamoisi . . ."* opens the river fragment with the sound of the river's flow.) These sayings are relatively self-contained; there are none of the connecting "therefores" and "if . . . thens" of science and mathematics.[3] He himself writes that "the Oracle of the God, at Delphi, neither affirms nor denies, but gives a sign . . ." and "the Sibyl with raving lips says unornamented words that are heard for a thousand years. . . ." These quotations suggest why Heraclitus chose the oracular epigram as his model for philosophic communication.[4] It is an unusual choice, not repeated in the West until Nietzsche's *Thus Spake Zarathustra*.

Everywhere Heraclitus sees cosmic order as resting on eternal flow, tension, and strife: "All things flow . . ."; "Strife is father of all and lord of all . . ."; "Opposition unites . . ."; "All things are changed for fire and fire for all things . . ."; "From tension comes concord, as with the bow and the lyre"; "The name of the bow is life, but its work, death"; and many more.[5] He has a low opinion of the mass of mankind in general ("Bias of Priene was wisest because he said, 'Most men are bad' "; "The Ephesians ought to be hanged . . ."), and a low opinion of the scientific and religious leaders of his day.[6] Thus he writes, "Much information does not teach wisdom . . . else it would have taught Pythagoras . . . who, from his polymathy, made up an art of mischief"; and, further, "unholy, they think to purify themselves by sullying themselves in blood . . ."; "Night-walkers, bacchants, magicians . . ."[7]

And yet, from the purposeless, cyclic flow of time, there does result a *logos*—a formula, word, ratio, cosmic order. There is a cycle of transformation by which the exchange of fire and earth and water takes place, an "upward" and a "downward" way.[8] But as soon as we think that at least here we have a clear proposition of Milesian physics—odd as the choice of fire is for a basic stuff—we read that "upward and downward the way is one and the same."[9] The *logos* "steers all and runs through all . . ."; "Hearken, not to me, but to my *logos*"; man can find the *logos* in something that is "common," not in the private worlds of opinion and dream.[10] In governing the world, the lawlike character of things is described in a manner reminiscent of Anaximander: "The sun will not step beyond his bounds; for if he did, the Furies, agents of Justice (*Dike*) would hunt him out."[11] But time is not neatly measured, as it was in Anaximander's world where each thing has its allotted "day in court"; rather, "Time is a child playing at checkers . . ."[12]

In psychology, too, we find the self treated in this same puzzling way. "Men and gods . . . dying in one another's life, living their death"; "The dry soul is the wisest and the best"; "Men should hold fast to the common, as a city to its laws"; "Man's character is his fate"; "There awaits us at death what we neither expect nor think."[13]

By selecting these sayings and arranging them in different orders, one can interpret Heraclitus in various ways.[14] Aristotle, for example, concentrated on the analogies of the universe to a restless flame and classified Heraclitus as just another Ionian materialist who had perversely made his *arche* fire.[15] (But he was always uneasy about this classification; he suggested, in his logic, that Heraclitus was not really a philosopher at all. In his *Ethics*, he wondered whether some defect of character must not be the explanation of Heraclitus' "absurd" sayings. In the *Poetics*, he said that after all many of the problems in Heraclitus could be solved by attention to the punctuation.)

The Roman Stoics thought that they were following Heraclitus. They made the *logos* a material breath or spirit present throughout the universe. By identifying this with God, they combined materialism and pantheism (the view that all things are part of God).[16] Philip Wheelwright, the modern scholar and literary critic, argues that Heraclitus is in fact a poet, using "plurisignation"—a deliberate use of many meanings simultaneously—to express his philosophy.[17] British scholars (at least, some of them) defend an interpretation that makes the presence of a single cosmic order, the *logos*, behind and above chaotic process, Heraclitus' central discovery.[18] Plato thought Heraclitus intended to equate reality with flow. He summarizes Heraclitus' whole philosophy in the epigram *"panta rhei"*—"all things flow." The exact opposite of Plato's own formalistic philosophy, this sounds as though it were a direct quotation from Heraclitus himself. It expresses the same idea as Heraclitus' famous river imagery in his sayings, "You cannot step into the same river twice . . . ," and, "Into the same rivers we step and do not step; we are and we are not. . . ."[19]

In the light of this range of interpretation, it may be both interesting and helpful to look again at the experience of paradox Heraclitus is describing and at the reasons that underlay his choice of oracular epigram as his means to describe it. When I "listen to the *logos* . . ." of Heraclitus, I am sure that I am not listening to a textbook of propositions that form a "polymathy . . . an art of mischief"; and I do not find the kind of serene eternal order that the Pythagorean concept of the *All* as a cosmos reflected.

I find a similar sense of paradox in the poetry of Bashō, a Japanese Zen Buddhist of the seventeenth century. Bashō is the great master of haiku poetry—the evocative three-line, seventeen syllable form.[20] And his poetry is in part a sharing of his philosophy. Consider the following three poems:

I

An ancient temple pond; jump of a frog; the sound of water.

II

A solitary crow on a bare bough; evening in autumn.

III

Wild seas tonight; past Sadō island stretches; The River of Heaven.

In each of these, and in his other poetry, the imagery has a peculiar felt significance. The brief lines give us directly a superimposition of some finite, noisy or black or rocky, isolated event on the background of some unruffled river of stars or ancient pond or pink, smoke-filled autumn twilight. This is the philosophic paradox of Bashō's own Zen Buddhist position: that being or reality, calm and eternal, can yet contain beings that are ephemeral, isolated, and noisy. The dark, small island set between the restless sea and the unchanging river of stars, the huddled-up lonely little crow, standing out black against the evening—these are what he thinks it philosophically important for us to see and share. Not to think about abstractly, but to experience directly; and only by poetry can he hope to share with us *immediately* his own experiences and sensitivity.

I find it illuminating to compare Bashō with Heraclitus. They share the sense of paradox in a world of transient individuality. They are not in complete agreement: Where Bashō's "River of Heaven" suggests that reality lies with the stars, Heraclitus is unable to tone down the wild sea's flow. Where Bashō communicates directly in sharp visual imagery, Heraclitus uses assonance, pun, epigram, explicit verbal contradiction. Yet they do share a fundamental sense of paradox and the belief that philosophy, if it is to be true, must not be taught indirectly and abstractly; it must be expressed directly. Furthermore, this comparison leads us to see something about contemporary existentialism. Often existentialists don't write conventional works of "polymathy" but novels, poems, plays. Is this also because they have a sense of paradox which they intuitively feel can be communicated only by literary telepathy? Or, to take another example of existential thought, are Heidegger's marvelous, if fanciful, "etymologies" doing somewhat the same thing as Heraclitus' unexpected turns of language?[21] The question is not meant to be rhetorical, though I obviously think that yes is the answer.

The ever-living, restless fire and the common *logos*, the strife and tension of opposites and the resulting harmony, the abstractions wise men devise and the concrete lives they lead, unordered time and unsleeping justice—these are themes that are central in Heraclitus. The attempt at direct communication of some concrete insight surely explains the choice of oracular form: the saying short enough to have its direct impact, the plain language and puzzling meaning that continue to be heard after two thousand years.[22]

Heraclitus added a new dimension to philosophy. Because it was a new dimension, not merely a new doctrine of a familiar materialist or formalist design, it is hard for us to say what he meant in any familiar way. What, for example, does he mean by *pyr*? Is fire simply a Milesian material stuff? Hardly. The material nature of *aer* was not yet established, and *pyr* would be much further from a sensible choice of material substratum![23] Is it simply a symbol for incessant transformation, for hot, violent change? It does, indeed, have peculiar power as a symbol: witness the recent study by the French philosopher Bachelard, *Psychanalyse de Feu*, or the line by Jack Kerouac that my students quote as an opening for their term papers on Heraclitus, "I burn, burn, burn!" But a living fire that supplies the driving force of a universe in endless change is something more than a symbol; it is a physical cause, at the very least. And the upward and downward way suggest some regular cycle of physical transformation as part of Heraclitus' view.[24]

I think that Wheelwright is right in believing that all the

meanings the term *pyr* can have are meant to be fused together.[25] But if we insist absolutely on keeping together *all* of the overtones of the marvelous cosmic fire in every context, it is only in creative poetry, not in nature or in science or in philosophy, that this can possibly be done. Perhaps the simplest thing to say is that Heraclitus is trying to express both the tensions that lead to harmony and the tremendous energy that flows through reality in his fire imagery: it is energy, not matter, that is most important for him.[26] Aristotle could not imagine energy without some material thing that was energetic—although in terms of his own philosophy, this should have occurred to him as a possibility. Perhaps it is only with such recent developments in Western thought as Einstein's and Whitehead's replacement of Aristotelian substances by events and processes as the elements of nature that we can see further than Aristotle. For today we can recognize as a genuine and interesting possibility a process philosophy in which physical reality is, not matter, but power.[27]

In some ways, Heraclitus seems to have stepped backward into the age of mythology. But what gives his sense of paradox a new vividness is the background of being, revealed by the question Thales had asked. Without that background of some unchanging reality, we have pathos rather than paradox in the poet who sees the generations of men "falling as leaves do from the trees."[28] Yet when reason becomes enchanted either by mechanical models or mathematical maps and forgets the concrete fact of change, the strife and individuality that are the very stuff of our experienced world, it needs an oracle once more. The vision of someone with acute aesthetic and metaphysical sensitivity is needed to show us that the tidy cosmos of our models and equations is not the world of existence which we know. Neither mythology nor abstract reasoning can divine its nature or give philosophy a final answer.

"This world, the same for gods and men, no one has made; but it is an eternal fire, kindling in fixed measure, and in fixed measures going out," wrote Heraclitus.[29]

VI. PARMENIDES

Logic and Mysticism

Only Being is; not-being cannot be. . .

PARMENIDES

A native of the city of Elea in southern Italy, Parmenides was greatly influenced by the Pythagoreans. He invented formal logic by applying their mathematical methods of proof to the philosophical problem of the natures of being and not-being. Presenting his argument in the form of an epic poem, he used logic to show that being is unchanging and uncreated. This conclusion denied the possibility of any appearance of variety or change. A corollary to this positive, if mystical, conclusion was that human reason has the power to understand reality.

Interestingly enough, Parmenides also wrote about astronomy, biology, and other sciences. Yet if his main insight was sound, the many changing things these sciences study could not be real. Vividly aware of change and individuality in the world they observed about them, the Greeks tried to find ways to keep Parmenides' logical method but to avoid his mystical conclusion.

P A R M E N I D E S presented his ideas in an epic poem, a form that had been used by Orphic poets for recording revelations. By great good luck most of the first part of this epic, "The Way of Truth," has been preserved. A few scattered fragments of the second part, "The Way of Opinion," also remain. The poem opens with a prologue, in which Parmenides journeys to the palace of the sun, where a goddess greets him and instructs him.

The horses that carry me bore me far as I desired
Having set me on the mystic way
That takes the man who knows through all the towns of men.
On this way was I borne; and the horses that bore me,
    well counselled,
Drew the chariot while the Maidens led the way.
The axle in its tree shrieked,
Glowing (as it was driven by the circles at each end),
When the Sun-maidens, hastening to lead me to the light,
Quit the house of night, throwing back their veils
    with their hands.

There are the gates to the ways of Night and Day
With lintel above and threshold of stone.
The great doors themselves reach high in *aither;*
And to them Vengeful Justice holds the turning keys.
Her did the maidens persuade, cleverly with soft words,
So that she threw the gate-bolts back
Without objection. The great gates opened, gaping,
As the doorposts, with their fittings of bronze,
Shrieked in their sockets;
Their bronze shoes turning as the gates swung wide;
Through these, on a broad way, the Maidens led the
    steeds and car.

The Goddess greeted me, taking my right hand in Hers
And spoke thus to me:
Oh youth, whom immortal charioteers
Have brought, with thy horses, here to My home:
Greeting! No evil fate has sent thee on this way
(Though it lies far from travelled paths of men)
But divine will and justice.
It is fitting that you shall learn all things,
Both the constant heart of encircling Truth,
And also mortals' thoughts, where not one true belief lies. . . .[1]

The goddess then proceeds to develop the way of truth; her
central theme is that "only Being is; not-being cannot be."[2]

This "Being that is" turns out to be a single, undivided whole, alike in every direction and throughout, one and unchanging. It can be grasped by reason, perhaps supplemented with a kind of intellectual intuition; but it cannot be observed in our common-sense world or expressed in ordinary language.[3]

To prove that such is, indeed, the way of truth, the goddess considers the alternatives. There are "only two ways; it is or it is not." The goddess knows the right way; but "mortals wander, turning back, undecided."[4] She now brings to bear an abstract logical argument to show why no one can follow the second way.

Suppose someone assumes that being is divided into many separate beings. Then what is it that separates them and holds them apart? It cannot be being, for then all of the parts would still all be together in one totality, and not be distinct. On the other hand, if one says things are separated by not-being this leads to absurdity. For not-being, if it is the opposite of being, can only be a void, a kind of pure nothing: if one says that not-being *is* a separator, he is treating it as being, which by definition it is not. If one says that though it is nothing, it still separates the parts of being, this is the same as saying that "nothing separates being into parts," which in fact is a statement denying that the parts are separated. How can nothing do something positive? The idea is self-contradictory.

The goddess is an excellent logician. By the same sort of reasoning she shows that being can have had no beginning: "For from what could it come to be? From nothing, nothing can arise; but if from being, then it did not come to be, but was already." It is changeless, indivisible, eternal; this is the final truth about reality.

The ideas involved are abstract and unfamiliar; and it is helpful, in appreciating what Parmenides has said, to examine his use of formal logic and his doctrine of the nature of reality separately, before turning to the third topic his poem suggests, that of the status of "the opinions men hold."

The city of Elea was close geographically and politically to Crotona, and Pythagorean ideas must have been influential there. If, among these ideas, Parmenides knew the Pythagorean proof that the diagonal of a unit square is incommensurable with the

THE CHARIOTEER OF DELPHI

Commissioned to commemorate a chariot-racing victory by Gelon of Syracuse in the sixth century B.C., this tamer of horses comes from the same part of the Greek world, and the same time, as Parmenides with his poem of the chariot journey to the truth. (Photograph courtesy of Greek National Tourist Organization.)

side, we can imagine how he came to generalize this proof-schema into pure logic. For what he actually did was to extend this type of indirect proof from relations of quantity to philosophy. Where in mathematics there are variables, the x and y of our equations, that stand for "any number," formal logic extends the range. In such logic, x and y stand for "any individual things," whether those things are quantities or not. Some redefinition of operations, of addition, product, and so on, is necessary; the new system is too general for the standard rules of mathematics to hold. But there is a very close analogy. Thus, Parmenides' reasoning is an extension of the Pythagorean proof. That proof shows that assuming a rational diagonal leads to the conclusion that "a given number is both odd and even." Since that conclusion is absurd, one must reject the assumption. In the same way, Parmenides shows that some philosophic assumptions—for example, that "being is many"—lead to the conclusion that "a given thing both is and is not."

This conclusion is absurd. Parmenides is explicit in saying why. The most important line of "The Way of Truth" for the history of Western science and logic is the remark of the goddess, in dismissing the false way, that ". . . it is the same thing that can be thought and can be."[5] Here is an explicit recognition of the power of human reason to penetrate the structure of existence. All of man's reasoning rests on the notion that what is reasonable or even clearly thinkable must be consistent. A flat contradiction, such as "the number x is both odd and even," is absurd: we can form no clear idea of such a number. Further, we are sure that there *is* no such self-contradictory number, and that if someone offers a proof leading to this conclusion, some of the steps or assumptions of that proof must be mistaken.

In explicitly recognizing that noncontradiction is a fundamental property of existence, as well as of thought, Parmenides hit upon a most important principle. Once it is recognized that only consistent entities can exist, the truth of generalizations can be tested by examining their consistency. Not only in mathematics, where the Pythagoreans had already developed *reductio ad absurdum* proofs in their exploration of quantities, but throughout nature—in philosophy, physics, everywhere—it became possible to show simply by examining their logical consequences that some generalizations cannot be true. Whenever precise deduction leads to a contradiction, we can be sure that the initial assumption is wrong. Being cannot tolerate anything internally contradictory. There are general forms of reasoning that show exactly what consequences do follow logically from given starting points: twentieth-century algebraic logic has been able to isolate these forms and make them stand out clearly. But it was Parmenides that first formulated the essential rule.

The effect of Parmenides' revelation was to reinforce philosophical formalism by showing that there is a close connection between reality and abstract logical form, and to make philosophers more conscious of the methods by which they arrived at their conclusions. Greek thinkers after Parmenides—and his student Zeno—appreciated the value of precise logical form.[6]

Turning from logic to philosophy, we may wonder whether any human being can believe these conclusions. Instead of Heraclitus' sense of tension, power, and paradox, Parmenides offers a vision of permanence, of an absolute in which differences and change are unreal. I don't suppose anyone could be convinced of this by pure argument, unless there were also some mystical experience to make the argument seem to fit the world. (By a mystical experience, I mean a vivid intuition of the oneness of all reality.) Probably this is one reason for Parmenides' choice of a poetic form and a goddess to reveal this doctrine.

But it is possible to have an intuition of the unity of all things, and a sense of transparent unreality about the particular items that appear. The school of Advaita Vedanta in India rests on exactly this insight, and teaches a doctrine almost identical with that of Parmenides.[7] The greatest philosopher in this tradition was Shankara, who concentrated on proving the unreality of all appearance. The story is told that one day, during a parade, an elephant rushed into the crowd and Shankara ran behind a tree. "Why do you run from the mere appearance of an elephant?" a friend asked him. The philosopher answered, "I only appear to run." But where in India this conclusion was accepted as a final doctrine, in ancient Greece the reaction to Parmenides was to accept his logic, then use it to see what was wrong with his philosophic argument—for later thinkers had little doubt that something *was* wrong with it, somewhere.

The awkward thing about Parmenides' way of truth is, that if it is so, there *are* no appearances at all. No goddess, no philosopher, no mystic way, but only the unbroken crystalline sphere of being itself. Appearances don't even appear, for they are pure nothing. And the Greeks, with their vivid appreciation of the world around them, could not believe a truth that so obviously denied the very possibility of the most evident facts of experience. Unfortunately, Parmenides' argument has some of the properties of the "universal solvent" of medieval alchemy. This solvent was a chemical that would dissolve anything it touched; one wonders what the alchemists, who were looking for it, thought that they would keep it in, if they ever found it.

There is no way around the problem of appearances if one sticks tightly to Parmenides' text and discovers its intention. The statement that the only choices are being and not-being raises a baffling problem in philosophy and logic. Before Parmenides, it was by no means clear that not-being would prove just as hard and provocative to define as being itself. Today it is still not clear whether the law of excluded middle—the logical rule that states, "Everything is either A or not-A"—applies rigorously to the world of fact. We will find with Plato and Aristotle that their analysis of the concepts of being and nothing made it possible to preserve Parmenides' rigorous logic without having to accept the philosophy he thought must follow.[8]

"The Way of Opinion," which is the second part of the poem, is known to us only through the introduction and about fifteen scattered quotations. The goddess begins this part of her speech by saying, ". . . here I cease the way of truth . . ." "Mortals go wrong in naming two forms, one light, the other dark . . . of which only one is proper to name," she states. But Parmenides is to be taught these opinions, so that "no opinions of mankind will outstrip you . . . ," and from the quotations that remain, the goddess then apparently proceeds to summarize Pythagorean science, beginning with the contraries of their philosophical table. Her criticism is that the Pythagoreans, when they include "void," "night," "the indefinite," in their table, are assuming the existence of kinds of not-being. This assumption has already been shown to be absurd by the goddess in her introductory criticism of "mortals" who "name two forms."[9]

But why this second part of the poem at all? Scholars have wondered about this question for a long time and have suggested many explanations. Does the fact that Parmenides treated opinion in detail mean that somehow the world of appearance is a projection or breaking-through of the pure reality that exists alone in the first part? Plato's *Parmenides* treats the relation of appearance and reality in this way; but Plato has a much more sophisticated philosophic position that recognizes degrees both of being and of nothing, and this Parmenides certainly does not have: "It is, or it is not." Was the second part intended as a textbook of contemporary science, written in poetic form, so that Parmenides' students could easily remember the incorrect expert opinions of the day? It may have been, but there was certainly no precedent in Parmenides' time—unlike our own—for anyone to write a compendium of ideas he thought all wrong or even to write a textbook at all. Did Parmenides change his mind about the nature of appearance between the two halves of his poem? If he did, there is no internal evidence of it. Or does he, perhaps, want to share with his reader the irreducible absurdity of a universe in which reason and experience cannot be reconciled, so that both parts are on the same footing, and the real excitement and novelty lie in the inconsistency between them?

All of these suggestions, and many more, have been made.[10] The interpretation that seems best to me is somewhat less imaginative. "The Way of Opinion" can be read as a straight-forward attack on the reliability of Pythagorean science with its explanations of the world in terms of the opposed principles of limit and indeterminate, number and void, form and field. When a Pythagorean offered an elegantly ordered explanation of phenomena of astronomy, or physics, or psychology, or genetics, this was attractive, and it was not at all evident that his whole procedure rested on a philosophical inconsistency. If the goddess is able to show with incisive logic that the existence of not-being is one of the assumptions made by *all* the more detailed Pythagorean work in science, she has kept her promise to Parmenides, and refuted the most plausible opinions of the day for him in such a way that there could be no escape from his critique.[11] And this is what the second part of the poem seems to me intended to do.[12]

Parmenides' combination of logic and mysticism had a profound effect on subsequent Greek philosophy. His pure logic was appreciated and adopted. His argument that "nothing can come from what is not" challenged generations of philosophers trying to explain the nature of change.[13] His unwelcome conclusions provoked later thinkers into new and more precise explorations of the concepts of being and not-being. Later thinkers were dissuaded from trying to identify being with any one single stuff or matter by his proof that, in a universe made of some *single* stuff, there could be no *real change* (since each thing would really be the same after changing as it was before). After Parmenides the exploration of being and change shifted from *monism*, the attempt to find a single identical underlying reality, to *pluralism*, the attempt to explain the world as made up of many different elements, material particles, or other kinds of being.

VII. ZENO OF ELEA

The Paradox of Motion[1]

If at each instant the flying arrow is at rest, when does it move?
ZENO

Zeno of Elea, follower and admirer of Parmenides, had a precise sense of logical form and a feeling for appropriate (and witty) illustration, a combination that has seldom been equaled in philosophy. Zeno accepted both sides of Parmenides' thought: (1) the philosophical conclusion that plurality and change are unreal, and (2) the new appreciation of formal logic as a method of testing theories by examining their consistency. Setting out to prove that Parmenides was right, he demonstrated the absurdities of the opposite view (that the world really contains plurality and change). His most successful effort in this direction was the set of four riddles he devised to illustrate the unreality of motion, by showing that neither common sense nor Pythagorean science can define motion without running into inconsistency or impossibility.

A MODERN LECTURER on Zeno might well begin, in Zeno's own spirit, by saying:

"It may seem so preposterous to be told that today I have a proof that you cannot possibly move from your seats to the door of this hall, that perhaps all of you who are sensible will feel a sudden impulse to move, to that door, and through it, and keep going! But this is in fact what I intend to prove. . . . I will offer four arguments, which, taken together, will show how muddled and unreasonable your common sense is, and why it is absurd to try to define motion. . . ."

[59]

Zeno's work did not convince his successors that Parmenides had been right but rather made them appreciate the value of precise formal logic. It strengthened formalism by establishing that fields as far apart as mathematics and contract law have identical patterns of logical form. It compelled philosophers to ponder more carefully the definition of not-being and being, and of their relation to the definition of change. Zeno showed the mathematicians, once and for all, that the Pythagorean program of building *continuous quantities* out of finite series of *discrete units* ran into impossible inconsistencies. The Greek philosophers and scientists after Zeno reacted to him as they did to Parmenides. They did not accept the doctrine that reality is a total, unmoved absolute; instead, they set about trying to show how, in the same universe, formal logic could be valid, reason reliable, yet multiplicity and change possible. We can see his influence on all subsequent Greek thought.

Zeno's reason for putting his criticism of motion into puzzle form was that he intended to attack common sense and technical mathematical views alike. The puzzles, taken concretely, posed a problem that forced common sense to admit that its own unclear ideas might not be so sensible after all. At the same time, taken as special illustrations of more abstract criticism, the puzzles showed that the technical assumptions about points and moments on which they depended for their baffling effect would lead to strict logical inconsistency. The four cases were chosen to show the Pythagoreans, admirers of mathematics and familiar with indirect proof, that their definitions of motion were unsuccessful. Plato quotes Zeno as "repaying the attacks of those who made fun of Parmenides, and with interest." Let us look at this counterattack.[2]

The paradoxes of motion are four stories. It was because Zeno needed to eliminate four different possible definitions of motion that he chose this particular number of cases; but, first, here are his four stories, which have continued to fascinate children, mathematicians, and most ordinary hearers, ever since he first devised them.

The first paradox is known as the bisection. Suppose you are in a stadium at a given distance from the exit door. Then you can never get out of the stadium, because before you reach the door you must reach the point halfway there. But before you can reach the halfway point, you must reach a point halfway to that. And since it takes some finite interval of time to move from one point to another and there are an infinite number of halfway points, it would take you an infinite time to pass through them all and get out. What is wrong with this argument? It doesn't seem sensible but, How do you get out of that door?

However, if you are unconvinced by the bisection, Zeno has a second puzzle, that of Achilles and the tortoise. In this, you are to imagine yourself, again in the stadium, to watch a race between Achilles and a tortoise. Since the tortoise moves so much more slowly, Achilles agrees to give it a head start. But that is his mistake; having done this, Zeno says, he can never pass the tortoise. For by the time Achilles reaches the point where the tortoise started, it will have moved ahead to a second point; and by the time Achilles reaches this, it will have moved ahead yet again. So Achilles can never overtake the tortoise. Zeno's Greek audience, no doubt, reacted to this at first by saying, "But we know perfectly well that in a real race, Achilles *would* pass the tortoise and win"; and then, on second thought, as they reflected a little more, "Yes, of course, he would pass it. But how?" Since we cannot be easily persuaded that what is logical leads to a conclusion diametrically opposed to what is actual, Zeno's challenge to explain how passing the tortoise is possible becomes provoking. We go back to the story and even draw a picture of the race as Zeno describes it to see where he has made some incorrect assumption about distance, speed, or motion. The diagram looks like this:

$$T_1 \text{ -------- } T_2 \text{ -------- } T_3$$

$$t_0 \text{ -------- } t_1 \text{ -------- } t_2$$

$$A_1 \text{ -------- } A_2 \text{ -------- } A_3$$

$$t_0 \text{ -------- } t_1 \text{ -------- } t_2$$

ZENO'S ACHILLES AND THE TORTOISE

A_1 is Achilles' starting line, T_1 where the tortoise starts. By the time Achilles has run from A_1 to A_2, the tortoise will have moved ahead to T_2; while Achilles runs from A_2 to A_3, the tortoise again plods ahead from T_2 to T_3; and so on indefinitely. The diagram still seems to prove that the tortoise wins the race.

Zeno's third paradox, that of the arrow, is the simplest of the four, but historically it has proven to be the most provocative. It asks, very simply, "If the flying arrow is at every instant of its flight at rest, in a space equal to its length, when does it move?" Well, when does it? This question is a good one to ask mathematicians or physicists when they begin telling us we cannot understand them, because they are talking about "states" or "moments" that represent "things in an unextended instant." How one can build motion from such static snapshots of rest is a question that they, and anyone else, should find interesting.

Zeno's fourth puzzle about motion takes us back to the stadium once more. Achilles and the tortoise have left—perhaps, in spite of Zeno, they have made their way to the door—and instead we have three moving "solids"—carts or chariots— arranged in a pattern. One is at rest; the second is moving past it. How long does it take the second chariot to move one chariot length? This depends on the speed of the moving chariot, of course; but whatever speed we imagine, we are asked to take "passing through one chariot length" as the unit of time. (We should note that to the common-sense Greek, fond of chariot racing, one chariot length is a natural measure either of the distance by which one chariot leads another or of the *time* by which it finishes faster.) But now, suppose the third chariot is moving as fast as the second one, in the opposite direction. When these two pass, the time each needs to pass one chariot length is only half of the original unit. Hence, as Zeno concludes his paradox, half the unit of time is equal to the whole unit of time. Once the argument is grasped, it is really puzzling to anyone who has always taken it for granted that there is an absolute difference between motion and rest. The ideas we ourselves at once supply have come into our common sense from relativity theory. We see that, of course, motion is relative to a frame of reference, so that the same chariot has different speeds depending on the way speed is measured. This idea was not familiar to Zeno's audience at all. In fact, if Zeno had said as his conclusion, "Therefore the same moving body has different velocities at the same time," his audience would have found this just as absurd as the one he presented: that the whole time equals its half.

While it is clear to the modern reader that Zeno has, in fact,

AAA

← — BBB   ● turning-post

CCC — →

ZENO'S STADIUM

The A's are at rest, the B's moving away from the turning-post (●), and the C's moving toward the turning-post at the same rate of speed. If we take "passing through one chariot length" as the unit of time, measured by B's motion relative to A, B passes a C in just half this time. This contradicts the notion that the initial time unit chosen was indivisible: the argument can be applied to show that there can never be an indivisible least moment of time.

hit upon an important truth, our twentieth-century common sense has become so used to the relativity of velocity that this fourth problem is less interesting to us than the other three. However, when we look at these paradoxes as criticisms of the "scientific" accounts of motion the Pythagoreans offered, we find that Zeno has hidden another problem in this last of his four paradoxes.

When Parmenides and Zeno lived, the Pythagoreans were the scientific and mathematical experts of the Western world. Are the four problems Zeno posed effective as criticism of the more precise notions of space, time, and motion that were then current?

The Pythagoreans seem to have agreed that the physical world, including space and time, was built up from separate "points," and "moments." They would, therefore, have defined motion much as we do velocity today: as passing through a number of spatial points during a number of time moments. The Pythagoreans also agreed, as a postulate of physics and geometry, that any continuous stretch—of a line, for example—could be bisected. But beyond this common agreement, there was no accepted school-wide doctrine as to the size of moments or points; they might have *no* size at all, or they might have a minimum but finite duration and extension, respectively. There was no agreement, either, as to whether a line made up of or determined by points should be thought of as points "next to" each other, or as points marking off segments with some kind of void or space "filling in" the intervals between.[3]

This lack of agreement on exact details meant that Zeno had to consider four possible cases to show that *no* exact description of motion could avoid inconsistency. He seems to have felt that Parmenides had already proved the absurdity of trying to have some void fill in the intervals between points.[4] Such a void would be a form of not-being, and since nothing can do nothing and has no properties, it would be illogical to think of it as holding points apart or connecting them. Therefore, the only possibilities free from logical objection were those in which the parts of space (and time) came next to each other.

The four cases, which include the possible ways a Pythagorean description of motion could have been given, form two sets: It is logically possible either (1) that the parts of space and those of time are not alike, or (2) that they are alike. If (1) they are not alike, either (1a) the parts of time may each have some length, but those of space be unextended; or (1b) it could be the other way around, with points having some least finite extension, but moments having no duration. If (2) space and time are alike, either (2a) the elements of both are without any extension at all, or (2b) the elements of both have some least finite length. [i.e., either $T = 1, S = 1$; or $T = 0, S = 0$.][5]

It is these four assumptions that are used, in order, in the four paradoxes of motion. A table may help to visualize this compactly.

ASSUMPTIONS	PARADOXES BASED ON EACH CASE	
Likeness or Difference in Space and Time Parts	*Size of Points and Moments*	
Case I: Different	Moments are extended; points are not	Bisection

Case II: Different	Points are extended; moments are not	Achilles
Case III: Alike	Neither points nor moments are extended	Arrow
Case IV: Alike	Both points and moments are extended	Stadium

First, going back to the bisection problem, notice that the puzzle assumes that the space between you and the door exit can be divided without limit: for both Zeno and the Pythagoreans, this was thought to mean that spatial points had no extension. At the same time, however, when Zeno said, "It takes some time to go through each point of space," he was assuming that the moments of time all have some "length" to them, so that an infinite time would result if an infinite number of moments were added together. The contradiction comes from applying to *space* the Pythagorean postulate, That any continuous quantity can be bisected, while applying to *time* the other Pythagorean theorem, That a continuous quantity consists of a finite number of separate parts in series. (Arithmetically, since the points of space have no extension, hence equal zero, adding them together will not produce a sum greater than zero. But, since the moments of time are enduring, any sum of them will be greater than zero. If motion is now described as a ratio of distance to time, s/t, we get the stationary result, 0/t.)

With the Achilles, the opposite assumptions hold. When he says Achilles can *never* overtake the tortoise, Zeno is evidently talking about a time that can be bisected indefinitely, and that is therefore made up of unextended moments; but he is assuming that some finite interval of space is passed through in each moment of time. In this case, every motion turns out to have an infinite velocity, for the ratio of distance over time (s/t) is s/0. Aristotle thought the Achilles paradox "childish," because "it is evident that the space is divisible in the same way as the time." But Aristotle did not understand that Zeno was using the Achilles paradox to destroy one of the set of logically possible Pythagorean explanations. (As a matter of fact, the first two cases that Zeno considered were never seriously entertained as scientific hypotheses until our own century; but a Pythagorean *could* have held them, and Zeno therefore included them in his over-all attack.) [6]

The assumptions in the paradox of the arrow are evident and straightforward enough: if neither the elements of space nor those of time have any extension whatever, the ratio of distance to time will always be 0/0—a meaningless expression. The reason the Arrow problem raises such fundamental difficulties is that we often want to divide space and time into knife-edge moments and states: a long and interesting chapter in the history of mathematics has to do with the various strategies that have been tried for fitting these sections back together into a continuous whole again.

Finally, the fourth problem, with its chariots in relative motion, assumes that points and moments have some extension, but a minimal one, so that they are *extended but indivisible*. (If they were not indivisible, then by repeated bisection they could be divided down to nothing, and we would once more have the case of the arrow.) But the assumption of indivisibility breaks down at once when we see that the fact of relative motion makes it necessary to divide moments or points into smaller parts, unless we accept Zeno's own, "So twice the time is equal to all of the time." It is typical of Zeno that his word for the objects moving in the stadium is *onkos*, a bulk or volume; an ordinary audience would at once imagine carts or chariots as the things intended; but *onkos* was also a Pythagorean technical term for "solid," and the more sophisticated reader might picture the vast stadium with diminutive Pythagorean points as the moving *onkoi*. [7]

Zeno's four paradoxes do very nicely what he set out to do. They show with logical rigor that something is wrong with the Pythagorean set of notions about motion, space, and time. And although they did not persuade later thinkers to accept the conclusions of Parmenides, Zeno's demonstration made them admire formal logic and see new potentialities in its application. A further effect, naturally, was to make later thinkers try to reformulate the Pythagorean notions in a way that would avoid the inconsistencies Zeno had shown. This took several forms:

the notion of separate points was given up in favor of pure continuity by Anaxagoras, arithmetic treated as entirely distinct from geometry by Aristotle, a sharp distinction of physical and mathematical "divisibility" introduced as a foundation of the atomic theory.[8]

VIII. EMPEDOCLES

Too Much Imagination

Heads without bodies,
Trunks without limbs,
Falling down awful heights of Air . . .
EMPEDOCLES

Empedocles of Acragas, which is a city on the south coast of Sicily, was an important doctor as well as a poet and philosopher. To account for change, without assuming that "something comes from nothing," he introduced the idea of a plurality of "elements," which mix in different ratios but themselves remain unchanged. However, both the form and content of his poetry suggest that Empedocles was more interested in interpreting the vivid world of our senses than in finding some other reality behind appearance. He had an imagination able to combine the most divergent notions—so much so that many later readers have been unable to appreciate the originality of his work. Those of his ideas that were most philosophically influential were his notion of a plurality of "elements" and a theory of natural selection in biology. But what is most interesting is the way his work combines the keen observation of Greek poetry and medicine with imaginative speculation.

ONE OF the most important human needs, Whitehead has written, is the need for adventure. Encountering the minds of persons different enough from ourselves to be stimulating is a mild case in point, whether they are from our own or another time. Whitehead does not say anything about encountering someone as different from ourselves as the proverbial man from Mars, but I suppose he would have thought it an excellent experience, because of the new possibilities of behavior and thought such a being would reveal to us. In many ways, Empedocles, the ancient Greek doctor who lived about 440 B.C. in Acragas, strikes me as being as different from our modern world as any Martian. He is so different that scholars have found it hard to believe in him—let alone appreciate him. Perhaps the poets have, once or twice, come closer. There is Matthew Arnold's poem *Empedocles on Aetna*, based on the legend that Empedocles, wishing to strengthen the belief that he was a god, committed suicide by leaping into the volcanic Mount Aetna. And, in a more serious vein, half a century after Arnold, William Ellery Leonard claimed in the introduction to his translation of Empedocles that in his work he recognized the great cosmological poetry of a Lucretius or a William Blake. Leonard was an exception to the tradition among earlier literary critics who, beginning with Aristotle, have had nothing good to say for Empedocles' poetry.

Empedocles is amazing to a modern reader because of his versatility, his occasional incisiveness, and his normal failure to recognize what we consider the most obvious and necessary of common-sense distinctions. Empedocles had been trained in and contributed to the Greek tradition of medicine in Sicily, admired the Pythagoreans, cured a plague at Selinus, and believed in reincarnation.[1] Empedocles also claimed to be a god, wrote lyric poetry about natural selection, first introduced a precise concept of "element" into science, and described the "first real experiment" in the West. He apparently identified *philosophy* with his own brand of *inorganic chemistry*, which was equal parts analysis and poetry.[2] Empedocles contributed to the fields of philosophy, genetics, literature, chemistry, public-health medicine, scientific method—an innovator in all but mathematics. Perhaps if we had nothing but a list of his discoveries, we would admire him more. Unfortunately, we know a little too much about his work in every case. (This is partly due to the fact that Aristotle, himself a doctor's son and a biologist, repeatedly quotes Empedocles, though he is repeatedly irritated by him.)[3]

In trying to understand Empedocles, I began by wondering why he expressed his thought in an imaginative but precise meter and imagery which is almost that of modern lyric poetry. I went on to wonder why he overlooked arguments that seemed obvious to his critics, and why there are such opposed judgments about his skill in science. My own notion is that, partly consciously and perhaps partly unaware, Empedocles held a view different from any other philosopher of the time about the relation of appearance to reality. This may be wrong, but it is a way of directing attention to something that has real philosophic interest and that I do find in his poetry.

All of the thinkers we have met so far have emphasized the great difference that separates *reality* and *appearance*. In various ways, they have sought insight into something beyond the ordinary world of touch and sight, whether underlying permanence or perpetual fiery flow. If there is such a difference between what things *are* and what they *seem*, two ways are open to the philosopher. Those who think that what things really are can be discovered by man's reason share the constructive speculation that characterizes the central tradition of Greek thought.[4] The Sophists, later, are representative of the other dissenting group, who agree that things are not what they seem but are skeptical of man's ability to determine what they really are.[5] There is, however, a third possibility: one can deny that there is any deep-hidden reality underlying appearance and argue that truth is to be found in close observation of what we can see or touch or imagine vividly. Someone who takes this standpoint will be less trustful of appeals to mysterious "realities," to highly abstract arguments, than he will be to more vivid items of experience. It may be useful to consider Empedocles' approach in this way.

Following the example of Aristotle and subsequent historians of philosophy, we shall begin our account by looking at Empedocles' discussion of the *arche*, the fundamental principle of all things. Coming after Parmenides and Zeno, Empedocles was willing to adopt their logic to reinforce his own conviction that *real change* requires more kinds of being than one. Given this, we might expect any of a number of things, ranging from some new concept of nature alive to a stolid return to the "four basic kinds of stuff" that was the common-sense of the day. What we find, however, is a fusion of philosophy and chemistry, pleasing to neither chemists nor philosophers. For Empedocles frequently writes that all things are composed from *six* elements: these elements are earth, air, water, fire, love, and hate![6] He takes the attractions and repulsions of things as a fact as direct as our experience that they are hot or cold, moist or dry. Sometimes he personifies all six of his elements as gods, sometimes only the last two.[7] The first four of his kinds of stuff come in particles with determinate shapes and sizes: this is why the Pythagorean discoveries hold, why number applies to nature.[8] The *formula* of a compound—"three parts earth to one of water," for example—determines its qualities and the tightness with which its "molecules" are packed together. These small, indivisible packets of the elements are the "letters" of an alphabet of nature. (Empedocles called them "roots"; "*stoicheia*," "letters," is used in this sense for the first time by Plato.[9]) Since these diverse kinds of elementary particles are of different shapes and sizes, they pack into arrangements of lattices or other designs with "pores" between them; particles that are fine enough can pass through these pores, but they stop larger elementary or compound particles. To show how this happens, Empedocles takes a familiar example:

> As when a man, thinking of a journey through a winter night,
> Kindles a lantern, a shining fire;
> And fits plates to it, which keep out the breath of wind;
> While the light passes through them, being finer,
> And shines across the threshold, unwearying:
> So at that time did fire conceal itself in the pupil of the eye. . . .

Because of its fine particles, this fire can issue from the eye through the pores in the water and tissue. This is a good scientific illustration of the point; it is also typical of Empedocles. He seems to have felt that understanding his pore-and-particle theory partly depends on imagining the golden beam of light, the sharp wind's edge as the threshold is crossed, the dancing lantern in the night.[10]

However, Empedocles did not have any empty space in his system; the pores were filled with a sort of fluid set of smaller particles of other kinds, and thus change occurred by reciprocal displacement, rather than by some sort of motion through a void. And, having appreciated the Eleatics, Empedocles was firm upon this point: empty space would be a pure nothing, imperceptible, impotent.[11] All elements take up space, have a determinate extension of their particles, and have resistance. The status of *aer* which has been hovering between a genuine physical substance and an abstract construct akin to "the boundless," was finally fixed by an experiment of Empedocles' design, which is discussed below.[12]

Philosophically, Empedocles' notion of tightly packed elements seems unsatisfactory, at first. For since the elements are defined by extension and shape, this seems to suppose that there is a common matter that "supports" the qualities we perceive and the shapes we infer. If there is such a common stuff, aren't we again forced, by Parmenides' line of reasoning, to deny the reality of change? But that was what starting with four or six elements instead of one was designed to avoid. Parmenides' logic is inescapable unless we assume that common sense is more trustworthy than highly abstract theory. If, with Empedocles, we do assume this, then we can be *certain* of the fact of change and the diversity of primary qualities in the world. We can be fairly certain (because it is a direct consequence) of a plurality of "roots," and wholly certain (because counting and measuring actually succeed in practice in finding laws and regularities) of some mathematical substructure in nature. But for such abstract generalizations as the arguments of Zeno and Parmenides, we have no test in our own experience that can give comparable certainty: how elements can be *both* extended and indivisible, how common matter taking on diverse shapes can really change, are puzzles for logicians that common sense seems content to let alone.

Even looked at scientifically, as distinct from philosophically, the merits of Empedocles' theory are controversial. The value of his notions of *chemical elements* and *chemical formulas* is indisputable. And yet, his way of determining what elements there are seems unreliable. For, instead of the *analytic* method that we would instinctively choose and expect, Empedocles uses what we might call a *projective* technique: he takes his subjective awareness of his own reactions as a starting point and projects this into the world. For example, the relative violence of hot, cold, dry, and wet seem to him reasons for his choice of earth, air, fire, and water as elements; and his direct feelings of love or hate seem just as elementary, vivid, and real as such physical sensations as hot and cold. Further, when other things attract or repel, one can understand this by thinking that they too must feel as we do when we tend toward or away from persons and things around us. Empedocles would, therefore, think the modern chemist's talk about the "attraction," "capture," "sharing," "giving up" of electrons both good literal description and scientifically respectable; the chemist would rather get along without it.[13] This raises an interesting general question, still much discussed in connection with scientific method. How far should or must a scientist depend on his imagination to supplement and go beyond direct observation? For example, if I judge that "this sugar is soluble in water," am I simply reporting or am I drawing on my memory and imagination? It must be the latter, because "a disposition to dissolve" or "solubility" isn't the sort of property anyone can *observe* until the sugar is actually dissolving in the water. But if judgment and interpretation go well beyond direct observation in such an obvious factual case, where shall we draw the line between fact and fancy? And this is a line we must draw if we want to maintain that "Hydrogen loves Fluorine" is unscientific poetry.

Empedocles' combination of imaginative projection, fondness for mythology, and precise observation led him to attempt to create a great poetic cosmology. He wrote his history of the universe in terms of a great cycle: in "the Sphere," Love is at one time dominant, and all things are attracted to each other and fused together tightly; but then Strife enters and "increases in the limbs of the Sphere," and separation and differentiation of parts and regions begin.[14] The poet continues, with a fusion of scientific insight that rivals Darwin and a mad creation of a world that matches Blake, to explain how, as things became separated, "heads without shoulders, bodies with no limbs"

[73]

appeared and fell (as Leonard translates it) "down awful heights of Air"![15] Love still retains some power, and we picture these various organs meeting and recombining by pure chance in a matrix of monstrous and arbitrary organic collage. There result "men with bulls' heads . . . ," and so on; the minotaurs, centaurs, sphinxes, sirens, and chimeras of Greek mythology now appear as lost species, in what seems to be an account of natural selection.[16] That it is such an account is clear as Empedocles goes on to describe these random combinations: "Of these, most perished, through being unable to assimilate food . . ." Even fewer were able to reproduce their kind. A few that were best adapted were, however, able to reproduce and to survive. Thus chance combination gives the look of reasoned purpose to the beings that survive the screening process of the cosmic age of increasing strife.[17]

Aristotle, as great a biologist as there has ever been, reacted violently to this Empedoclean science in technicolor.[18] He dis-

SIRENS: A BY-PRODUCT OF EMPEDOCLEAN NATURAL SELECTION?

In Empedocles' poem on Nature, when Strife grew strong, the air was filled with headless bodies and bodiless limbs falling down awful heights. But Love, having still some power, united limbs and organs at random as they fell. These Sirens illustrate one result. They embellish an Attic vase now in the National Archaeological Museum in Athens.

[74]

liked mixing poetry and zoology, and after getting the two sorted out, devoted a large part of his introductory lectures on natural philosophy to a defense of purpose in nature as against Empedoclean "chance" or "mechanical necessity."[19] But, as we have noted, and as a look at the source of the *Fragments* attests, Aristotle could not resist an impulse to insert quotations from his predecessor.

Finally, in Empedocles' cosmic epic, there comes about the hostility and separation of all things, when Strife completely rules in the cosmic cycle; but, in this state of total separation, Love once more arises and begins to increase, so that the universe once more becomes organized and unified.[20]

Empedocles' work thus presents new ideas of cosmological cycle and of natural selection, ideas with extraordinary precision and power, in a poetic medium that gives the monsters of myth a status in zoology. The poem, further, presents the subtle stages of organic adaptation through the picture of a gaudy combination-matrix of "heads without bodies," "limbless shoulders," and other such separate specialized organs—which, of course, as Aristotle sourly observes, could only have come into being at all as parts of complete organisms![21]

Elements and evolution do not exhaust the enigma of Empedocles. What place should he be given in the history of experimental science? In explaining respiration, for example, he offers a marvelous image to show that air takes up space and is resistant to other matter. When the lungs are filled, the air in them excludes and holds out the other "elements" that might otherwise rush in: "As when a maiden, taking a bronze tube to the spring, covers the end and dips it in the clear water, the tube is not filled up because of the resistance of the air therein. . ."[22] The maiden and the spring remind one, perhaps, of modern television; science is being made glamorous by the beautiful young laboratory assistant, as irrelevant logically and essential rhetorically as the girls in bathing suits in advertisements for cigarettes are.

But is this science at all? Professor Arthur H. Compton, a Nobel Prize winner for his own experimental work in physics, once told me that he thought this passage was the first account of any controlled scientific experiment designed to establish the corporeality of air. David Furley, a philologist and historian, has recently written a detailed article to show that the passage is rather a poetic simile, which Empedocles need not have thought of as a controlled experiment at all, but simply as a homely model of a familiar organic process.[23] In the light of Empedocles' other work and ideas, both authorities seem right. I think what is described is a hard-headed enough crucial experiment, with special apparatus selected (from the hardware of an ordinary ancient kitchen) to force nature's alphabet to spell out the answer to a particular question; but without the girl, the spring, and the application to breathing, it probably would never have interested Empedocles enough to find its way into his poem concerning nature.

Empedocles' other notions and adventures, such as combining medicine and magic, incorporating Orphic-Pythagorean beliefs about metempsychosis into his system, or accepting "as is only proper" the honors paid him "as to a god," present the same sort of problem in interpretation.[24]

Idiosyncratic as he was in some ways, certain things about Empedocles are characteristic of Greek thought. It is characteristic of the philosophy and science of the classical period that even the idea of evolution is still pictured *within* a view of time as a closed cycle; a genuinely open, emergent time does not appear until much later in Western thought. It is characteristic that the scientist has at once a universal range of interests, sharp powers of observation, and (even in Empedocles, on occasion) respect for clear logical argument. It is also characteristic that what seem to us not only reasonable but inevitable distinctions are not clearly recognized as such, or are not recognized at all.

In his own age, Empedocles had more influence on medicine and biology than on philosophy. Though some of his ideas have remained a permanent philosophic contribution, he is interesting for philosophy today primarily because of the central question his work poses: Are we being realistic or merely arbitrary when we draw sharp lines between subject and object, observer and world observed, science and mythology, experiments performed and experiments imagined? Can we argue, as some modern philosophers have, that man is continuous with the rest of nature, hence that our conscious feeling and thought must have some counterpart, however dim, in the existence of a fish, an amoeba, or even an electron? Should we be satisfied with the knowledge that change and plurality are *actual*, even though we can't out-argue a Zeno who proves that they are unreasonable and, hence, *impossible*?

But even our contemporary philosophers who raise these questions have failed so far to recognize Empedocles as an interesting predecessor. He had too much imagination![25]

IX. DEMOCRITUS AND THE ATOMIC THEORY

Materialism

There is no chance, but all is from necessity.

LEUCIPPUS

Nothing exists but atoms and the void.

DEMOCRITUS

Applying the logic developed in the Eleatic school by Parmenides and Zeno to the ideas of matter that had been formulated by the Milesians, Leucippus and Democritus produced a new philosophy—materialism. Their thesis was that all reality consists of hard indivisible particles, moving and colliding in empty space. This was the first philosophical or scientific statement of the atomic theory. But in this Greek form, the theory is somewhat different from later versions. And it is important not to confuse it with later philosophical ideas or with the theories of twentieth-century atomic physics.

W H E N Democritus of Abdera was a young man, he journeyed to Athens, hoping to talk with Anaxagoras, the leading scientist and philosopher of the circle of artists and intelligentsia that Pericles, the Athenian statesman, had gathered around him. But the eminent older man had no time for a bright young theorist from a foreign city and did not see him. Disappointed, Democritus wrote, "I came to Athens, and no one knew me."[1]

[78]

How different he would find the trip today, where the main approach to the city from the northeast runs past the impressive "DEMOCRITUS NUCLEAR RESEARCH LABORATORY." The name is a reminder that ancient Greece was the original home of the "atomic theory," and that Democritus was its first great developer. It is to variations on the theme of Democritus' ideas that modern science and technology owe much of their spectacular development; and it was atomism that provided the final concepts needed for materialism to appear as a powerful and coherent system of philosophy.[2]

Credit for the invention of this theory is given to a philosopher named Leucippus, but we know almost nothing about him, and it was in the systematic explanation and applications of Democritus that the theory became stabilized and influential.[3]

Democritus of Abdera lived about 400 B.C. He lived at the same time as Socrates, and we are therefore ignoring chronological order when we follow the accustomed practice of discussing him as a pre-Socratic philosopher. But in a way it is entirely reasonable to do so, for Democritus represents the final synthesis of ideas that brought to systematic completion the Milesian effort to understand the underlying material components and mechanisms of nature. Socrates began a revolution in thought by rejecting the claim that science can answer all questions of ethics, human life, and philosophy.

There is something not unlike William James's division of philosophers into "tough- and tender-minded," in the ancient world's contrast of Heraclitus and Democritus as the weeping and laughing philosophers: "Heraclitus weeps, and Democritus laughs, at all things."

Of the events of Democritus' life we know little; the one personal item is his remark quoted above: "I came to Athens and no one knew me"—a clear record of unappreciated genius that has been sympathized with by many a later scholar. Of his thought, we know a good deal, for his atomic theory was criticized extensively by Aristotle and quoted approvingly by Epicurus (whose extensive philosophic "Letter to Herodotus" has been preserved in the medley of lives and opinions in Diogenes Laërtius' book).[4]

The atomic theory as Democritus developed it was a combination of the Milesian science, Eleatic logic, and probably the development of technology that preceded it.[5] Long before Leucippus or Democritus developed the notion of atoms, others had suggested that the physical world is made up of small particles. Empedocles had suggested that each of "the elements" comes in small particles of definite size and shape. This idea in turn traces back to the Pythagorean notion of small "regular solids" as the "molecular parts" of nature. Earlier, the Pythagorean attempt to bring mathematics and physics together by building a physical world out of points led in this same direction. Most important in the background of this theory, however, must have been the use of mechanical models to study natural process, which was introduced by Anaximander. In the model, a natural phenomenon is duplicated by the mechanical interaction of small, separate "parts." Therefore, it is tempting, when one wonders *why* model-building works, to test the hypothesis that the model is like nature because nature, too, is a complex combination of small parts that interact mechanically. This notion gains plausibility when technology shows that mechanisms can perform functions of a much more complex kind than earlier thinkers had imagined.

The essential ideas of Greek atomism as a physical theory are four: first, that matter comes in separate, smallest particles which are "uncuttable" (*atoma-* "unable to be cut"); second, that an empty space exists, in which these particles move; third, that the atoms differ only in shape and volume; fourth, that all change is the result of transfer of momentum by the moving atoms and such transfer can occur only by contact—there is, of course, no "action at a distance" in this scheme.[6]

The atoms of this theory are small, hard chunks of being (which, like the One Being of Parmenides, are indivisible, because there are no inner veins of not-being along which they could be "cut"). They have none of the "secondary" qualities—color, flavor, and so on—that we experience, but only shape and extension. (The idea of a qualitatively neutral matter is finally clearly formulated here.)

The atoms differ from each other, singly and in their combinations, "in shape, position, and order." Thus, A differs from B in shape; N from Z in position; AZ from ZA in order.[7] These particles come in all sorts of shapes, for, as Democritus argues, "There is no reason why they should have one shape rather than another." They have always been in motion, and as they move about they collide; sometimes they "interlock" and hold together; sometimes they "rebound" from a collision.[8] (The Roman poet Lucretius, trying to present a popular, imaginative picture of atomism, pictures "hooks" on the atoms that fasten them together.) All change is ultimately, therefore, change of place and transfer of momentum among these hard particles, and all objects are aggregates packed together in more and less stable patterns.

This notion of all change as a transfer of motion or change of "packing" among differently shaped, hard particles offered an immediate and satisfying explanation of many phenomena that physics wanted to explain.

First of all, consider condensation and rarefaction, changes that have continued to play a central part in physics ever since Anaximenes. If density depends on the relative amount of empty space between the particles of a substance, it is easy to see how pressure leads to condensation, while bombardment by small "fire" particles will spread the atoms apart, leading to rarefaction. And, in principle at least, science has found no more satisfying explanation of differences and changes in density.

The Ionian accounts of the formation of the world by a "spinning vortex," in which different elements collect in different levels because of their respective mass, worked excellently when the vortex was reinterpreted as made up of many fine particles. It could be argued, with close analogies to experience, that collisions would tend to make the smaller atoms "rebound" further, gradually forcing them to the outside. Empedocles' analysis of "pores and effluences" could be taken over, and was much more satisfactory when the pores were genuinely "empty spaces" in latticeworks of atoms. Anaximander's "models" were, of course, the strongest argument in favor of this new approach to physical reality; for the atomic theory could explain the fact that nature behaved like a machine because it really was a complex mechanism.

So far, the new theory could synthesize and improve on all of the developments of physics up to its inception. There seemed no sharp limit to the phenomena it could explain. In principle, the atomic theorists believed that physics was identical with philosophy: that to the question, What is being?, science had finally found the answer, "In reality, nothing exists but atoms and the void."

The logical and philosophical background of this new theory played a crucial part in the emergence of atomism as a systematic materialistic philosophy, rather than a specialized physical theory. The scientists of Ionia and the logicians of Elea were almost equally responsible for this. Tracing the line back to Parmenides, the reasoning leads directly to atomism, in the following way:

1. Parmenides had shown to the satisfaction of the atomic theorists that the existence of change, or even the appearance of change, required that being be many, not one; and, if many, divided by not-being into its separate parts;

2. But common sense and Ionian science made it clear that "nature" does change, if not really, in some abstract sense, at least apparently;

3. Therefore, reality must be divided into many parts; and not-being must exist as their separator.

(As a matter of fact, this line of argument, which Democritus accepts, had already been outlined by Melissus of Samos, a philosopher who followed the ideas and methods of Zeno and Parmenides, but Melissus had gone on to reject the conclusion as absurd, since it asserted the existence of not-being. Leucippus and Democritus, on the other hand, accepted the conclusion as actually true, since it was a necessary condition for the appearance of change.)

This Eleatic ancestry also shows in the clear, rigorous logic by which the characteristics of atoms and space are deduced. The atoms are in fact small chunks of Parmenidean "being," and each one has the properties of *indivisibility, homogeneity, qualitative neutrality* that Parmenides had ascribed to his One Being. If they were otherwise, the atoms would necessarily have some not-being within them, and so would be, not single particles of matter, but collections of several parts. Empty space is Eleatic not-being: it is defined as having no resistance, density, or cohesion: it cannot, therefore, *do* or *transmit* anything, since "nothing comes from nothing." Any interaction must be the result of two units of being coming together.

The theory thus synthesizes earlier traditions into a new philosophy that has methods and logical rules of its own. The way to understand a subject matter, it assures us, is to analyze every subject matter into its least parts and to find their pattern of combination. If the theory is right, there will always be such parts, and phenomena can always be explained and duplicated by study of their mechanical interaction.

The proponents of the atomic theory further claimed that it could be used to explain medicine, psychology, ethics, and the theory of knowledge, as well as physics and chemistry. In these extensions it sometimes ran into difficulties—for example, in ethics its idea of absolute determinism was hard to adapt to the notion of freedom of choice. But it also had some remarkable successes. For example, in medicine, the doctors and surgeons of that day found that the atomists' idea of treating the body as a complex machine fitted their own practical knowledge of the body's mechanics. It was clear that the workings of the muscular and skeletal system, the ebb and flow of blood (they did not, of course, know of its circulation), the effects of damage to the brain could all be mechanically explained. The processes and functions involving an interaction of the mind and body were obviously more complex. For example, there were patients who complained of pain, though physically there was nothing wrong with them; their trouble had a psychological origin. It was not clear then—and still is not clear today—how such phenomena as these could be reduced to mechanical explanation. But that they could, somehow, be so reduced the atomists were certain.

The old indecisions about *psyche*, reflected in attempts to make the soul *pneuma* or *aer*—but still to hold religious views that would make it immortal—or to make *psyche* a part of the regular order of the physical world—but still have it initiate motion by a kind of "free decision" to act—had found a decisive resolution. The self was no exception to the total structure of reality; it was corporeal and part of nature, and only illusion and wishful thinking had led mankind to believe in its freedom or immortality. The soul, because of its sensitivity and activity, was supposed to be made up of particularly small, mobile atoms (probably spherical to account for their mobility), which responded by inner movement to the impacts of sensation from the outer world.[9] When, after a disturbance, the soul moved back into equilibrium, its motion was amplified and transmitted to the body, and also was transmuted into consciousness and thought.

The theory provided a new tool for exploring the mechanism of sensation. Since all "action" is the result of contact, sense perception was explained as the impression made on the senses by atoms from outside. Visible surfaces, for example, radiated atomic films that moved through the air and struck the eye. The clarity of vision depended both on the strength of this constant radiation and on the state of the medium. If the air atoms between the observer and the object were moving violently, the image would be distorted. Even if it were not moving violently, there would be some friction. The corners of the film traveling from a square tower would be knocked off; the eye would receive the impression of a round tower. For transmission and distortion of visual images and sound, for an analysis of touch and taste, the theory gave new precision to accounts of sensation and illusion. Philosophers have never forgotten the new sharpness which this application gave to accounts of the work of the senses, and of the different "perspectives" that objects present to us under different conditions of observation.[10]

Consistent with their philosophical position, the atomic theorists treated so-called secondary qualities (warmth, weight, color, taste), not as objective properties of things, but as a subjective contribution by the observer. All of these exist only "by convention," writes Democritus. "By convention"—here is the opposite of existing "in reality" or "by nature." The phrase extends the notion of social custom and law—distinctively human constructions—to the senses of the observer who clothes the neutral outer world, which consists of "nothing but atoms and the void," with its apparent qualities. There are some early and rather unsatisfactory suggestions in Democritus' fragments of the way in which different "colorless" or "black-and white" configurations of atoms are perceived as having color.

In the field of ethics, the price of consistency seems rather high. Since all events are the mechanical result of physical chains of causality (one of the two surviving fragments of Leucippus

says, "Nothing occurs by chance, but all is from necessity"),
there is no place for human freedom in this scheme. Neither is
there any way for a purpose to be explained, and there is no
assurance, on the basis of this theory, that observations from the
past will have any relevance in the future: the theory will accept
only direct observation as evidence, and the future can never be
directly observed. On the other hand, the theory was an excellent
antidote to the superstitious component of the then current religious notions.

Various sayings, attributed to Democritus, show how atomism was able logically to connect itself with ethical recommenda-
tions. According to these, the soul will either be disturbed, so
that its motion affects the body in a violent way, or it will be
at rest, in which case it regulates thoughts and actions harmoni-
ously. Freedom from disturbance is the condition that causes
human happiness, and this is the ethical goal. A society in which
individual men meet and associate like atoms will be stabilized
when collisions are kept to a minimum.

It may seem strange to find, in the ethical fragments of
Democritus, statements about what we *ought* to choose or to do,
for the theory leaves no place for human freedom of choice.
Sometimes this problem is met by saying that because of our
ignorance, we seem to have freedom, since we do not know all
of the small contributing causes that made a given decision inevitable. In the light of our illusion, we make moral judgments,
administer justice, and feel responsible for our own destinies.
(To dismiss human freedom, in order to keep the explanation
of reality simple and precise, is not satisfying to those for whom
ethics is the most important part of philosophy. Later, Epicurus
and his school added the notion that the atoms sometimes
"swerve" unpredictably, in an attempt to give freedom and
chance some foundation in natural science.)

Ethics and politics based on an atomist philosophy are clear
and realistic; it is tempting to develop them in this way. Nevertheless, throughout the history of Western thought, no one has
satisfactorily reconciled his notion of human nature with rigorous physical necessity. Materialism as a philosophy, based on
atomism as its scientific application, has remained ever since
Greek times an important and attractive speculative synthesis.
There was a period of eclipse during the Middle Ages, because

materialism so evidently went contrary to the Christian religion, but there have been three different versions of the theory: the Greek original, the later Roman adaptation of Epicurus and his school, and our contemporary interpretation. The following table shows where the Greek original agrees with and where it differs from these two later versions, our ordinary notion of the atomic theory being actually a composite of elements from all three phases. What is particularly interesting about these three variations on a philosophic theme is the different excellences of each version: Democritus' atomism is, of the three, the most clear and rigorous in its logic and its deductions; Epicurus' atomism is less interested in logical elegance than in the *ethical* implications of atomism, and the theory is reconstructed around these ethical applications; our contemporary concern is less with the logical rigor, or the moral impact of our theory, than with the *physical* applications for description and control. We may now be moving toward a theory that will combine the excellences of each of these three.[11]

Greek	*Roman*	*Contemporary*
Atoms are hard pure being.	Same.	Atoms are soft.
Necessity of causality.	Atoms swerve unpredictably.	Probability, rather than necessity or spontaneity.
Atoms have volume, but weight is a derivative property.	Atoms have weight as a primary property.	Atoms have mass as a primary property.
Weight results from centrifugal force in a cosmic vortex.	Weight results from a tendency of atoms to fall downward through space.	Weight results from gravitational fields.
The basic quantity is a unit of momentum.	Same.	Units of force are basic.

Greek	Roman	Contemporary
Space equals pure not-being.	Same.	Space equals a field which conducts as well as insulates; it has some positive properties.
Atoms are mathematically and physically indivisible.	Atoms are physically, but not mathematically indivisible.	Atoms are both physically and mathematically divisible.
The strongest points of the theory are its simplicity and clear logic.	The strongest points are its ethical implications.	The strongest points are its experimental confirmations in physics and chemistry.
Strict conservation of matter and energy.	Conservation of matter; but the "swerve" precludes strict conservation of energy.	Conservation of mass and energy taken together, but of neither separately.

We could extend this list considerably; but these points bring out, perhaps, the blend of incisive logic and complete objectivity that make Democritus' theory unique. Notice, in particular, how the Roman version muddles its ideas with imaginative picture-thinking, and how the modern loses the sharpness that made the classical theory particularly clear and satisfying. Four more specific criticisms might also be noted here as suggesting limits to the theory—and criticisms continue to be made.[12]

First, there is the criticism that in an atomist's universe, there can be *no theory* at all.[13] For to claim that a theory is generally true and that people should believe it, presupposes a theorist who has examined the evidence and chosen the best explanation from among alternatives. But if "all is from necessity," including all psychological processes, what any man thinks is simply a necessary, mechanical outcome of previous conditioning. The objection, notice, is not that someone who believes the atomic theory is *wrong*, but only that he is inconsistent in holding that this belief can represent more than a personal reflection of his past experience and that he, therefore, has no right to say that anyone else ought to agree with him.

Second, there is the question of whether the so-called secondary qualities can really be relegated to existence "by convention."[14] To explain how a black-and-white world can appear colored, for example, scientists have devised excellent laboratory experiments in which patterns built from colorless elements show how the observer perceives color. But it is sheer Milesian absentmindedness to think that this explains how I perceive color. The scientist, treating his experiment as a model of the brain, forgets his own part in it. He can show, granted, that a pattern of colorless impulses can look colored, but he has not shown how the observer knows it has this color. What, in the model of the brain, corresponds to the experimenter in the laboratory, who "sees" the color emerge from the neutral pattern?

Third, there is the question of whether "empty space" is an intelligible scientific concept at all.[15] If like Democritus we treat it as pure not-being, then can we say that it "separates" the atoms that move about in it? This third objection does not apply, as the first two do, so directly to our modern theory as to the two older versions.

Fourth, there is the objection that there is our own awareness of our freedom, responsibility, and sensitivity to value and purpose. Here the atomic theory may be in the same position that Eleatic philosophy confronted with its denial of motion. Even if ultimately these things are an illusion, isn't it necessary for an adequate theory to show how it is possible for the illusion to appear? And can this be done by any theory that supposes at the outset that there is no place in reality for freedom or value?

Perhaps the first atomic theorists were too optimistic in thinking that their ideas could answer all of the questions of philosophy. In the following chapters, we will see how a new attention to the human observer led to the different speculative synthesis of Platonic idealism and the final attempt of Aristotle to combine Platonism and materialism, which ends the Hellenic epoch of Greek thought.

As a final comment on the relation of technology to the atomic theory, I should like to note that the atomic theory has always been useful when applied to experience. It is a particularly useful view for the inventor or engineer who wants to get a set of mechanical parts to work together automatically and perform some useful function. Would the theory have seemed plausible and remained so intellectually important in a culture with no technology to give it imaginative plausibility and concrete illustration? One would certainly think not, and the fact that in ancient India atomism was thought of as a theoretical position but discarded as implausible matches this expectation.[16] But until recently we had no notion of the true ancient Greek attitude toward technological gadgetry. Classical literature offered several references deprecating arts and crafts and almost no passages describing inventions or equipment. On the basis of this evidence, we would have had to picture the classical atomist as a very strange human being, able to be as fascinated by abstract mechanical design as we are but without any concrete experience with mechanisms.

New archeological evidence shows, however, that by the time of Leucippus and Democritus there was enough use of mechanism to make the analogy of ancient and modern atomic theorists plausible. Factors partly of custom, regulating what themes were or were not the sort of thing to put in book form, partly of supply and demand, determining what available written works would be best sellers and hence recopied and preserved, operated to cause a gap in the older picture. For a clear, demonstrated tradition of scientific apparatus, we are still about fifty years short of closing the gap between Hellenistic and Hellenic periods. But for the discovery of a number of more modest devices that show exactly what we want to know, 1957 in the Athenian Agora proved a decisive year.[17]

Aristotle in his *Constitution of Athens*, itself not recovered until the turn of the present century, describes the equipment and procedure used in impaneling jurors and deciding cases in court. His description has overtones of a Rube Goldberg dream. In 1957, archeologists first discovered ancient equipment that confirms Aristotle's statements. Let us look at one or two of these applications of mechanical ingenuity to insure legal impartiality. The American voting machine will be seen to have an interesting Athenian ancestor, both in the problem necessitating its invention and the lever-gear-and-wheel solutions.

AN ANCIENT SECRET BALLOT:
ATHENIAN JURY BALLOTS

These ballots show how the Athenians used their ingenuity to insure secret votes in jury trials. The wheel-shaped ballots look identical, but their hubs are different: some solid and some hollow. A solid hub stood for acquittal, a hollow one for conviction. To cast his vote, a juror, holding a ballot between thumb and fingers in each hand, dropped the one representing his decision into the official box and the other into a discard bin. As a further precaution, the official box had a shaped slot in its cover which admitted only one ballot at a time. (Photograph courtesy of Agora Excavations, American School of Classical Studies at Athens.)

AN ATHENIAN LOTTERY MACHINE *(Kleroterion)*

Although we tend to think of the ancient Athenians as men who spent their days in high-minded discussion, they were in fact flamboyant, passionate people. This is an allotment machine invented to make the selection of juries random, and so prevent bribery in the courts. The tickets (see small photo) fitted into the slots of the backboard shown; each was inscribed with the citizen's name and a letter indicating his place of residence. Drawing of black and bronze balls determined which rows of tickets would, and which would not, serve on juries for that session. When the custom of paying jurors began, many who had previously been apathetic became eager to serve the city. (Photograph courtesy of Agora Excavations, American School of Classical Studies at Athens.)

A secret ballot was essential, if jurors were not to be criticized, intimidated, or assassinated for voting the wrong way. And a single ballot for each juror was similarly essential if someone with a dozen extra ballots up his sleeve was to be prevented from dropping them all in the box. The Greeks devised voting tokens to meet the first requirement. Identical in appearance—round wheels, with short shafts sticking out at each side—were these "pebbles" (a name preserved from a simpler time) used in voting. They differed only in that the shaft of one was solid, that of the other hollow: the juror was required to hold his tokens with thumb and finger over the shafts, so that no one else could see the difference. (A further refinement is still not wholly understood: the clerk was required to put the two ballots "on a lampstand" from which they were picked up, in the manner just described, by the juror.) Second, to insure that only a single vote be cast, the voting cask had a top with a slot exactly designed to admit only one disk-and-shaft token. The essential principle of the coin-operated slot-machine or telephone has thus an ancient Athenian ancestry. A special tally board was used to count the ballots, and a courtroom water clock officially measured pleading time.[18]

The Greeks took it as a practical axiom that, if anyone knew who the specific jurors would be, no case would be impartially decided. To rule out the possibility of coercion a splendid selection-by-lot mechanism had been invented and mass-produced: twenty were required in preparing for a day in court. So far as I know, no actual traces of the other courtroom devices have been found: a hundred hoppers holding acorns, each lettered from A to L; colored staves used to route jurymen to the courtroom where they were allocated; tokens entitling jurors to payment on surrender to the court; some way of standardizing fractions of a day that allowed for case presentation as between the day-lengths of December and July. But even without these, the documents and finds to date confirm the philosophically interesting hint: that the Greek world, at the time of the atomic theory, had enough mechanical ingenuity and gadgetry to give some concrete content to the vision of reality as a large congeries of small indivisible wheels, slots, and shafts in some magnificent machine.

⌂⌂⌂⌂⌂⌂⌂⌂⌂⌂⌂⌂⌂⌂⌂⌂⌂⌂⌂⌂⌂⌂⌂⌂⌂⌂⌂⌂

ATHENS

The School of Greece

W H E N Socrates went about the Agora asking questions about
what constituted human excellence, he found many experts; each
was a specialist who knew some particular art or craft—poetry,
politics, pottery-making—and each expert tended to be satisfied
with his own knowledge. Only under Socratic questioning did
it become clear that wisdom in some specialized area cannot
adequately answer questions about final goals and values. Such
questions were of importance to all of human activity, but
refused to be put into some tidy compartment where one could
hunt up the appropriate expert and copy down his answer.

After two centuries of philosophical exploration had been
carried on, as we have seen, at the boundaries of the Greek world,
Athens rose to her period of greatest brilliance, and it is there
that the second part of our story of Greek thinkers takes place.[1]
During the fifth century, Athens emerged not only as the capital
of Greece but as the center of an unparalleled level of culture
and creativity. No other Western city has ever rivaled her excellence.

This creative expansion began after the defeat of Persia in
479 B.C. Her naval power enabled Athens to build an empire
in the islands of the Aegean Sea; expanding commerce made
her a central shipping and marketing center and brought increasing economic prosperity. Incomparable new temples rose on the
Acropolis to replace the old shrines that the Persians had destroyed. The theater was the scene of plays by Aeschylus,
Sophocles, Euripides, and Aristophanes. Sculpture had Phidias
and his associates. Scientific history, oratory, coin-design, pottery

[93]

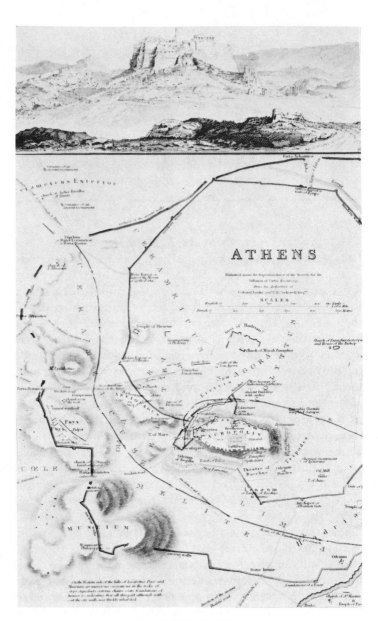

CLASSICAL ATHENS

This map of ancient Athens includes some Roman antiquities. (Map Collection, Yale University Library.)

[94]

—in every field Athens reached a new high point. And along with military, business, and artistic growth went the development of Athenian philosophy.

This extraordinary cultural explosion gave the rise of philosophy in Athens the background of adventure that new advances seem to need.[2] It was a city where everything was exciting, and where all new developments met together. Political experiments, moving from an older aristocratic structure to a new town-meeting type of democracy, kept the Athenian citizen excited and engaged; commercial expansion, as a great mercantile center, added to the sense of excitement, of activity and innovation. The defeat of Athens by Sparta, which ended the Peloponnesian war in 404 B.C., did not stop Athenian artists and writers. Both Plato and Aristotle made their contributions in the following century, while drama and sculpture went on with the same excellence as before.

The increasing prosperity and class mobility of Athenian society was like a magnet, attracting artists and thinkers. The Athenian leader Pericles gathered a circle of authors, sculptors, and poets around him, his patronage increasing the attractiveness. To Athens there came for the first time acquaintance with Ionian science at first hand, in the person of Anaxagoras, a brilliant young astrophysicist whom Pericles invited.[3] To Athens there came also the Sophists, that group of traveling teachers of rhetoric and law, who were distinctly limited in their patience with "impractical speculation" but startlingly effective in their tutorial training for young men eager to get ahead.[4] The meeting of science and sophistry in Athens led to Socrates' concern with the nature of the human self, which revolutionized the course of Greek thought.[5] The Athens of Socrates with its new artistic frontiers was the background against which philosophy took on systematic form at the hands of Plato and his student Aristotle.[6]

The problem for the earlier Greek philosophers had been one of insight and radical innovation. In Athens, nature no longer played a crucial first-hand role in daily life, since technology had brought a new independence from the immediate demands of natural environment. The tides of the market had thus become as relevant as those of the sea; the torch and water clock as influential a measure of time as the circling of the stars; the bath and shaded portico moderated the violence of the seasons for the city-dweller.[7] Thanks to the work of the Ionian and Italian pioneers, the natural world and the abstract world of form were no longer hidden beneath a fog of tradition, waiting to be glimpsed for the first time. Bit by bit, new breaks with custom and new moments of vivid insight had illuminated this unknown domain, as science, mathematics, astronomy, technology, formal logic were discovered. What was now needed was an extension and consolidation. A constant evidence of this must have been Athens itself, where specialization had separated "speculation" in its business and in its intellectual sense in a way that was certainly not true at the time of Thales. Athenian politics was the resultant of many special interest groups. Central leadership, except for two decades under Pericles' direction, was never adequate to the task of holding together the centrifugal forces of commercial advance or of harnessing the new cultural achievements effectively.

The first major extension in the scope of philosophy came when Socrates observed that, in their concern with the outer world of nature or the outer world of practical advantage, the scientists and teachers up to his day had neglected the human observer. Socrates recognized the difficulty and importance of understanding human nature, with its peculiarly complex self and its almost paradoxical awareness of life's short duration and vision of immortality. From Socrates on, Greek philosophy never forgot that "the world of reality" which it needed to explain must not only include the observable physical order but must also account for the observer. It must also give some responsible explanation of how the impersonal concourse of physical fact and the engaged human pursuit of value could exist in a common reality together.

The great Athenian philosophers, Plato and Aristotle, were constantly aware that reality has many dimensions and that exclusive attention to one dimension makes specialization possible. Other philosophers have usually been far less comprehensive than Plato and Aristotle in their notion of the extent of the reality they must comprehend. This is true not only of the earliest times but in the medieval and modern periods as well. New insight into any one aspect of reality demands extraordinary genius and originality. Athens itself was a setting in which philosophy could at the same time share the adventure, optimism, and creativity of the other arts and be constantly reminded by the vivid achievements in each domain that there must be room for such divergent areas as theater, market, Acropolis, and school in the final system of reality.

This rise of specialization made philosophers aware of a new place for philosophy. Of course, it was necessary to expand the field, including new questions about things and areas that the earlier philosophers had not asked. But it was equally important for philosophy to fit the many specializations together in some coherent plan. Poets, merchants, politicians, athletes, doctors, each was concerned exclusively with one dimension of reality. Philosophy was responsible for their integration. The great educational inventions of Plato and Aristotle were partly a response to this demand. The Athenians were experiencing one of our own most urgent and pressing problems: how to communicate and cooperate across narrow specialized fields without giving up the value of specialization.[8]

Only the briefest stay in modern Athens is needed for it to become plainly evident that ancient Athens did indeed offer its philosophers unforgettable lessons in the importance and vitality of the several worlds—of commerce, art, religion, politics—that came together in the city sometimes in cooperation but often in collision.

On the southern slope of the Acropolis, the Theater of Dionysus still stands.[9] From any seat, beginning with the handsome stone chairs reserved for religious officials, whose offices were carved into each, stretching on up to the top tier, where seats were free to develop popular support for the theater, you can imagine the chorus bouncing across the stage, as Aristophanes in his comedy *The Clouds* makes fun of the new ideas that he finds unwelcome importations; or, with a change of mood, you can imagine the Furies pursuing Orestes to his final trial; or the chorus of Trojan Women, as Euripides adapts history to comment on Athenian foreign policy; or Oedipus about to "make dark things plain." In this city, philosophers could not ignore, fate, myth, imagination, and whatever kind of truth and power reside in poetry.

THE THEATER OF DIONYSUS

This theater saw the productions of the plays of Aeschylus, Sophocles, Euripides, and Aristophanes. Its ruins can still be visited on the south slope of the Acropolis. In the front rows religious and civic dignitaries sat in reserved stone thrones with backs; in the front row center was the throne reserved for the priest of Dionysus, patron god of the theater. (Photograph courtesy of Embassy of Greece, Press and Information Service.)

On the opposite side of the Acropolis, at the foot of the north slope, are the Temple of Hephaistos and the ancient Agora.[10] The world of the Agora is public, competitive, practical—a center of crafts and trade, where coins, weights, standardized measures, clocks, money-changers' tables try to channel competition within the limits of a public world where business ethics hold sway. It is also a world of gadgetry, infinite inventiveness expressed in new tools for doing things from wine cooler to jury-selecting machine.[11] It is different in texture, sound, significance from the theater altogether: decrees of fate are less heeded than laws of supply and demand, and it is not the mad hallucination of pursuit by Furies that the Orestes of the Agora sees, but rather pursuit by his creditors.

OSTRACISM BALLOTS *(Ostraka)*

*These inscribed pieces of pottery are souvenirs of the rough-and-ready politi-
cal life of Athens. Contests between leaders of rival factions were decided by
vote: the leader receiving most ballots was exiled from the city. The ostraka
in this photograph are inscribed with the names of Aristides, Themistokles,
Kimon, and Pericles. A whole box of ballots found with "Aristides" written
on each in the same handwriting suggests that some ancient political club had
found a way to save the less literate voters trouble. Against this background,
the training the Sophists offered can be seen to have had survival value; it
was not merely a status symbol. (Photograph courtesy of Agora Excavations,
American School of Classical Studies at Athens.)*

Beyond the Agora, past the old Dipylon Gate, the avenue of
the Academy runs westward through the Ceramicus cemetery.
It was once a wide, tree-lined street with memorials along its
length to the Athenian dead; and beyond it, beside a large public
garden and gymnasium, the foundations of Plato's Academy
have been uncovered.[12]

Rising above this city of many aspects, the Acropolis must
have seemed then, as it does now, the embodiment of an ideal,
providing a focus outside of time, ordering and recalling the
pattern of the life below it.[13]

X. ANAXAGORAS

Mind Orders All Things

In one world, things are not cut off
from one another with a hatchet.

ANAXAGORAS

*Anaxagoras' acceptance of Pericles' invitation added a young
scientist and philosopher to the brilliant circle of artists and
statesmen in Athens.[1] Anaxagoras contributed three new ideas
to Greek philosophy. First, he developed the view that matter is
a continuum. This is one way to escape Zeno's paradoxes, since
it gives both space and time the property of infinite divisibility.
Second, he presented a new concept of mind and its place in the
cosmic scheme, maintaining that although all other things mix
together, mind remains pure. This was not yet a mind-matter
dualism, but it was an important philosophic contribution.
Third, Anaxagoras formulated a new way of relating these two
dimensions, using mind as the motive power that sets matter in
motion.*

A N A T I V E of Clazomenae, Anaxagoras advanced the theory
that the heavenly bodies are stones, kept revolving around the
earth by their rapid motion. The idea was, apparently, fairly
widely known and considered ridiculous—How could there be
stones up in the sky? But, in 467 B.C., when a tremendous
meteorite fell in Sicily, at Aegospotami, this seemed tangible
proof that there was something to be said for the young man's
strange theories, and he was given credit, in some quarters, for

having predicted the meteorite. Probably it was this event that made Pericles select this young Ionian—still in his twenties—as the "consulting scientist" for his Athenian group of cultural leaders.[2]

For thirty years, Anaxagoras lived in Athens until, as Pericles' political fortunes declined, an accusation of impiety was lodged against Anaxagoras forcing him to withdraw to Lampsacus. The various biographical anecdotes we have of him give a picture of a research scientist who had very limited patience with people or social commitments that interrupted his work. We know that he talked with Pericles, with Euripides, with an enthusiastic Athenian named Archelaus who was later to found a school of scientists in Athens. On the other hand, Socrates—then a young man and fascinated by the new Ionian ideas—seems never to have met him; and when Democritus came to Athens, Anaxagoras had no time to see him.[3] Nevertheless, in spite of this personal aloofness, his ideas in a popularized form attracted general attention in the city, and the new "science," with its challenge to tradition, provoked opposition and discussion.

Anaxagoras' ideas are a formulation of the insights into the continuity of changing process that Heraclitus expressed epigrammatically. He also extended Ionian science from its exclusive concern with matter and its motions to a broader field of inquiry that included mind, as well as matter, and tried to explain the relation between them. These ideas of mind, of matter, and of their relationship were the central contributions of Anaxagoras to the history of Greek philosophy. For the first time, we can see, looking back, an anticipation of the dualism of matter and mind[4] that has been a central problem in Western thought from the late Roman period to the present day. Anaxagoras himself did not hold the very sharp mind-matter distinction that emerged in later thought: his concept of mind was still, in some ways, too material, his concept of matter too spiritual, for them to fall into sharp opposition with no bridge between them.

In his reformulation of Heraclitus' intuition that "all things flow," Anaxagoras was careful to meet the logical difficulties raised by Parmenides and Zeno. Matter is continuous: it is not built of separate points or particles; it moves by flowing, not by jumping from one point to the next. Anaxagoras' matter is a mingling flow of qualities, not an icelike extended "stuff" that "supports" qualities. If everything were really such a spatially extended, supporting stuff, change could not be real. Whereas the atomists were to allow for change by having not-being— pure space—as well as being in their system. Empedocles seemed to run into a logical contradiction. His four roots differed in their shapes and sizes, and yet those shapes and sizes were shapes and sizes of some stuff common to all the roots. Anaxagoras avoided this difficulty.

Finally, impressed by Parmenides' statement that "nothing can come from nothing," Anaxagoras held that matter changes only through a different mixing of qualities which all things share. There is never a sudden bursting into being of something that was nothing just before. Instead there are changes in intensity of the mingled qualities that flow from one place to another. The qualities themselves, once they have separated out of the primordial state when "all things were together," are conserved, not created nor destroyed.

It is a subtle analysis, and it seems unlikely that his Athenian colleagues were able to understand it. At any rate, when Athenian scientists defended materialism, they introduced a much simpler concept of matter than Anaxagoras' own.

Let us now consider the Eleatic objections Anaxagoras avoided in a bit more detail. If matter, space, and time are defined as both continuous (therefore indefinitely divisible) and discrete (made up of a finite set of successive points or other smallest parts), there is bound to be, as Zeno's paradoxes show, some logical flaw in the theory. Anaxagoras, however, answered Zeno's critique by giving up the assumption that particles of matter, space, or time are discrete, while keeping continuity and indefinite divisibility. There is no logical problem in assuming a physical world where everything is divisible indefinitely, though there is a need for some new mathematical ideas to express the relation of wholes and parts in such a fluid cosmos.[5] In Anaxagoras' world, motion is like the flow of a river, not the bounding of a grasshopper. We do not need to make an infinite number of jumps from each point to the next to get from here to the door, since there are no such separate points to reach and no spaces between each point and the next to be crossed.

In addition to avoiding Zeno's paradoxes of motion, however, Anaxagoras wanted a world in which *change was real*, and so he had to take into account two of Parmenides' arguments: The first is that if the world is made of a single "stuff," there can be no real change; the second, that "real" change leads to the impossibility of "something coming into existence from nothing." The first of these objections holds whenever the matter that gives things their reality is treated as a glasslike extension, taking up space but having no other qualities of its own. This is the kind of matter found in the atomic theory, where the reality of change can be affirmed only by saying that not-being exists and separates the atoms of being. This concept of matter is also what Empedocles' theory of elements, with particles differing in shape and size, seems to presuppose. Anaxagoras, however, nowhere used such a notion of matter. Instead, his world is made up of opposite qualities—hot and cold, moist and dry—and these qualities are not qualities of some other stuff that "supports" them; they *are* the matter of the world, and their changes are ultimate facts of nature, not mere reflections from the surface of a frozen sphere of filled extension.

A third property of Anaxagoras' matter, that "in everything, there is a part of everything," states his solution to Parmenides' denial of any process in which "something comes from nothing."[6] Changes are not sudden jumps from not-being to being but changes in relative intensity of qualities in mixtures. The contrary qualities are never pure but always mixed together: Snow has *more* white and cold than black and hot, but when it melts into water, it has simply added *more* hot and black to a mixture that already contained some of each. The result is that, when snow melts, there is not the sudden creation of something from nothing but an increase in degree. This notion has not always been clear to Anaxagoras' readers, because his own statements—such as, "For how can what is not-flesh become flesh?"—are often misleading. That saying used to be taken to mean that there actually are small particles of human flesh and bone in any food that nourishes us; this is picturesque enough, but it is also absurd. However, if it is held to mean that there are *qualities common to food and flesh*, so that the two can mix and produce new assortments of quality, the doctrine is a sensible one. We can also see that Anaxagoras' peculiar form of statement is designed specifically to answer Parmenides' objection: he takes "flesh from not-flesh" as a special case of "something from nothing."

To build the world we know from these insubstantial, inter-penetrating qualities, Anaxagoras introduced stages of qualitative mixture and composition. Some fusions of quality are "tighter" than others; so we read of "shares" that melt together into "seeds," which in turn fuse to produce "things."[7] Perhaps because he was so concerned to avoid any technical objections from the Eleatics, his theory of matter is also highly technical. At every point, one is tempted to fall back on common-sense notions of objects and extended stuff in interpreting what "things," or "seeds," or "opposites," are for Anaxagoras. But every time one does this, the theory ceases to be sensible. Anaxagoras is thinking of the physical world in another way; his concept is much closer to Heraclitus' fire and flow.

As he moved from pure theory to an account of the formation of the cosmos and detailed scientific study of its mechanisms, Anaxagoras evidently felt able to reintroduce into his work more familiar Ionian words and ideas. His Athenian admirers, who could not make much sense of a discussion of qualitative materialism, could understand and appreciate the combination of clear deduction and brilliant conjecture with which he described how the world came into being.

Anaxagoras' cosmology is of the classical Milesian type, though he carries it several steps further. In the beginning, "All things were mixed together"—except mind, which set the mixture in motion in a spinning, expanding vortex.[8] As a result of this spin, the opposites separated out: heavy particles tending to drift to the center, forming our earth, and lighter particles—including a very great quantity of air—being forced to the outside.[9] So far, this could be a mixture of the ideas of Anaximander and Anaximenes. There are "many worlds," but that conclusion had already been anticipated by Anaximander and had continued as a standard idea of Ionian science on into the atomic theory.[10]

Yet Anaxagoras saw that this classical model of separation as the result of rotation could not account for the world as he observed it. A "giant vortex," working mechanically, would have to arrange things in homogeneous layers, sorted by density; there would be no sun, moon, and planets formed in the upper strata.[11] Hence he added to this account his own notion: that great masses of stone had been thrown out from the center and were kept from falling back to it by the speed of their motion. The sun, moon, and planets were such hot stones in the sky; the meteorites were smaller pieces that had fallen to earth when they lost the speed that kept them up in the sky.

Anaxagoras had some other suggestions that must have been startling; they seem original even today, when we are used to science coming up with odd theories and discoveries. For example, he thought that there were inhabitants on other worlds; that life, in a simple form, had originally reached the earth "by falling from the sky" and had then developed in complexity; that the Nemean Lion, a monster slain by Hercules, "had fallen from the moon."[12] These notions combine the mentality of a scientist and the imagination of a top-flight author of science fiction. Perhaps this combination explains why Euripides and Pericles enjoyed the company of their Ionian colleague.

The Athenian public *could* understand this new cosmology, and it scandalized them. The sun, moon, and stars had always been worshiped as gods; to have them demoted to hot stones came as such a shock and challenge to religious feeling that it still offended public opinion half a century later. To explain changes in nature—rain, seasons, lightning and so on—by purely mechanical causes seemed equally irreligious to those accustomed to picturing each such happening as a special divine dispensation. The Athenians had become accustomed to the idea that ritual and sacrifice were necessary to secure or avoid rains, earthquakes, good winds, and similar occurrences. If Anaxagoras were right, they saw, their whole traditional set of beliefs would have to be discarded.

Nor did Anaxagoras' speculations about *Nous* ("reason" or "mind") reconcile the Athenians to his view. There was, he held, a mind that remained "unmixed and pure," that saw and knew all things, and this originally had set the universe in motion. All things had some share of this cosmic mind, man, in particular, having a large share. The unmixed character of mind does involve a sort of mind-matter dualism. On the other hand, its operation as a motive force and its description as "dispersed in shares" through all things remind us that there was as yet no sharp distinction between corporeal and incorporeal; without this, it is impossible to define mind as an incorporeal entity. But this cosmic *Nous* obviously could not have a human body. What we view today as provision for a deity and religion in Anaxagoras' system seemed to his contemporaries merely another example of atheism. Few Greek statesmen, businessmen, housewives, or poets had ever thought of the gods except as real and undying beings. They thought anyone could see what the gods looked like from their statues on the Acropolis, or as they were represented on the stage in Aeschylus' or Euripides' tragedies.

The reason that in Anaxagoras' scheme "mind alone remains pure" is that it must be possible for mind "to know all things" without actually *becoming* them. If mind were like the other qualities in the world, mixing with each thing it touched to produce a new compound, it would lose its own distinctive nature with each passing sensation or encounter. Anaxagoras has mind set the cosmos in motion, because he sees the need for some kind of *energy*, or *force*, in addition to *matter*, to make a logically satisfying physics. The fact that mind seems to be able to move the qualities in the world by a direct pressure reflects Anaxagoras' attempt to stay within the framework of materialism. His *Nous* is still close to a vital breath or "fine current," and he probably would not have welcomed the modern suggestion that it is incorporeal.

How active a role mind actually plays in the world of Anaxagoras has been often debated. Later Greek philosophers thought that he introduced *Nous* only because he needed something to start the world in motion, that he was really treating it as another piece of materialistic machinery. Some modern scholars take his statement, "Mind knows all things," more seriously and credit *Nous* with foreseeing the development of cosmic order. The correct interpretation probably lies somewhere between the two.

Anaxagoras is interesting and important for a number of reasons. Historically, he woke the Athenians up to what had been going on for some time in the centers of thought on the frontiers of the Greek world. He represents a transition point in the tradition of science. His discussion of *Nous* extends the interest of the scientist from matter in motion, as we observe it, to the human observer as well. The effect of his ideas of matter on later thinkers able to appreciate their subtlety was to direct attention to the continuing changing flow of things, counteracting the Eleatic and Pythagorean tendency to view the world as static form.[13] His rigorous logic and arresting imagination make him an interesting figure in his own right in the history of science and philosophy.

The most direct and immediate effect of Pericles' young scientific protégé was to provoke admiration in some quarters—to the extent that his admirers founded a sort of scientific research society—and criticism in other, more conservative quarters—to the extent that his critics charged him with atheism, so forcing him to leave the city.[14]

In Lampsacus, where he went from Athens, he was well received and honored as an important citizen. The work of Metrodorus of Lampsacus gives us an idea of the effect Anaxagoras had on popular beliefs. Crediting Anaxagoras with the idea, Metrodorus set about giving popular mythology a naturalistic interpretation. In this interpretation, the gods were equated with familiar phenomena and elements, the fall of Phaëthon being taken as a description of a daytime meteorite, for example.

Instead of being memorialized by a statue or commemorative inscriptions, Anaxagoras asked only that the anniversary of his death be given to the school children as a holiday, a request that was honored.

Perhaps the reason that today it is generally held that Anaxagoras has been too little appreciated is because later philosophers, before Whitehead in our own century, did not follow out the line of thought that led him to view the world as process, rather than matter.[15]

XI. ARCHELAUS

The First Athenian
Scientist

Zeus is no more; the whirlwind reigns instead.

ARISTOPHANES

Archelaus' place in the story of Greek thought is that of a teacher, rather than of an original theorist. If the new ideas of science were to take root in Athens, attract public attention, and have an impact on the course of philosophy, it was necessary that Anaxagoras' difficult ideas and aloof personality be made more popular and more practical. Archelaus, in seeing the implications of the new methods and ideas of Anaxagoras, performed exactly the service that was needed to give them impact and effect. The enthusiasm he seems to have inspired, the steps he took toward establishing a genuine research center with his school, and the concreteness with which he restated the notions of Anaxagoras' cosmology make him a successful popularizer and teacher. And though we remember Archelaus best because of his prize student Socrates, who became disillusioned with science when he found it had no answers to what he believed were the most important questions, his influence should not be rated too low. After all, some of the most original and most detailed work in the history of science took place in Athens in the generation after Socrates; and some of the ideas and enthusiasm of Archelaus' school doubtless remained enough in the air to have their influence on the Academy of Plato and the Lyceum of Aristotle.[1]

THERE IS general agreement, and some contemporary evidence to support it, that Archelaus was a pupil of Anaxagoras and later his close associate. According to some reports, he left Athens with his teacher when the latter was forced into exile.[2] But this does not mean that Archelaus had his students study the philosophical work of Anaxagoras as their source of ideas or methods. On the contrary, we have Plato's report that Socrates, one of Archelaus' students, not only had never met Anaxagoras but did not read the latter's book until after a long period of scientific study.[3] There are several possible reasons for the fact that Anaxagoras' book was not used as a text: perhaps Archelaus considered it too technical for his students (which would not be surprising); perhaps he thought it better teaching to attack problems directly; almost certainly he thought that Anaxagoras' ideas were too speculative at some points and in need of correction at others. Probably all of these considerations are relevant.[4]

Although Archelaus followed Anaxagoras in his key notions of a distinction between mind and matter and of the continuity of nature, his particular interest was the detailed application of his scientific theories to medicine and psychology.[5] Archelaus found the very abstract concept of *Nous* hard to imagine or work with experimentally. He had to translate the idea of a cosmic creative force unmixed with any other qualities into some more concrete form before he could measure and manipulate it. He did this by identifying *psyche* with air, much as Anaximenes had identified air with "the boundless" years before.[6] In this he may have been influenced by a minor contemporary figure, Diogenes of Apollonia, who also used air as the basic stuff of his scheme; but this did not involve any break with the ideas of Anaxagoras since for him, too, the first stage in cosmic evolution, once rotation has begun, is a phase with vast quantities of air. Perhaps both Diogenes of Apollonia and Archelaus thought that, by making air both the element that composes *psyche* and the basic physical stuff, they were improving on the analysis made by Anaxagoras.[7]

Archelaus' air served three functions: It was, at one and the same time, the neutral state of matter from which other qualities separated themselves out; a governing principle of things, that is, air had the power to start cosmic motion; and "the vital stuff" composing soul and mind. There was nothing truly original about these ideas. Air as *psyche* had been anticipated as far back as Homer. Air as primary matter was the theory of Anaximenes. The role of respiration and whether various diseases were due to excess or deficiency of air in the body were familiar medical topics. Archelaus himself was particularly interested in this medical line of thought. He disagreed with Anaxagoras' view that *Nous* is shared throughout nature, holding instead that only animals have any part of it. Plants do not breathe, he thought, and do not react intelligently; thus he was unwilling to credit them with any share of soul or mind.

This reinterpretation of Anaxagoras, identifying *Nous* with air and limiting its presence to animals, had the effect of translating what had originally been speculative philosophy into much more specific physiological problems of the kind dealt with today in biochemistry.

In both Aristophanes' *The Clouds* and Plato's *Phaedo*, there are accounts of Socrates, during the early "scientific" phase of his career, when he was concerned with the questions that particularly interested this Athenian pioneer research group. Their interests were *astronomical* and *medical*, and Socrates is shown as wanting to know the shape and position of the earth. Is it flat or round? Is it at the center of the cosmos or perhaps moving about the center? He also wants to understand the nature of thought: Do we think with the air in us (this would be Archelaus' notion), or with fire, or perhaps with the brain? Are the natural phenomena—rain, clouds, whirlwinds, and the like—to be explained as processes of air in various states of density, moisture, and motion?[8]

According to Plato, it was only after he had spent considerable time in working with these questions that Socrates encountered Anaxagoras' book. He heard someone reading from it, and was particularly struck by the phrase, "Mind orders all things." In that case, thought Socrates, mind has surely arranged things with some purpose and value in view. In that case, he thought, one could decide between scientific hypotheses by seeing which was the "most reasonable" arrangement. He bought a copy of the book at once, and read it. To his disappointment, it seemed to him that Anaxagoras used mind only as a concept to explain the beginning of motion, and for the rest talked only in terms of mechanical causality.[9] In spite of this disappointment, Socrates' encounter with Anaxagoras' book was the beginning of his realization that science as Archelaus taught it was limited in the problems it could effectively deal with and solve.[10] The result was that Socrates turned from science to other inquiries, and we have no further record of what happened to the school.

XII. THE SOPHISTS

How to Succeed
in Athens

Nothing exists; but even if it did, we
could not know it; and if we did, we
could not communicate our knowledge.
GORGIAS

Justice is the advantage of the stronger.
THRASYMACHUS

*The emergence of the Sophists, a group of professional itinerant
teachers, challenged Greek philosophy in a new and important
way. The early philosophers, in concentrating on the natural
world, had tended to overlook human affairs. Some thinkers,
like Heraclitus and Empedocles, were exceptions, but even they
seem to have been more interested in questions about the outer
world than in subtle analyses of the inner self or even of society.
The Sophists, who were engaged in training young men to live
successfully, suggested that rhetoric—the art of persuasive discourse—not philosophy, should be studied.*

THE IMPRESSION the Sophists made can still be glimpsed
in our idea of sophistication. The "sophisticated man" was
what their training set out to produce; and we still have schools
today that aim to produce a similar product. Such a man is a
good conversationalist; he is adaptable and has traveled enough

to be acquainted with the customs of more than one place; sure of himself, he is polished and not easily embarrassed. Stephen Potter's "lifeman" is a paragon of sophistication with his tactics for "winning in the game of life without actually cheating."[1] Athenians were, however, far less hardened than we are today to lifemanship. Not only the theory but the practice was new; and the young man who could apply his intelligence to finding ways of making a good impression had a great advantage over his competitors in politics, law, and social life. The new concept of a sophisticate came into being to characterize this tactical skill.

Athens needed something like the Sophists as a progressive force. Its sudden expansion as the center of Greek civilization required new ideas to replace the inherited ideal of a gentleman, derived from Homer's tales of chivalry in the Mycenean Age. It needed continuing class mobility, but to displace the outmoded monopoly of property and prestige was difficult. It needed a new degree of political adaptability; its administration was badly hampered by traditional conservatism.

But, naturally enough, although in certain ways Athens needed the Sophists, not all Athenians welcomed them. The very success of their education provoked resentment and envy among those who could not afford it and antagonized the more conservative aristocrats—Aristophanes among them—by challenging their monopoly on cultivated, snobbish gentility.[2]

The more serious thinkers in Athens were dissatisfied as well. Socrates and Plato both felt that there was a fatally short-sighted superficiality in the assumptions that underlay sophistry. They believed that life was something more than a perpetual social round and that to measure success in life merely in terms of wealth or prestige was a goal that was unworthy, both of society and the individual. But neither did they overlook the positive side of this new educational movement; Plato devoted four or five of his dialogues to portraits that give a kind of "Who's Who in Athenian Education," and this certainly indicates that he did not dismiss the Sophists lightly.[3]

Although there was a wide range in the interests and methods of these traveling teachers, they had the collective effect of challenging science and philosophy, by offering an alternative kind of education. Their interest in practical effectiveness led, inciden-

THE PNYX: MEETING PLACE OF THE ATHENIAN ASSEMBLY

The art of rhetoric taught by the Sophists was essential for citizens making political speeches. The stone steps in this photograph are the rostrum of the Pnyx, which was the meeting place of the Assembly in Athens. (*Photograph courtesy of Embassy of Greece, Press and Information Service.*)

tally, to many improvements. The art of rhetoric gained a new precision at their hands. They introduced the "adversary system" into the study of law. They recognized the conventional character of language and studied grammar, dialects, and etymologies. They applied formal logic to trial law, debate, and public speaking, offering new standards of clarity and new subtleties of fallacy. Their insistence that ethics and politics were based only on convention, not on nature, provoked three generations of Athenian philosophers to a more exact examination of human nature and behavior. Perhaps as important a contribution as any of the others was their demonstration that good manners and the proper accent could be taught; Greek aristocrats had thought before that gentlemanly behavior was inherited, so that the *status quo* truly seemed to rest on "nature." Finally, we must credit at least some of the teachers of this school with a new interest in the arts and crafts, which had come to be looked down on by the intelligentsia of Athens, though this had not been the case in the earlier periods of Greek history.

On balance, the Sophists did not offer a major constructive advance in Western philosophy; their effect, rather, was critical. They made the sharp break with tradition that was necessary as a prologue to new studies of social phenomena. But they did not trust general theories far, and their use of rhetoric, with which they persuaded their hearers that science and philosophy are impractical, was an alternative to philosophy, not a contribution to it.

One of the earliest and greatest teachers of the Sophist group was Gorgias of Leontini. He improved the art of rhetoric by applying formal logic to debate and oratory. Against a background of pleas and speeches that rambled on almost anyhow, Gorgias first began to use the rhetorical figures, the prose rhythm and alliteration, the sharply indicated topical outline that have been the tools of oratory ever since. (Or, if not ever since, we must, at least, admit that it has taken twenty-five hundred years for the West to get familiar enough with these Gorgian innovations to try to avoid them.) His effect on his Greek audience, fond of argument, conversation, and public speeches, was magical. Gorgias was a great success as a diplomat when he was sent to Athens from Sicily; the Athenian poets and statesmen began to imitate his style. He set up a statue of himself at Delphi, and the base of another erected by a relative of a later generation has also been found there.[4] We have several of Gorgias' speeches preserved; to us, they seem rather artificial and trite in their construction. For example, when we read in the "Funeral Oration": "For what have these men left undone that should have been done, or what have these done that should have been left undone," we feel that this is an artificial cliché.[5] But it was not a cliché when Gorgias introduced it, and its impact was extraordinary. In his speech "In Defense of Helen of Troy," Gorgias digresses for a moment to praise the power of words; and the passage shows his own attitude and interest.[6]

But Gorgias did not trust ornament alone to give his speeches their power. The organization of his two display pieces defending the legendary Homeric characters Helen and Palamedes

before imaginary courts reflects the work of one who has appreciated the sharp logic used so effectively by Zeno. Helen, the
defense goes, deserted her husband to go with Paris of Troy for
one of three reasons: it was *either* because of Fate *or* irresistible
passion *or* overpowering persuasion. But if it was Fate, Helen
did not have any choice in the matter and, therefore, is not
guilty of willful desertion; if it was love, a force stronger than
human will was also responsible; and the same holds true of
persuasion, since words have the power to master both mind and
will. Consequently, concludes Gorgias, we have shown that
Helen was not wicked; she did not desert Menelaus willfully;
and she deserves our sympathy rather than condemnation.[7]

Gorgias was not alone in recognizing the usefulness of this
new logic for organizing legal cases, political talks, and dramatic
soliloquies. It spread through Greek drama, law, politics, debate,
and even private conversation. He was, however, one of the first
to apply Eleatic formalism to practical concerns, and, it must be
said, he was not very gracious toward the Eleatics to whom he
was indebted. One of his rhetorical displays was a logical dem-
olition of all speculative philosophy—that of the Eleatics, in
particular. With some of Zeno's own imaginative ingenuity, his
speech is organized to prove three things: first, that nothing
exists; second, that even if something did exist, we could not
know it; third, that even if something did exist and we could
know it, we could not communicate our knowledge.[8]

The defense of the first thesis shows his technique at work:
If anything exists, it must be either finite or infinite; Parmenides
has proven conclusively, from the assumption that "only being
is," that it must be finite; but Parmenides' later follower
Melissus has shown that being must be infinite, using the same
assumption and equally conclusive reasoning. Only a false proposition can lead to such a contradiction; therefore, nothing exists.[9] This is a type of argument often repeated in the history of
thought: that contradictions between great philosophers show
philosophy itself to be purely verbal, or untestable, or beyond
the reach of a human mind. It would be true if there were
no way of reconciling apparent contradictions, either by new
distinctions (for example, between the meaning of finite in
Parmenides and in Melissus) or by new syntheses (for example,

by showing that one level or dimension of being is in fact infinite, but another is determinate and finite). Gorgias' speech reflects his attitude; he did not teach his students science or philosophy.[10]

Since the skills important to a young Greek eager to get ahead in the city-states of this period just after the Persian War were public speaking and legal ability, all of the Sophists taught these subjects as part of their training. Some were concentrated exclusively on them; others included law and oratory in a more general education. The great legendary lawyer of the Sophist school was Protagoras of Abdera, who was able to win either side of any case in a jury trial. He shocked the Athenian public by training his students to argue both sides of each legal case, a procedure that has since had its value recognized and become standard practice in the teaching of law.[11] But to the man in the street of ancient Athens, it was a demonstrable fact that every lawsuit had one just and one unjust side: to put the two on an equal footing went counter to the notion that a jury would have an intuitive sense of justice and could determine a right judgment of every cause. Expressing the scandalized reaction to Protagoras' new approach, Aristophanes in *The Clouds* created a great debate between Just and Unjust Discourse. In the play, the two are wheeled onstage dressed as fighting cocks. Unjust Discourse, defending the wrong side of each case, comes out the winner.

From other documents, such as the "Double Arguments" (*Dissoi Logoi*), it is plain that some of Protagoras' imitators were not very bright. This book is a collection of opposed arguments to prove such theses as, "The just and unjust are the same" and "The just and unjust are different." Protagoras himself, however, had the great legal knack of presenting each case in a way calculated to gain the jury's sympathy for his client and win the verdict he wanted.

Protagoras, like Gorgias, had no patience with the abstract speculations of science and philosophy. One of his most famous sayings is, "Man is the measure of all things; of things that are, that they are; of things that are not, that they are not."[12] Whether he intended this to mean that each man or society collectively is the measure, the proposition reflects a new notion of truth as relative to culture and the individual observer. He also wrote, "Concerning the gods, whether they exist or not, I do not know, because of the difficulty of the topic and the short-ness of human life."[13] Piety, justice, truth, and so on, were not natural to man but were rather conventions devised by society. The next generation of Athenian lawyers were outspoken in stating one implication of this view: that it was impossible to say which side of any case was "just" until a court decided it; for the law was simply "what the courts have done"; justice was "what the courts will do."

Another Sophist, Prodicus, best illustrates the new attitude toward language, as tool, not magic. This is a very important change. Someone who has grown up in a community with a single pattern of speech, particularly before the invention of grammar, will not realize that he is speaking *a language* at all. It will seem to him that his form of speech is natural and a di-rect communication of truth and meaning. Such an uncritical attitude can be dangerous; and Prodicus' work is a service to Western civilization. His classification of the parts of speech— into names, articles, verbs, participles, and particles—was the beginning of scientific grammar in the West. His discrimination of meaning between near synonyms fascinated his contem-poraries. He was also the first to study differences of dialect and the history of words.[14] Prodicus' lectures on language were well known; Plato pictures Socrates apologizing for his lack of skill in words, because he was able to afford only Prodicus' cheap lecture and not the expensive "complete course in language."[15] At the same time, if Plato's portrait is at all correct, Prodicus was a pedantic scholar, quick to draw distinctions between words whether the distinctions were relevant or not, and capable of interpreting the line of poetry "It is hard to be good," as "the good is bad," after detailed word-by-word etymological scrutiny.[16] But, pedant or not, after Prodicus, Greek thinkers had to be conscious of language and take some definite stand on such questions as the adequacy of ordinary language to describe the world, the need of philosophy for a special technical vo-cabulary, the safeguards needed to distinguish real from purely verbal reasoning and refutation.[17]

Hippias of Elis is known to us mainly through two dialogues

written in Plato's Academy; the reaction he provoked reminds one of Heraclitus' reaction to Pythagoras: that much learning does not always make wisdom, but may be a "polymathy and an art of mischief."

For Hippias was indeed a polymath; he knew everything. He invented a so-called art of memory, and used it to advantage by putting on and starring in his own "quiz program" at the Olympic games.[18] He was a competent mathematician and astronomer, and also interested in arts and crafts.[19] One of the Platonic dialogues shows us Hippias as he describes how he appeared at the Olympic games, with clothing, shoes, a ring, all made by himself. To complete his versatile performance, he read poetry of his own composition.

The Sophists' appreciation of the power of "convention" to direct and shape human behavior could have been suggested, and was partly confirmed, by the developments of technology in the Athenian Agora. In Hippias' appreciation of "knowing how," we have clear evidence of the part this interaction of technology and thought played in the development of sophistry. But, if we can place any trust at all in the *Greater Hippias* and *Lesser Hippias*, the Academy's portraits of this expert in action, Hippias knew all the facts but was incapable of any kind of generalization or of any appreciation of humor. It is exasperating to see him—in caricature, but probably with some verisimilitude —pompously offering to decide which is right in a subtle philosophic debate between Protagoras and Socrates; agreeing that with spoons, poems, and a host of other examples, beauty equals functionality, but unable to see that this suggests a universal correlation between beauty and function; encountering Socrates' sharp irony and, wholly unaware that he has been transfixed by its shafts, continuing to identify intelligence with information.

Such were the teachers among the Sophists of the older generation. They were urbane, courteous, held responsible political offices, and for the most part behaved as gentlemen were expected to. Protagoras, for example, though he was not sure whether the gods existed, was certain that they should be worshiped; the sense of piety reinforced by civic religion was an important part of the civilizing influence needed to tame human nature. Gorgias had worked out a sort of table of etiquette, indicating what behavior was correct for each social situation, age, sex, and status.

But this cultivated gentility underwent a complete change in the younger teachers who were the Sophists of the next generation.[20] From the new notion of the importance of convention in structuring social behavior and creating the values of a society, they went on to draw abrasive conclusions, dismissing all standard values as entirely arbitrary and conventional. Critias, better known for his later career as unprincipled interim dictator than for his intellectual achievements, represents this destructive criticism applied to all religion: the gods, he says, were invented by shrewd politicians to frighten the masses of mankind into good behavior. Thrasymachus, a hard-bitten lawyer, summarizes his experience with courts and cases in the outspoken statement that justice is simply a name given to whatever action furthers "the advantage of the stronger and the ruler."[21] Antiphon is sure that injustice is not unnatural because it is followed by no pain unless detected and punished, whereas actions that "go against nature" always have harmful consequences. An unknown author draws up, in the "Double Arguments" (*Dissoi Logoi*), a general pattern for arguing both sides of any case, including examples to show how to prove that the same action is good, bad, and indifferent. The list can be extended, but these examples show how the later Sophists generalized and made explicit some of the less acceptable and, in fact, less credible implications of the ideas of their teachers.

One thing that helped make sophistry widely known and led to exasperation with it in many quarters was the new emphasis on debate. Hippias' appearance at the Olympic Games to perform feats of intellectual athleticism by answering any and every question hurled at him typifies the fact that conversation was coming to be more and more regarded principally as an opportunity to match wits, as a form of intellectual contest. The Greeks liked a good argument, and an interested audience could be gathered to listen to a duel with words. Aristotle later wrote his analysis of logic and language, in which he summarized the aims of these "debates": Those who fight with words aim first to refute their opponent. If that is impossible, they aim to trap the opponent into asserting a paradox. Failing this, they try to get him to commit a fallacy which can then be exposed to his discredit, or to perpetrate solecism; if he is forced to speak ungrammatically, they can claim that this shows his illiteracy and incompetence. Finally, if all else fails, they try to reduce him to babbling!

One of Plato's dialogues, the *Euthydemus*, shows Socrates caught up in such a combat to the death with words. His opponents are two visitors to Athens, Euthydemus and his brother Dionysodorus, who have "given up fighting in armor in favor of fighting with language." Caricatures of contemporary debating heroes, their mixture of bad manners and verbal victories gives the modern reader some sympathy with the conservatives who, like Aristophanes, were outraged by this side effect of the new higher education.

In Plato's dialogue, Socrates, when he asks the visitors about the nature of virtue, is told that he already knows the answer:

"Then do you think it is possible for any of the things there are, whatever it happens to be, not to be what it is?"

"No, by Zeus, I don't!"

"And *you*," he said, "know something?"

"Yes."

"Therefore, you are knowing . . . And isn't it necessary, since you are knowing, that you have knowledge of all things?"[22]

Socrates thinks that this is untrue; but Euthydemus has a ready answer. Untruth would be "saying a thing that is not"; but, "Not-being can neither be, nor be thought, nor be spoken," so falsehood is impossible! This irrelevant introduction of Eleatic logic is followed by a misuse of the answer-yes-or-no technique of legal cross-examination that the Sophists had perfected, mixed in with personal remarks that, while they leave Socrates impassive, come very close to giving one of his younger companions apoplexy.[23]

The Sophists were a colorful group and one that philosphers could not ignore. Their proposal to forget about philosophy and accept rhetoric instead was a challenge that had to be met. Their conventionalism and relativism directed attention to important limitations in previous scientists and philosophers who had assumed, without recognizing that they had done so, that human nature and society were simply special cases of the system of nature—chemicals, seasons, and stars. Their new awareness of the instrumental character of language and their discoveries of the properties of this most wonderful instrument were arresting and permanent contributions to Western culture.

But it was not the second generation of Sophists who saw the relevance of these new ideas to philosophy; that younger group seems to have substituted slogans for responsible speculation. It was rather the serious critics of sophistry's challenge who set about re-examining the relation of human existence to being and nature as a whole, and to exploring the very significant philosophic question of the relation between nature, fact, and value.

The influence of sophistry in Athens was widespread: it was reflected in the plays of Euripides, the great orations of Pericles, the less great orations of other speakers, the debates in the gymnasium. But the Sophists were not universally popular. Conservative Athenians—for whom Aristophanes was a spokesman—resented their challenge to traditional values; some less conservative Athenians, unable to afford the high fees charged, resented the advantage this higher education gave. The story that Protagoras' book was burned and he himself forced to leave Athens in 418 B.C. appears to be apocryphal, but it rests on the historical fact that, for all their attention to ways of attaining popularity, the Sophists did not win over all of the Athenians.[24]

After the Sophists, Greek philosophy altered. It was forced to be much more self-critical and circumspect. The Sophists had shown that language is a tool of man's invention, not an infallible replica of reality. They had argued convincingly that in society and law there is at least a very large element of convention; this made it impossible to assume that the behavior of one's own community was "just human nature." And, doubtless to the annoyance of philosophers, there was Gorgias' speech designed to show that past speculation about reality had only led to contradictions, whereas the useful arts showed consistent progress in *their* history.

XIII. SOCRATES

The Search for the Self

The unexamined life is not worth living.
SOCRATES

Thales' answer to the question, "What is being?" led Greek thinkers to examine the world about them. The disciplines of physics, mathematics, logic, and zoology developed in response, producing partial answers. Socrates' question, "What am I?" led to a new phase of inquiry. Early fascinated by the ideas of Ionian science, Socrates came to realize that neither scientists nor Sophists nor ordinary common-sense Athenians could explain the human self. He recognized the need for ethical inquiry and inspired new approaches to politics and education. Greek philosophers were confronted with the new problem of reconciling natural science and human values within a single system of reality. The very example of Socrates' own life and death reminds us of the importance of human intelligence, and of the freedom to use that intelligence.

''W H E R E are you going, men? Ignorant that you do nothing you ought, wealth and its gaining are your sole concern. As for your sons, to whom this will be left, you take no care whether they have the knowledge they will need to use it justly. You do not seek teachers of justice for them, if this can be taught; nor, if it is rather by practice and by training that it comes, for adequate trainers and instructors. You do not even make a beginning by mending your own ways in this respect . . .''1

The speaker is Socrates in the Agora, and with Socrates Greek philosophy was given a new direction.[2] His concern with the nature of a human self, his persistence in trying to get his fellow citizens to think less about how to make their children rich and more about how to make them better, his critical deflation of politicians and Sophists, who claimed to know what virtue was and how it could be taught, redirected the attention of philosophers from the world as observed by man to man as its observer. They began to see that philosophy has implications for everyday social and political practice, and that its pursuit of truth might come into collision with tradition or political expediency. In one of the most dramatic scenes in Western history such a collision did occur. This moment was the trial of Socrates in 399 B.C. When the political leaders of Athens found that the questions he was asking undermined the uncritical support they thought they needed, they tried to force him to leave the city, or at least to stop talking. Brought to trial, accused of impiety and of being a subversive influence, Socrates refused to be intimidated or to compromise. He argued in his defense that he had a duty to inquire, to keep the Athenians aware of the important questions they would perhaps prefer to ignore. He claimed to be a public benefactor, not a criminal; and, given a chance to propose a counter-penalty to the death sentence asked for by the prosecution, he said that if he got what he deserved, it would be permanent board and lodging at public expense. Socrates was condemned and executed; but throughout Greece his interest in the human self and his spirit of impartial inquiry found many admirers who continued his work; and, to the present day, his example reminds us of the importance of intellectual freedom, and the right and duty of the individual to engage in intelligent inquiry.

It is usual to divide Greek philosophy into a pre-Socratic and post-Socratic period; for after Socrates, Greek thinkers could never forget the question, What am I?, which proved as tantalizing and important as the older question, What is being? with which Greek speculative thought began.

Socrates himself wrote nothing, and when we try to reconstruct his ideas, we find a different portrait of Socrates from each man who gave an account of him. The main schools of Greek philosophy claimed, all of them, to be Socratic, carrying on the work and sharing the goals of Socrates himself. His friends Xenophon and Plato have left us literary portraits; and we also have the caricature of Socrates from the pen of Aristophanes. We find in Aristophanes a Socrates who is a shyster and a charlatan; Xenophon pictures a sensible retired soldier. The Cynics, one of the Socratic schools, saw a man unwilling to put up with social conventions, who lived "according to nature." The Megarian school's Socrates is a formal logician. The Cyrenaic school thought his main lesson was the ethical doctrine that a good life consists of the "intelligent pursuit of pleasure."[3] To the present day, this combination of shared admiration but diverse interpretation continues; thus, in our own century, Socrates has been treated as an existentialist, a political liberal, and a Hindu guru.[4]

There are two reasons for this multiplicity of interpretations. The first is a result of Socrates' belief that people must do their own thinking: he usually presented himself as one who did not know the answers to the questions he was asking, but would be glad to be a critic and share an investigation with his conversational partners. It is therefore not easy to make out a list of Socratic doctrines, even if one wants to do so; and it is easy to see that as items in a textbook list, Socrates' ideas would lose their intended force and meaning. The second reason for there being so many views of Socrates is that later philosophers all recognized his life as a proof that man's ideals can be the cause of his behavior. Socrates' example showed that there were times where someone would choose to do what was right, even though that choice went against all his selfish interests and was made at the price of life itself.[5] And, naturally enough, each later group of philosophers, recognizing Socrates as an idealist, read its own notion of the ideal human life into its interpretation of Socrates. The history of Western ethics can be read as a continuing debate between these various visions of the Socratic ideal. Each has its own attractions but also its own limitations; and probably nothing would have pleased Socrates more than knowing that his example would be so convincing that it would direct future ethical inquiry, yet so enigmatic and challenging that it would continue to make people criticize and question each solution that was proposed.

We will want to follow Socrates' career in some detail, seeing his early enthusiasm for natural science, his discovery of the need for ethical inquiry, and the story of the Delphic oracle that strengthened his determination to play gadfly to his fellow Athenians. Further, we will see that he did arrive at constructive conclusions, in spite of his claim not to know anything with certainty. Finally, we will see that his very trial and execution proved the futility of attempting to use intimidation to curb human intelligence and curiosity.

As a young man, Socrates was fascinated by the new ideas of Ionian science and was a leading member of Archelaus' school. In fact, for a time after Archelaus left Athens, Socrates himself was the school's recognized leader or director, the role he plays in Aristophanes' *Clouds*.[6] But in Athens in this period, it was impossible for an alert young man to pay attention exclusively to one set of new notions. Socrates had many interests and acquaintances outside this scientific circle. For example, he attended Prodicus' "less expensive" lectures on language; he was acquainted with some younger Pythagoreans in nearby Thebes; he had been impressed by a meeting with Zeno and Parmenides.[7] And, from his own skill in cross-examination, we can be sure that he was an interested listener whenever one of the Sophists gave a major speech or argued a case in court. He had read the manuals of rhetoric then current, but didn't think much of them. He served in the army with distinction, attended the theater, went to the public assembly, and carried on conversations in the local gymnasia. All of these activities influenced him in developing the qualities that marked his later career: his appreciation of new ideas, his sense of humor, and his serious conviction that intelligence and justice were necessary qualities of a good society and of a good life.

When he was about forty years old, Socrates discovered that science could not answer the questions that had come to interest him. These questions were about the nature of the human self, what is of worth and value in the world, and the definition of human excellence. Earlier thinkers had also searched for the self. Heraclitus had written, "I sought for myself"; "KNOW THYSELF" was one of the three sayings inscribed on the temple of Apollo at Delphi; the salvation of some sort of psychic self was the aim of Orphic and Pythagorean religious practice; and the

COOKING BELLS

Pottery ovens were placed over the dough and then surrounded with coals. Aristophanes, making fun of the new science and its models, wrote (in The Clouds, *referring to Socrates' Thought-Shop)* :

> "*That is the reflectory of wise souls.*
> *In there live men who state convincingly*
> *That heaven's a cooking bell which sits*
> *Around us and we, within it, coals.*"

(Photograph and quotation courtesy of Agora Excavations, American School of Classical Studies at Athens.)

relation of fate to self-knowledge was a theme emphasized in history and tragedy. But Socrates was the first to discover an answer to this riddle by critical intellectual inquiry, going beyond mythology, epigram, and poetry.[8]

We can even see, looking back at Archelaus, how the new science of the day could have led Socrates to raise this general question. One of Archelaus' main interests was to apply science to human physiology and psychology. As a student in the school, Socrates must have been fascinated by such questions as, "Whether we think with the air in us, or the blood . . . or perhaps none of these, but rather with the brain."

But Archelaus was also a scientist in the Milesian tradition, and that tradition, with its stress on objective observation and description, left no room for study of the subjective experience of the observer, nor for evaluation.[9] When he realized this,

Socrates may, at first, have thought that the Sophists were closer to the approach he was after. But if he thought this, he quickly changed his mind. For sophistry was so concerned with "realistic" tactics for amassing property and gaining prestige that it overlooked both the possible part ideals could play in human life, and the possibility that prestige and wealth were not intrinsic goods for a human self. The sophistic "self" was a rather simple amalgam of natural greediness and conventional habit. Self-knowledge interested this group no more than it did the general public or the preoccupied politician of the day.[10]

The story of the oracle at Delphi and the part it played in leading Socrates to go about Athens asking his critical questions is probably a true one, and it is wonderfully characteristic of Socrates in its combination of humor and passion for knowledge.[11]

Socrates' friend Chaerephon on a visit to Delphi, had asked the oracle of Apollo, "Is any man wiser than Socrates?" and the oracle had answered, "None!" Socrates was astounded, for he was just beginning, he said, to realize how many things he did not know. He determined to set out looking for a man wiser than himself, so that when he found one, he could go to Delphi and cross-examine the oracle to find out what Apollo really meant. (It is, of course, typical that Socrates did not accept the compliment by settling back complacently as an authority, but instead interpreted it as a command, or a riddle, designed to encourage him to go out and ask questions.)

The result was a surprise. Starting with the most likely candidates—educators and politicians—then going on to poets and craftsmen, Socrates pursued his search for a wiser man. But each expert, although he thought he knew all about human excellence, justice, courage, good social policy, turned out when Socrates questioned him to be, "Just as ignorant as I was myself!" So Socrates asked himself, "Whether I would rather be as these men are, ignorant but fancying that I know, or as I am, aware that I know nothing; and I decided that I would rather be myself!"

Meanwhile, those experts whom Socrates had shown to be ignorant were not grateful for the demonstration, particularly since an audience often enjoyed the exhibition. We can get an idea of this reaction if we imagine Socrates cornering a senator who has just finished a speech on the injustice of some new legislation and asking him what he means by "justice," then showing with a few sharp questions that the speaker has only the most vague and muddled notion of his meaning!

So Socrates moved through Athens, wondering, thinking, and questioning. During this period, he arrived at some preliminary conclusions of his own, which were positive and which he found unassailable. Sometimes he would even state these as his firm beliefs, though more often we find him defending them indirectly, offering them as hypotheses or asking them as questions.

Later writers agree in attributing to Socrates the statements: "Virtue is knowledge"; "The virtues are one"; "A just man harms no one"; "It is better to suffer than to commit injustice"; and "We shall be better men if we inquire than if we do not; that is a belief for which I will fight in word and deed."[12] All of these positive views have their origins in a new constructive insight into the self and human value.

All these ideas are closely connected with Socrates' discovery that values can be classified as either *intrinsic* or *instrumental*, and that his fellow citizens usually made the classification in exactly the wrong way.[13] The things that have intrinsic value are the qualities of being that make a person excellent and happy. Things that may be used as means to this end but may also be misused have instrumental value—they are prized because of some further use they can be given. Property, physical beauty, and strength fall in the instrumental category. Neither wealth nor physical fitness can in itself make its possessor either a good person or a happy one. Wisdom, justice, and courage, on the other hand, have intrinsic value. Someone who knows what these virtues are will prize them for themselves, not as means to some other goal.

The ordinary Athenian, Socrates saw, set up his scale of values in exactly the opposite way. He commended justice because it was a means to a good reputation, which in turn was a means to political and financial success. Or else he told his sons they should be just because they would be punished—by human law courts, or by the gods—if they were not. The ends for which virtue was commended as a means were exactly those that were really external to happiness and true character: money, beauty, strength, prestige, and so on. Socrates found that the reason for this fundamental error in evaluation was ignorance: ignorance of the true nature of the soul, and ignorance of the true dignity that realization of an ideal brought to its possessor. And so Socrates was convinced that "virtue is knowledge" and that "the virtues are one." Anyone who knows the good—in Socrates' sense of knowledge, which involves really evaluating a thing itself, not just memorizing a slogan about it—will always choose it. And, in every situation, human excellence results from "knowledge," that is, from intelligent evaluation.

Since virtue is a condition of the inner self and this alone is intrinsically good, the popular notion that a person can be harmed by being deprived of property or of physical comfort is mistaken. The only real harm that can befall is for something to occur that will make one a worse person: and this can only be the result of a mistaken choice that leads one to give up dignity and act wickedly. Consequently, Socrates argued, faced with the choice, it is better to be treated unjustly than to act unjustly oneself.

Socrates believed that the only hope for Athens lay in correcting the ignorance of the Athenian statesmen and their followers. The history of Athens during his life showed the need for such a correction. Athenian expansion had collided with Sparta and her allies, and for many years the long, drawn-out Peloponnesian War continued, ending finally in 404 B.C. with the defeat of Athens. An interim dictatorship of thirty oligarchs established itself, led by the Sophist Critias. They drove out the leaders of the democratic faction and, for a time, subjected Athens to an unprincipled reign of terror.[14] In 403, however, the democratic group invaded the city and drove out the Thirty. The democratic leader Anytus had a law passed that no one could be prosecuted for actions before this democratic restoration, and the democracy tried to sustain its precarious position and regain some of the lost power and trade.

Socrates' first encounter with a government that wanted him to stop talking occurred when the Thirty were in power. Presumably some of his comparisons of their behavior with that of bad craftsmen angered Critias and his colleagues. At any rate,

Critias took Socrates aside and told him to "give your cobblers and donkeys a rest . . ."—that is, stop talking! (My own guess would be that Socrates compared the Thirty to shepherds who spent all their time barbecuing the sheep they were guarding.) This warning was not heeded, and presently, in an attempt to implicate him, they ordered Socrates to help arrest a wealthy man, Leon of Salamis—an arbitrary arrest prior to the assassination of Leon and the confiscation of his property. Socrates quietly went home; and only the return of the democracy saved him from assassination by the oligarchic dictators.

But, in spite of the moderation Anytus showed in his law of general pardon for earlier offenses, he too found Socrates a public danger and brought charges against him intended to frighten him into leaving Athens or to stop criticizing the democracy. Anytus had some justification for his feeling that the democratic government in Athens was in a precarious position and that Socrates' criticism was not the sort of uncritical patriotism that Anytus wanted.[15] But obviously Socrates, convinced that intelligence was the only hope for human improvement, could not agree to give up his mission for the sake of the government's ideas of temporary expediency.

Anytus made the same mistake about Socrates that many other Greeks did: he assumed that Socrates did not really believe what he said. The city was full of people who *talked* idealistically, but who *acted* to increase their own property and comfort. But Socrates did, in fact, believe that it was better to suffer injustice than to commit it. He believed that his questions were essential and beneficial to society, and that he would be wrong to run away or keep silent.

And so Socrates stood trial, was condemned, and was executed. Plato in his three famous dialogues, the *Apology, Crito,* and *Phaedo,* re-creates the trial and death of Socrates in some of the greatest writing in classical literature.[16] Plato has recorded Socrates' speeches to the court, in which, instead of apologizing and promising to reform, he claims to be a public benefactor. The story of the Delphic oracle is told by Socrates to explain why he inquired so persistently and why Anytus and others found his questions so offensive. We have his concluding speech to the jury, ending with his statement of his own conviction,

"That no evil can harm a good man, in this world or the next."

Finally, in the *Phaedo*, Plato shows Socrates on the last afternoon of his life, discussing with the friends who visited him in prison the nature of the human soul and the evidence for its immortality. Calm, critical, and friendly, he explained to his friends how he came to realize that the human soul was more valuable and more complex than poets, scientists, or practical men had thought. And he told them why he found grounds for the hope that a soul able to know eternal truths and to reflect in itself the image of the ideal would have immortality. Like Socrates' proof that men could be motivated by respect for justice, which did not entirely convince his friends, the abstract arguments—which Socrates urges his friends to examine and criticize—may not carry conviction to the reader. Plato's dialogue, nevertheless, convinces every reader of the immortality of Socrates.

As the sun began to sink in the west, Socrates drank the fatal poison and died. "So died our friend, of all the men I have known the best and most just," is the concluding sentence of the *Phaedo*. And the judgment of history, reversing the verdict of the Athenian court, has upheld Plato.

XIV. PLATO

Order, Fact, and Value

Plato is philosophy, and philosophy is Plato.
PLUTARCH

*Endeavoring to answer the questions that concerned both Thales
and Socrates, two great creative Athenians brought together all
the earlier insights of Greek philosophy and science into two
marvelous speculative systems. These men were, of course, Plato
and Aristotle.*

*If any one idea can be said to stand for Plato's system, it was
his notion of the good. This value principle is, in a way, the
goal of all inquiry, and it provides the order for Plato's new map
of reality.[1]*

*Within this map, Plato located the earlier insights of Greek
thought. He tested the system by applying it to various problems. In particular, he applied it to the questions that had inspired him to take up philosophy: the nature of the self, and its
relation to society.*

*Plato's career may be considered in four stages, with corre-
sponding growth and change in his thought. He moved from the
poetry of his Socratic dialogues to practical action, from practice
to speculative thought, from philosophic vision to precise testing
and criticism.*

*His ideas, too, have had an interesting career. Many later
developments in philosophy possessing certain common features
are termed "Platonism."*

*Whitehead once characterized Western philosophy as "a series
of footnotes to Plato," and this is hardly an exaggerated ap-*

praisal. Plato, with his speculative vision, gave the West a tradition it has never lost and a goal it has never realized.[2]

IN DISCUSSING Plato and Aristotle it is important to get some notion of the over-all patterns and key themes that made it possible for them to see and present the vast scale and complexity of all being and all knowledge as a single ordered whole. To do this briefly is difficult, and leaves too little room for illustrations; but, fortunately, both Plato and Aristotle took as their starting point the history of philosophy that we have just finished tracing, and perhaps the earlier chapters will supply some of the appraisals, examples, and suggestions that are relevant to Plato's idea of form, and Aristotle's notion of causality.

After Socrates, philosophy in Athens was in a confused, chaotic state. Socrates had shown that "science," which provided the model for earlier speculation, could not account for the elements of value that played so important a part in human life. Gorgias and the other Sophists had shown that speculative philosophy, if one accepted the testimony of the philosophers themselves, led to contradictory, opposed conclusions and had not even given a consistent account of the world of fact with which it was concerned. The problems that had accumulated for three centuries of exploration and debate failed to fit together in any neat, credible scheme. Even with the force of Socrates' example, philosophers were tempted to substitute some other discipline—rhetoric, medicine, or physics—for philosophy, or to limit themselves to inquiries into logic or ethics. In those specialized areas, they did not have to face the baffling problem of trying to develop a complete systematic answer.

The synthesis of old ideas and new problems required a genius: someone who combined a poet's sensitivity and a mathematician's clear appreciation of abstract structure. But sensitivity and appreciation would not have been enough. These qualities alone might have only provided a blur of admiration. What was needed in addition was a flawless sense of coherence and form, an ability to see how the most intransigent parts went together. The genius of Plato in the Athenian setting was equal to the demand, and rescued philosophic speculation from the danger of neglect, trivialization, or rejection.

Plato became committed to philosophy as a result of the

execution of Socrates. Plato, at that time a young aristocrat, had planned to enter politics. He gave up that ambition, and wrote his Socratic dialogues, brilliant imaginary conversations and speeches with Socrates the central figure. His purpose was a double one: first, to defend Socrates against the verdict of the Athenian Court; second, to carry on Socrates' mission of inquiry, which the Athenian politicians had hoped to end.

We know very little about Plato's life before he was twenty-three. He came from a family long important in Athens. Socrates was a friend of the family, and Plato knew and admired him from an early age, though Socrates was probably not in any formal sense his teacher or tutor. Plato's stepfather, Pyrilampes, was politically active when Pericles was directing Athenian affairs; two of his other relatives, Critias and Charmides, were leaders of the powerful conservative political faction. It was therefore quite natural for the young Plato to take for granted his own political career, which is in accordance with the way he describes himself in his *Seventh Letter*. The story that his great ambition was to write poetry is hard to confirm but, in the light of his literary talent, possibly true. The two ambitions need not have seemed mutually exclusive.

Plato's first chance to take an active part in Athenian political affairs came when The Thirty established their dictatorship at the termination of the Peloponnesian War. Critias was the leader of this group, Charmides a member, and young Plato was invited to become one of them. But he waited for a time to see what they would do. He refused to join them when he found that their injustices and outrages made men look back on the war years as a happy time. When Anytus and his democratic group returned to power, the time seemed propitious for Plato to begin the career he had planned. Though an aristocrat, he was not in sympathy with the extreme ideas of the antidemocratic group; when Anytus came into power, he may well have hoped that he could be instrumental in re-establishing Athenian political unity.

It was, however, just at this time that Anytus, frightened by Socrates' freedom in expressing his ideas, arranged the indictment of false charges that led to the trial and execution of Plato's admired older friend. So once again, Plato put his ambitions to one side, disillusioned and outraged to find that in

Athenian democracy as well as oligarchy, injustice seemed to go hand in hand with power.[3] Whether this was a necessity that followed from the nature of society itself or whether there might be a social order in which a Socrates would be appreciated and justice respected was a problem that Plato continued to think and write about throughout his philosophical career. But whatever the theoretical answer, the actual political practices of the time convinced him that he could not be a politician, and he never tried to return to statesmanship as his own occupation.[4]

Immediately after Socrates' execution, Plato seems to have left Athens for a brief sojourn in Megara and to have begun writing his Socratic dialogues. He was passionately convinced that Socrates had been right: right about the intrinsic value of justice, right about the importance of inquiry, right about the need to make people stop and think seriously about what they were and where they were going. Plato did not intend to let the Athenians succeed in silencing Socrates by executing him. He intended to show that Socrates was, as he claimed to be, a public benefactor, not a criminal.

These imaginary conversations are models of literary and philosophic drama. The discussion of the nature of temperance in Plato's *Charmides* is a good example.[5] Socrates meets and cross-examines Critias and Charmides on the subject. Both are intemperate, yet each thinks he knows what temperance is. The reader, too, is likely to be persuaded that he knows and that he agrees with each in turn. Socrates, with his commitment to inquiry, shows both the reader and the characters in the dialogue that the obvious notions they accept are neither clear nor defensible. At the end of the conversation, Charmides and Critias have actually, though only temporarily, become more temperate and wise. At the end of the dialogue, they leave Socrates. The reader knows from Athenian history that they are to organize the intemperate reign of terror of The Thirty. A more vivid drama of interplay of ideas, characters, and actions cannot be imagined.

At the same time that Plato managed to re-create the Socratic passion for inquiry, he gave a portrait of Socrates in which he emphasized the point mentioned in the previous chapter, that Socrates' own life proved the truth of his thesis that sometimes men act as they do because of their ideals. Plato's re-creation of

Socrates' trial, imprisonment, and final conversation with his friends on the afternoon of his execution shows that Socrates was consistently acting on principle: a just man, he refused to compromise in any way with what seemed to him the right thing to do. Since some Athenians, including Socrates' friend Xenophon, had not understood why he was so stubborn in his refusal to compromise with the government, Plato proposed to enlighten them.[6]

The range of characters and topics in these early Platonic writings is wide: Socrates talks, not only with politicians, but with the leading Sophists of his time, with a religious fanatic, with young boys, with a polished but empty-headed youth who has just completed his education under Gorgias, the master Sophist, and with many others. Their discussions range from criticism of Homer through theories of language to the more frequent themes of wisdom, courage, temperance, and the definition of human excellence in general.[7]

These dialogues from the time they were written have had an almost magical effect. A rare combination of beauty in style and form with challenging content, they have been continuously copied, translated, commented on, and widely read.

Plato's choice of the dialogue as the form in which to write his philosophy was inspired. As we have seen, in philosophy's early stages there was no agreement that the vision of reality required one rather than another literary form. A philosopher's choice of form—whether epic, epigram, or diagram—seemed to depend on what aspect of reality he held most important. At the same time philosophers conceived their subject in such objective terms that Socrates could accuse them of forgetting to account for themselves.[8] For if reality is a single system, having nature and man related within it, philosophy should have, in both its form and content, a "proper distance" or "proper balance" of the impersonal outer world and the individual response of the observer.

Compared to the writings of most earlier philosophers, the dialogues of Plato achieved new standards of argument, evidence, and objectivity. They do not, like the lecture or technical work, cancel out the human interests, personalities, motives of audience and author in a dry selective focus on subject matter. In America today, an increasing use of discussion methods in teach-

ing and the continuing use of Plato as philosophic reading—
now beginning to extend from college level into our senior high
schools—may be signs that our own idea of philosophy is moving back toward some more engaged form, away from the lecture toward the dialogue once more where we are all participants
in the inquiry.[9]

Plato, with his dialogues, is one of the great literary figures of
all time; he is also with his new design for the Academy, the
first university, one of the great educational pioneers. He was
inspired by a combination of things: admiration for Pythagorean science, a new idea that perhaps "social science" could be
put on a solid foundation; and an awareness that some institutions for research were necessary if human society were to improve. His work has had an enormous influence: every later
college, university, and research foundation in the West is a
direct descendant of the Academy of Plato.

Just before he was forty, Plato again left Athens and traveled
to the western part of the Greek world. He wanted to visit two
cities: Tarentum in southern Italy and Syracuse in Sicily
(Egypt no longer was an important intellectual attraction).
Tarentum had remained a Pythagorean center. The political
revolutions that had destroyed the Pythagorean Order had not
occurred there or in neighboring Rhegion. The elected head of
Tarentum was Archytas, himself a Pythagorean, who had done
brilliant work in pure mathematics, had definite ideas about the
application of mathematics to ethics and the social order, and
had a reputation as scientist and statesman. He seemed just the
sort of person Plato wanted to meet.[10]

And he was not disappointed. The visit to Tarentum was as
valuable an experience as the traveling young author and philosopher had hoped: he formed a lasting friendship with
Archytas, and as a result of their meeting, clarified ideas for a
new kind of educational institution that he hoped to establish
when he returned to Athens.

His visit to Syracuse was another matter. Under the rule of a
succession of dictators, Syracuse had achieved an incredibly high
standard of living; its rulers had defeated the Carthaginians in
repeated battles, and attracted leading poets, sculptors, and
craftsmen to their court. At this time, under Dionysius I, Syracuse was at the height of its glory, and Plato had been attracted

by the accounts of this brilliant capital, both as a Western center of cultural leadership and as an example of dictatorship in its best and most successful form.[11] According to the story that has come down to us, however—and it is a story earlier and better accredited than most such accounts are—Plato so disliked the luxury and pointlessness of court life, and was so outspoken about it, that Dionysius I, in an outburst of bad manners and breach of hospitality, shipped Plato away to be sold as a slave in Aegina. Fortunately a friend of his was there to pay his ransom, and Plato returned to Athens as he had planned. This account may be exaggerated; but there is no doubt at all that Plato felt the apparatus of spies and secret police a sign that the state was not healthy; that he thought the court decadent and degenerate and its ruler paranoid; and that he concluded that "only a madman would choose to be a tyrant!"[12]

We are probably right in thinking that Plato had Archytas in mind when he wrote, later, about the need for "philosophic rulers"; and he certainly had Dionysius I in mind when he drew a scathing concrete portrait of a totalitarian state enslaved by a power-mad dictator.[13]

When Plato returned to Athens, he founded his Academy. A new type of school, this was a center of research and instruction on the level of higher education. Although inspired in part by Archytas, Plato was not willing to reduce all knowledge to mathematics, as Archytas advocated; Socrates had convinced him of the importance of other questions and methods. However, Plato had been looking for some way to carry on Socrates' program of applying intelligence to human affairs, ethical and political; and Archytas' suggestion that mathematics might serve as a model for social science he found an attractive one. If one could present political problems in the objective, neat, deductive form of geometric analysis, one could probably detect fallacies and ambiguities. Perhaps one might arrive at intelligent policy in this way, instead of by the usual guesswork and whimsy that swayed political decisions at that time.

Plato was convinced that it was possible, if difficult, to develop a new science of man. To do this, society needed some sort of community of scholars working together. The Pythagorean Order had already assumed that education beyond the elementary or secondary level might be necessary for its most talented members. Specialists in medicine had for some time received additional advanced education; and it was a natural consequence of Socrates' search for new kinds of expertness. But in Plato's time the idea was still not generally accepted. It was taken for granted that young men would and should learn by actually participating in business and politics. In the face of public opinion that such an enterprise was useless and unnecessary, and quite likely impossible, Plato needed both energy and conviction to implement his plan for an Academy.[14]

Of course, the idea of such a school did have some precedent in Greek history. From the informal master-student associations of ancient Miletus through the shared ethical and religious life of the Pythagoreans to the Athenian research group of Archelaus, a tradition had been developing of organized groups working together on problems in mathematics and science. Socrates, with his circle of friends, and the Sophists, with their classes of pupils, represented an extension of this practice to philosophy and the law. But it was Plato who first saw clearly that the research necessary for continued advancement of knowledge would be much easier if there were a specific institution designed for exploring, discussing, recording, reading, and perhaps experimenting.[15]

It is characteristic of Plato that he not only had this idea but promptly put it into operation. Later critics and admirers often overlook this intense engagement in the practical application of his thought.

Outside of Athens was a large public avenue and garden, named for the hero Hekademas, who was buried there. Plato established his educational center on the adjoining ground, and it was thus that it acquired the name the Academy.[16]

In selecting and inviting associates to his new school, Plato intended to have every branch of specialized knowledge represented. He wanted this because of his feeling for system, and the earlier Pythagorean success in finding the same laws in fine art and in nature may also have had their influence in this decision. For an ordered whole cannot usually be mastered piecemeal, part by part. Further, any advance of knowledge in one area or dimension will have implications for all of the others. To take a modern example, new discoveries in abnormal psychology have immediate relevance to criminal law; new studies of spiral structure in solid geometry may be exactly the tools needed to explain molecular behavior in organic chemistry. So the Academy was to be a "university": a small replica of the universe it was designed to study. Here again, Plato's design broke with tradition; for the schools up to his time had been either professional, as in medicine and law, or held together by unifying beliefs quite different from a common intellectual purpose, as the Pythagorean Order had been.[17]

In addition to its research scholars, Plato from the outset planned to have younger students as members of his group. The Academy was to carry forward Socrates' ideal of inquiry, and to insure a continuing group of inquirers it seemed desirable to give this school a teaching as well as a research function. The younger associates were probably expected to do some formal work in mathematics and science and some reading in poetry and philosophy, but presumably their main training was to come from sharing in the discussions of work in progress and assisting in its actual execution.

In passing, it is interesting to note that two women students were members of the Academy: the idea of collegiate coeducation proves, therefore, to be as old as the idea of a college itself. This, like the other new ideas embodied in the school, no doubt provoked criticism, for higher education for women went directly against tradition and seemed silly to the citizens of the time.

It is gratifying to see that the Academy was a great success. It quickly achieved a reputation throughout the Greek world, and beyond. Twenty years after its founding, Plato was so intellectually eminent that a visit from him was a source of prestige to the Syracusan court; the Academy seemed the logical place to send an unusually brilliant doctor's son from Macedonia to study. Cities revising legal codes or drawing up new ones for colonies asked the Academy to send consultants. And, final accolade then as now, comic poets satirizing notorious intellectuals ridiculed Plato and his school. Diogenes Laërtius quotes a number of these jokes (from comedies now lost) in his "Life of Plato."

At about this time, Plato began to see more clearly how his ideas could be combined in a new system of philosophy. His admiration for Socrates' idealism, his belief that nature forms an orderly cosmos which his meeting with Archytas helped to strengthen, his hope that an investigation shared by many intelligent specialists might lead to new advances not only were key ideas in the plan of the university but also seemed to offer keys for philosophy. In his great dialogues of this period, the *Phaedo*, *Symposium*, *Republic*, and *Phaedrus*, Plato shared this new vision with his readers. Plato's outline of this system, summarized in the *Republic*, will be discussed below.

Plato did not sit back complacently once he had what seemed to him a new, satisfying answer to the questions about reality and the self. Instead, he and the Academy began to test and criticize these new ideas, and to apply them. Plato's writings during this later period (the *Timaeus*, *Parmenides*, *Theaetetus*, *Sophist*, *Statesman*, *Philebus*, *Laws*, and probably *Epinomis*) are, as we would expect, much more technical and analytical than his early or middle dialogues; in fact, it is only in our own century, with the new development of "analytic philosophy," that they are finding readers who can fully appreciate them.

From the founding of his Academy in about 387 to his death in 347, Plato worked in his school, leading discussions, writing, and investigating. The only important interruptions of this scholarly concern began with an invitation that led him to undertake a second voyage to Syracuse. He had, on his first visit, formed a friendship with Dion, the brother of Dionysius I; and, on the death of the latter, Dion invited Plato to come to the court and educate his nephew, Dionysius II, who had succeeded to the dictatorship. This time the visit from Plato was a state occasion, considered a distinction by the court. But presently the young king became convinced that Plato and Dion were plotting to depose him, and both had to escape from Sicily. That was in the years 367-366. In 361, Plato went again to Syracuse to try to act as mediator in the feud that had continued between Dionysius II and Dion; but his efforts at reconciliation were not successful. In 359, against Plato's advice, Dion invaded Syracuse and forced his nephew to flee to Corinth; but in the following year, Dion was assassinated and Syracuse plunged into a chaotic political situation. This was one of the few projects Plato undertook where he was not successful. He later wrote in some detail two long "open letters" (*Epistles* VII and VIII) about his own part in the affair.[18] Some scholars think this experience was largely responsible for the new concern with exact practical

applications of ⌐   later Platonic writings
show, as oppose⌐

Apart from   ⌐t, Plato must have
been able to   work he had accom-
plished; but   no means complacent.
When h⌐ ⌐i⌐ ⌐⌐   ⌐s still hard at work on
the *Lav*⌐ ⌐ mon⌐   ⌐ legal code for cities of
the time.   ⌐'s importance in Western
intellec⌐ ⌐⌐   ⌐e facts that the Academy
continue⌐   until A.D. 529, and that
Plat⌐ ⌐⌐   ⌐esent day, one of the major
tra⌐

⌐la⌐   ⌐t ways of knowing, and the
d⌐ ⌐e⌐   n in each way, in a diagram in
Boo⌐   This diagram, which provides a
good introdu⌐   system, assumes that all of the kinds
of knowledge and u⌐ ⌐ ⌐nown are related to each other in a
great system, with a single highest form holding it together on
the top level. We must understand this scheme of "levels of
clarity of knowledge" if we are to understand Plato's political
theory. When he says that the only hope for mankind is to have
responsible intellectuals take over the direction of society, he has
in mind experts in a kind of "social science" and "general theory
of value" that he hoped could some day be found. The West has
yet to find them.

TO AGATHON (The Form of the Good)

BEING	Tested Theory	*Noesis* ("Knowing Why")
	Hypotheses	*Dianoia* ("Knowing That")
BECOMING	Techniques	*Pistis* ("Knowing How")
	Stories	*Eikasia* ("Guessing" or "Telling Myths")

PLATO'S DIVIDED LINE

Take a line, and divide it into four segments . . . these will be related to
each other as the relative clarity of four kinds of knowledge . . .

Republic VI. 511A.[21]

[143]

The kinds of knowledge run from least clear, at the bottom, to clearest, at the top. Plato's names for the four segments help to indicate what kind of method and certainty he thinks each way has. But the diagram can also be read as Plato's outline of the history of earlier philosophy, for he sees this, too, as a progress from a very unclear stage of prescientific folklore to the final synthesis that was his own. The "Form of the Good" at the very top of the figure is what Plato sees as his own final contribution to this history: it is his way of explaining how the four kinds of knowing, despite their differences in method and subject matter, fit together into a single coherent whole.

This diagram of "the Divided Line" has an intrinsic interest of its own: it is probably the most famous and most often drawn diagram in the whole history of philosophy. Plato here has evidently adopted the Pythagorean technique of teaching and investigating with the help of diagrams.[20]

He introduces it in the course of a discussion of political theory, in order to show what he means by a genuine political scientist as opposed to a practicing politician who has a wholly different method and different kind of knowledge. To make the point clear, four degrees of "clarity of knowledge" are arranged along a line (see the preceding diagram).

The bottom segment of the line is called *eikasia*, sometimes translated "conjecture," or "guessing." The name itself refers to a kind of picture-thinking; a knowing that is nothing more than fantasy and story. Perhaps "hearsay" is a good description of this, or possibly "guessing" in the American colloquial sense of "I guess so," said when we have *some* notion but can't pin down our reasons for having it.

The second segment, *pistis*, has a name that refers to faith or trust, meant to contrast with the untrustworthiness of conjecture. It is the kind of knowledge that a craftsman or technician has, dependable *"knowing how."* Plato's choice of a name suggests that such practical "knowing how" has a wholly different degree of reliability and clarity from guessing. Long human experience with centuries of trial and error lies behind the discoveries of the arts and crafts, just as a long period of practical training is necessary for each individual craftsman.

The third kind of knowledge is called "dianoia." "Understanding" or "knowing that," *dianoia* goes beyond *pistis* in clarity and certainty, since it not only is knowledge of how things work but also what they are. It is the knowledge of the chemistry student who can use the general rules summarized in his periodic table to predict and explain reactions, as opposed to the boy with a chemistry set who has learned some combinations that will produce explosions, invisible inks, and strange odors. The scientist of this type, like the chemistry student, has discovered by generalization the *general laws* and *kinds of things* of his particular subject matter—the law of gravitation, the classification of numbers into odd and even, and so on—and he solves particular problems by showing how these general rules apply. (When Plato wrote this passage, he thought that mathematics was already well developed in this *scientific* form, that natural science had made some progress toward it, but that in politics and ethics, the greatest experts of the day had gone no further than a muddle of "know how" and "guessing.")

But above *dianoia*, "knowing that," with its generalizations and deductions, Plato places a higher level: *noesis*, "knowing why." The difference between knowing that and knowing why is the difference between knowing one specialized set of rules and kinds, and knowing how these specialized sets fit together with one another in a systematic whole.[21] *Noesis*, knowing why, as the Greek name indicates, is knowledge by *Nous*, the mind that had already been so important in Greek philosophy from Parmenides to Anaxagoras. Plato himself describes the difference between "knowing why" and "knowing that" in three ways:

1. KNOWING THAT is satisfied with *partial* systematizations; KNOWING WHY involves complete systems;

2. KNOWING THAT uses hypotheses, generalizations, and tables that have predictive value; KNOWING WHY goes beyond hypotheses that work to *tested theories*;

3. KNOWING THAT has as its aim *exact description*; KNOWING WHY (as the notion of tested theories suggests) adds an *evaluation*.

The idea of *Nous* as a power of insight into the inner nature and ultimate order of things finds no obvious counterpart in our usual modern discussions.[22] Plato, however, contrasts "knowing why," which sees systems as wholes, with the more specialized "knowing-that," which is satisfied with explaining individual parts. It is only on the level of "knowing why," for example, that one recognizes that there is a serious inconsistency between a materialistic philosophy and a belief in the incorporeal soul of theology. Reason challenges us to reconcile these or to decide between them. But the physicist who is a materialist and the theologian, each within his own discipline, may be perfectly satisfied with the "knowing-that" explanations of souls or atoms which he has devised.

Another way in which this difference appears to Plato is that reason, "knowing why," is self-critical and *tries to examine its presuppositions*, whereas understanding, "knowing that," is satisfied when it *can make confirmed predictions*. Here the difference in the two kinds of knowing is like that between the theoretical chemist, who tests and criticizes the assumptions built into the periodic table of elements, and the chemistry student, who takes this table as given and is satisfied with it because he can predict and explain reactions.

Third, "knowing why" introduces considerations of value, whereas "knowing that" is only concerned with descriptions of fact. We can see this best by considering the scientist or philosopher who is comparing several alternative hypotheses each of which has generality and predictive power. He must *evaluate* these hypotheses and choose the best one, or combine them in a new theory that is better. Here Plato believed that the way we talk shows, correctly, that a final judgment of value is a necessary part of the world of fact.[23]

These three differences in clarity between understanding and reason, "knowing that" and "knowing why," prepare the way for the final passage above reason, to the very topmost term of the figure of the line, the special knowledge of the good.

At the very top of his diagram of the Divided Line, Plato locates "the Form of the Good." This idea goes back to the Pythagorean notion that value is realized through order—a *cosmos*, whether in the heavens, or in the individual soul, or in society. If the different dimensions of reality that philosophers have recognized were completely disconnected from each other, there would be many "worlds" and no single system, no *cosmos* of being.

Considering the connections that hold between different kinds and levels of the scattered set of "realities" listed in the outline that follows we discover that there is, in fact, only one world with its parts in systematic interconnection. For Plato, this was a carefully reasoned conclusion. Since his time there has almost always been this idea as an unconscious *assumption*, not *conclusion*, in the background of both our common sense and our technical scientific and philosophic thought. After all, in a world with many kinds of knowing and reality to be known, what ground have we for our belief that mathematics has anything to do with objects in space and time, or physics any relevance at all to the aesthetic world of religion and poetry?

PLATO'S NEW SYSTEM OF REALITY

I. The Problem

A quick schematic look at a map of ancient Athens gives us a picture of many different "worlds," each with its own kind of reality and its own frame of reference:

World of the
Assembly

World of the
Acropolis

World of the
Sciences

World of the
Theater

World of the
Marketplace

Plato had inherited from earlier Greek thought explorations of various components and kinds of reality, all of which deserved attention. This inherited philosophy included the list that follows:

Physical objects and processes (Milesians, Anaxagoras)
Unchanging numbers, shapes, etc. (Pythagoreans)
Social conventions (Sophists)
Changing flow, transient individuals (Heraclitus)
The complex human self (Socrates)
Ideals and goals (Socrates)

It also included the following suggestions:

There is some single plan of order in the *cosmos* (Pythagoreans)

There is some single highest reality (Parmenides)

Ideals act as causes in human life and in nature (Socrates)

Things as we know them may be quite different from things as they exist in fact (Sophists, especially Gorgias)

II. Toward a Solution: Classification

Plato, by the time of the middle dialogues, had worked out two four-part classifications of kinds of knowledge and kinds of things, ordered in terms of their *permanence, certainty,* and *completeness.*

It is this scheme that the Divided Line summarizes:

Knowledge	Things
1. True sciences	1. Systems, Ideals
2. Hypotheses	2. Abstractions and structures
3. Techniques	3. Physical objects; human societies
4. Stories, poems, painting	4. Fictions, shadows, reflections

At this stage, we know that these eight kinds are *different*; the problem now is to see if any systematic connection holds between them.

III. Thoughts and Things: The First Step

In the *Republic,* Plato argues that since what seems most reasonable to a human inquirer is also most true in the world of fact, there need not be a sharp distinction between human thought and the rest of the world. Both our minds and the outer world have the same shared order. If they did not, what seemed best in the order of thought would not be best when applied to fact. Thus, thoughts and things fall into the same pattern and contain the same kinds.

IV. Causal Connections: The Second Step

The Pythagoreans had shown that there are mathematical laws which apply to and explain the world of physical objects and techniques. They were convinced that in principle this also was true for human societies. This fact, that "generalization" explains nature, points to a causal connection between levels 2 and 3 of our scheme, above. That is, objects behave as they do *because* the unchanging types and laws are what they are.

But just as laws and objects stand in a causal relation, so do objects and "images" of them—reflections, shadows, snapshots, etc. The different successive "perspectives" I see as I walk around a desk are systematically related to it: they are perspectives *of* the desk. Fine art is a craft for selecting particular perspectives of nature or society: the artist's work "imitates" the social and natural world. The realm of "fictions" is, in this way, explained as *caused by* the realm of objects. It is true that we can be highly selective in picking out perspectives, and highly original in recombining them: but, ultimately, it is from the objective world that the artist gets his material to imitate.

Further, it is possible to go beyond separate special schemes of explanation ("hypotheses") to find larger systems which relate these as special cases ("sciences"). For example, number-theory goes "beyond" the multiplication table in this way: psychology tries to go beyond the standard lists of "types of audience" and "types of case" which the practicing rhetoricians used, to find out *why* just these types occurred and why the table worked. This possibility rests on a causal connection between the first and the second levels of the schema: complete sciences contain and explain the partial generalizations that serve as starting hypotheses.

It follows from this, if we agree that *causality* is transitive (so that when A is cause of B, and B of C, A is causally connected to C) that the four levels of the line are all causally related.

Further, although no one level of the scheme contains the human self, a "three-part" soul that has three levels seems adequate to answer Socrates' questions about human nature.

V. The Form of the Good: The Final Step

To explain *why* there are the systematic connections we have observed between the different types of knowledge and reality, Plato insists that there must be a *single form* which is the form that orders reality. This is his "Form of the Good."

Thus the final outcome is shown in the figure, below.

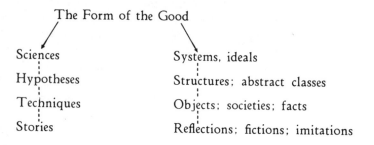

The Form of the Good

Sciences	Systems, ideals
Hypotheses	Structures; abstract classes
Techniques	Objects; societies; facts
Stories	Reflections; fictions; imitations

There is a cross-level causal connection, demonstrated by the fact that the higher level gives us an *explanation* of the lower (that is, a "because" answer). The Form of the Good is the highest form and cause; it operates both in our thoughts and in fact, and gives reality its complex systematic order.

So let us consider some of the kinds of relevance which confirmed this idea that there is only one world. The first striking evidence of connection holds between *our human way of thinking* and *the objective order of fact*. Theory-building by the method of generalization "comes naturally" to a human mind: we "know" more clearly when we find some single general rule or class, of which the many items we want to understand are special cases or instances. We go ahead, building abstract theories, with the blithe assumption that *simple* theories, *consistent* ones, *comprehensive* ones will explain the natural world. This is a large assumption, since that natural world is quite independent of our own psychological peculiarities and preferences. But it turns out that we are right: the kind of explanation that we "like" best is also the kind that has most predictive value when applied to nature. There must be a reason why this is so; one can easily imagine a world where *human prefer-*

ences have nothing to do with *objective facts*. Indeed, the erratic, cluttered world of mythology would be a world of just that kind: peopled throughout with unpredictable agents, no general theories could be trusted to apply to it in practice. Plato thought that the reason for our ability to know the outer world is that the same *simplicity* and *order* that please us in our *ideas* are also found in the *objective world*. These are properties that we use as criteria to choose best theories, and so are standards of value. Since they hold for the natural world as well as for the world of thought, *simplicity* and *order* must be guiding principles in nature. The good, as the highest value, including order and simplicity as special types, is present in thought, and in the world of fact as well.[24]

In summary, the way that our ideas relate to the world—both the world of nature and the world of form—is the first piece of evidence that there is a single ordered *cosmos*, in which idea and object, form and process, value and fact are related to each other. A second piece of evidence for the idea of a single system of reality is, Plato believed, given by the obvious but baffling fact that applied logic and mathematics do describe the operations of a world in space and time. Why do mathematics and logic, which describe relations in an unchanging realm of structure, also apply to the world of physical reality? This is not nearly so naïve a question as it sounds. The Pythagoreans tried to avoid any separation of pure and applied mathematics just because they wanted to explain *how* shapes and numbers relate to objects and processes, although in the end they did make the distinction. There is a causal connection here that shows the systematic plan of reality. In a Heraclitean world of strife and flow, if no *logos* governed constant change, *mathematics and logic would not work at all*. There might still be pure mathematicians and logicians, but what they studied would have *nothing* to do with what happened to them and around them. Plato tried by a simple example to show how his forms relate to physical facts. The logical relations of the forms *limit* possible causes and changes. For instance, the forms (that is, the abstract concepts) of hot and cold are mutually exclusive. Physical fire "shares in" (has as an essential property) being hot. We can tell *by formal reasoning* that a "cold physical fire" cannot be found in nature. More generally, the tables and rules that make "knowing that" possible, assume that in nature the formal relations of the science hold for factual relations of objects. In exploring the relation of the dimensions of reality that previous philosophers had discovered separately, this relation of logic and mathematics to physical causes and processes shows that the Pythagorean forms and Milesian material things are related, not opposed or indifferent.[25]

This is the second step of the philosophic argument. Given five different types of "knowing," with different kinds of "things" to match, Plato is exploring the way in which they fit together in a single order. The first step was to show that our subjective "mental world" is systematically related to the "world of fact." This second step has been to show that the "world of unchanging structure," which we refer to in "knowing that," is systematically related to the "world of nature," which is the world we are dealing with in "knowing how." The third step will be to see whether any similar systematic relation holds between the "world of nature," the public world of physics and technology, and the "private world" of appearance, "guessing," imagination.

And, indeed, a connecting relationship also holds between the public world of "knowing how" and objects and the "guess-work" world of reflections, shadows, imagination and myth. The "images" that we see or imagine are images *of* something, just as reflections in a mirror are reflections *of* some other thing. All of the different "snapshot views" we get as we walk around, away from, and back toward a castle tower are exactly related to the tower itself. Its image is progressively smaller as we go farther away from it, brighter or darker as we stand on the sunny or shaded side, and so on. When we can relate these immediate snapshot impressions to an object which is their cause, we find a systematic order in what would otherwise be a chaotic picture album of *different* small snapshots. Though it is much harder to trace poetry, myth, imagination to origins and causes in the world of nature or of form, there, too, the object-reflection relation shows the expected kind of causality.[26]

Two further kinds of connection remain to be considered.

The first is the relation between different values and some single form of value, ("the good"), which gives them their common nature. It is not an error or an accident when we call beauty, truth, human excellence, and social justice, "good." For in each case, the value results from a common kind of part-whole order. Beauty, for example, has as an essential condition an organization of parts, in which each fits together with the others in a harmonious whole. Truth, we have seen, attaches to a simple, consistent, comprehensive whole of general laws, in which no part contradicts any other, and in which we find single types or laws that apply to multiplicities of cases and instances. Human virtue, too, is a right ordering of the "parts" of the self: reason, ambition, appetite, have a proper order of subordination and each has a proper place in a good human life. In short, a necessary condition of value is that parts belong to a single whole, in which each part keeps its place and its identity. There is a loss of value, an injustice, if a part destroys the whole or if the whole crushes any part. This principle of harmony is given by the form of the good, which is the common source of the goodness we find in beauty, nobility, intelligibility.[27]

Plato showed that this principle of *harmony* gives direction to choice and change. In the physical world, the planets and stars change constantly according to a simple, "musical" plan. On the much smaller scale of molecules, the "regular solids" offer a satisfying model, since here stability and symmetry are found together. In the animal world, a sense of incompleteness leads to a desire for immortality; an instinct for the preservation of the species, a stirring of creativity. The instinct for self-preservation can also be described as a drive toward self-realization; and the attraction of an ideal gives this drive its direction. With man, consciousness appears, able to ask about its own nature and its sensitivity to ideals. In short, it is not just *definite* structure which gives a direction to nature but *systematic* structure which realizes completeness by an integration of parts into larger functional wholes.

How far our modern science and ethics agree with Plato's insight and how far they contradict it are very hard to appraise. This is partly because there are different theories within and between our sciences and ethics. The theory of evolution gives exactly the picture of some drive throughout nature for immortality and increasing complexity of organism which Plato's view proposed. Various of our philosophies of history find the same directed progress toward value and order in the course of human civilizations (Hegel, Spengler, Toynbee, et al.). In chemistry, there is no exact modern counterpart to the idea of "crystal-shaped" elementary particles. In physics and astronomy, the "evolution" of stars and galaxies has not shown the sort of conservation of value that would be expected in Plato's view. Natural science, however, has found that a single set of laws of nature hold for every observer, regardless of his relative rest or motion compared to other observers. In ethical discussion, freedom is the center of interest rather than self-realization. Philosophers from Kant through Sartre have essentially shared Plato's concern. But changes in language and style make it hard to appreciate Plato's way of describing the highest form in his system, which gives order and direction to that system as a whole.[28]

This demonstration that the kinds and levels of reality are systematically related, in such a way that the higher levels "explain" the lower, may seem unnecessary. Once Plato has traced out this system of the kinds and levels of reality, we can see clearly that our world is not four or five isolated dimensions, each off by itself. But it took this systematic tracing to make sense of the earlier history of Greek philosophy. If we now read this history as the successive discovery of new levels of reality, as thought moved from myth to final philosophic system, we can understand the appearance of inconsistency that the Sophists found so easy to satirize. The error of each earlier position, in this Platonic account, was *to mistake a part for the whole.* The resulting identification of philosophy with physics, mathematics, poetic paradox, technology, the pursuit of self-knowledge was in each case incomplete.

Probably it required the history of philosophy from Thales to Socrates to provide the materials Plato needed to create this account of reality. We can use the Divided Line as a guide in summarizing this history of philosophic discovery.

TABLE I: PLATO'S HISTORY OF PHILOSOPHY

Level of the Divided Line	Earlier Thinkers	Kind of Reality Recognized
5. TO AGATHON Final complete system	Plato	The Good as single ideal and ordering principle
4. NOESIS Testing and systematization; knowing why	Socrates	Ideals as causes and realities
	Anaxagoras, and some scattered earlier insights	Nature as a single ordered system
3. DIANOIA Generalization, classification, knowing that	Pythagoreans	Mathematical forms
	Eleatics	More general logical forms
2. PISTIS Technique and knowing how	Milesian science	Physical objects
	Sophistry	Human conventions
	Common sense	Techniques
1. EIKASIA Guess and story	Mythology	Stories of gods as causes
	Heraclitus	A feeling of dynamic cosmic flow

1. Before science, the desire to know found its sole expression in poetry and mythology, on the level of "guess" and "story."

2. The Milesians, in their discovery of the regularities of nature and their new use of models for explanation represent an advance to the level of "knowing how." So do the Sophists, in their discovery that by agreement we can create a public world of stable, impersonal standards and objects. (Notice the com-

paratively late date, in this history, at which study of society and man move above the lowest level, as compared with the study of nature.)

3. The Pythagoreans discovered the realm of mathematical forms, and the fact that there is some close connection between these eternal entities and the natural world. In particular, their development of methods of deductive proof gave a new model of "knowing that" to all branches of Greek thought. The extension of this method from mathematical proof to reasoning in general was the work of the Eleatics, Parmenides and Zeno.

4. Parmenides' insight that there is *one* highest form common to all of reality seemed to Plato a true and vivid intuition. But it was an intuition that Parmenides could not develop systematically. He refused to admit degrees of reality, and this left no logical place for appearance in his scheme of things. His one being, though he called it a whole, was a whole with no parts to relate or harmonize. The Pythagoreans and Eleatics represent the *dianoetic* ("knowing that") level of Plato's line, but *dianoia* with some awareness that a further idea—of *cosmos*, of *being*—was needed to complete their studies of abstract form.

It was at this point that the attention of the Greek thinkers and artists shifted so dramatically from the outer world to the human self:

(1) The nebulous, inconsistent notions of literature and common-sense of the time are presumably still on the lowest level, mere *eikasia*. (2a) Anaxagoras and Archelaus were both concerned with the place of mind in their scientific schemes of things; both tried to make the self a part of nature, but at the price of making it a physical thing. (2b) The Sophists challenged this view. They saw the self as formed by the public world of social convention, having by nature only drives for pleasure and security. This notion directed attention to the choices, habits, and motives, which the scientific approach had ignored. Both science and sophistry were still treating the self empirically and operationally, so that the kind of knowledge they represented falls on the second level of Plato's line.

(3) Socrates, through his inquiries into the human self, advanced ethical inquiry to new levels. We find him generalizing

current notions into *hypotheses*, deducing consequences, and rejecting as unsatisfactory all of the suggestions offered. This critical examination, applying techniques of logic and science to test
hypotheses about the self, moved the discussion to the stage of
generalization represented by *dianoia* ("knowing that"), though
Socrates found no ready-made periodic table that was satisfactory. (4) What he did find, however, was that the directing
and unifying part of a self was the ideal of self-realization, of
completeness, which was part of each human being. Existence,
for the self, is always a pursuit of value. Justice, courage, wisdom, and temperance have intrinsic value through the right order
they give to the combination of appetite, ambition, and intelligence which characterizes a human soul. This introduction of
value as a real attractive force in nature is an example of the kind
of explanation Plato located on the fourth level of his line. We
do not know how explicitly Socrates himself thought that his
ethical insight made it possible to fit together all of the earlier
notions in a coherent scheme. Plato, however, was sure that it
had this virtue, and on occasion he even tried to build the combination diagrams that show how motivation and insight interact to determine types of personality.

(5) In Plato's history of philosophy, the final advance came
as the result of Plato's extending what Socrates had found about
the self, that it is an ordered system of powers held together by
a common ideal aim, to apply to all reality. What had seemed
separate dimensions could in this way be ordered as higher and
lower, in a *hierarchy*. Each level is related to the one below it as
"a one over many." An object, for example, is the single center
and source of its many appearances, reflections, aspects. A kind,
such as "animal," is one unchanging form common to many
physical objects, the animals in nature, which "share" or illustrate it. An ideal is a form of system, in which some positive
value is realized through a proper part-whole pattern. (So
beauty, justice, truth, and symmetry, are *single* forms common
to the *many* works of fine art, societies, and scientific theories.)
Finally, the good, "like the sun at midday," is the single highest
form at the apex of the hierarchy, the common cause of goodness
reflected in the ideals, and the form which makes reality a single,

ordered system, with each dimension properly subordinated and integrated in the whole.

We can picture this by a diagram almost as universally used as the divided line itself, a figure showing the Platonic system as providing levels of unity, and converging at the top level. (See Fig. 1, which follows.) Shelley caught the aesthetic and religious feeling that this diagram symbolizes when he wrote:

> The One remains, the many change and pass;
> The light of heaven abides, earth's shadows fly;
> Life, like a dome of many-colored glass
> Stains the white radiance of eternity. . . .

Since the fourth century after Christ, Christian theologians have accepted this Platonic view of a hierarchically ordered, systematically connected world. Instead of the form of the good, they place God at the top of the hierarchy. The influence of Christianity, sometimes in the background, sometimes explicitly, has given us a "religious common sense" which *feels*, without arguing the point, the validity of this Platonic one-over-many world pattern.

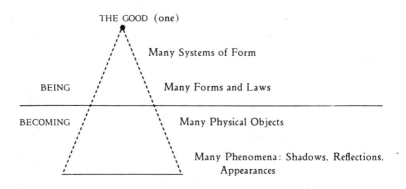

FIGURE 1. THE ONE AND THE MANY

Plato does not explicitly describe the present figure in his dialogues, but ever since Crantor, head of the Academy at the turn of the third century before Christ, such triangular designs have always been used to picture and explain Platonism to Western students and readers.

The triangle in this figure is another representation of the four levels of reality of the divided line. But the triangular figure suggests, as the single line did not, that as we move from appearance toward reality, we are also moving from multiplicity to unity, to *one* from *many*.[29] Thus a single physical object has many appearances. In the same way, a single type or law has many instances—the law of gravitation, for example, has as many instances as there are physical bodies attracting one another. And the many types and laws are themselves part of a single system, with one highest form.[30] The different paths leading to the true, the just, the one, and the beautiful all come at last to the good.[31]

This systematic vision of Plato's is not dead, not an out-of-date historical curiosity. Whitehead has used Plato's model expertly and systematically to interpret science and society. Many of our most pressing practical debates still center around the relevance and order of the same dimensions of reality that Plato marked out in his great outline.

PLATO'S IDEAS IN RELATION TO MODERN THEORIES OF EDUCATION

One test that Plato himself applied to philosophy was its *practical usefulness*. His discussion of the form of the good, in the *Republic*, ends with an ideal curriculum, a practical scheme to teach men to recognize this highest form. One question worth asking, therefore, is whether Plato's system can solve any pressing practical problems of today? As a test case, we will try to do for current discussions of American high-school education what Plato himself did with earlier discussions of reality. Using Plato's systematic map as our chart, we will find that it clarifies the relation between schools of theorists, and offers a program for bringing their insights together.

As we listen to contemporary discussion of high-school education, we find ourselves hearing an argument reminiscent of discussions of philosophy in the Athens of Plato's time.[32] To show "what Plato's philosophy means" by an example of "how it works," I will apply the system to education—not education in Plato's Athens, but in modern American secondary schools, starting just as Plato did in Athens, in the middle of an active public debate.

Among groups with definite ideas about what is needed today in our high schools, there are the formalists (sometimes grouped together under the name of Liberal Arts Humanists) who want the center of education to be development of intelligence by discipline and by contact with masterpieces of form—literary, mathematical, philosophical. Like the Pythagoreans, they have recognized the relevance of the third level of Plato's line, *dianoia*, to human inquiry and understanding.

But some currently fashionable educational theorists, whom we can classify as a family influenced by existentialism, have a different point of view. They question the value of *admiring* form, as opposed to *creating* it; they distrust any conditioning that trains the student to accept some social role. Their chief concern is to make the individual student aware of his uniqueness, his freedom, and the authenticity he can achieve. They seem to insist that *eikasia*, the vivid individual imagery located on the lowest level of the divided line, be given a part in educational practice and theory. Surely, this is a recognition of a truth that Socrates saw—without motivation and personal engagement, we may get memorization but not real learning or inquiry. It is not enough to have pure form without content; Plato himself always, by myth or concrete characterization, gives poetic, concrete vividness to even his most abstract formal ideas.

Progressive education is a name we can use for the set of ideas still dominant in American educational practice and theory. The progressive theorist believes that education should teach the student to use ideas as tools. The meaning of a word or an idea is, he believes, determined by its use; the purpose of school is to give the student skill, through experience, in tool-using. Pragmatism also emphasizes the importance of a social context. The individual self is largely a social creation, and the skills required for living in his society are among the most important skills a student should "learn by doing" while he is in school. Some modern pragmatists have admired the Greek Sophists, and believed that they anticipated much of pragmatism. As remarked in our discussion of Sophistry, when the uncritical opportunism of the Sophists is contrasted with the careful rationale of pragmatism, the resemblance becomes less close than it seems at first glance. The fact remains that the pragmatist, with his instrumental definition of knowledge and his emphasis on technique and practical aims, fits exactly where the Sophists do on the divided line. The main contributions of the pragmatist are his recognition that to be able to understand ideas one must see them applied and his further recognition of the crucial part skill and convention play in human behavior.

It is interesting for a Platonist to notice that our concern with education at all is the result of an idealism which all three of these groups share. They want full self-realization for the individual, progress and justice for society, and, in the long run, survival and betterment of the human race. Such a shared ideal evidently belongs on the top level of the Platonic line. Because the groups share this aim they can adjust their correct, but overly general, conflicting claims and work out a compromise position. And the Platonist offers as his contribution to the discussion the reminder that there is such an ideal, which is more important than any specific set of methods or subjects that relate to it as means to ends.

PLATO'S LINE AND MODERN DISCUSSIONS OF EDUCATION

Level of the Divided Line *Emphasized as Essential* *to Education*	*Modern Theories and* *Greek Counterparts*
THE GOOD: REASON	Idealism: emphasis falls on intrinsic value of education as a means for self-realization and human betterment. (The Academy.)
UNDERSTANDING	Liberal Arts Humanism: emphasis is put on models of good form—of thought, art, self-expression; discipline is

important. Stress falls on the intellectual and impersonal dimension of the self. (The Pythagorean mathematical studies.)

SKILL

Pragmatism: emphasis is put on skills, funded experience; an instrumental view taken toward words and ideas; stress falls on social adaptation and the social dimension of the self. (The Sophists.)

IMAGINATION

Existentialism: Emphasis is put on individuality, authenticity, freedom, motivation; stress on the vivid, but individual and private, dimension of the self. (Homer; Heraclitus.)

Note: To an observing Platonist, it seems that here each group of theorists has discovered the importance of one dimension of a reality which is complex. Each is right in emphasizing the necessity of that dimension for attainment of the common ideal; each is wrong in taking too narrow a view of the situation and believing that its own program contradicts or should exclude the others. Idealism, if it takes the form of laudatory speeches without paying attention to techniques of realizing the ideal, can be just as one-dimensional as any other theory.

Plato's philosophical sympathies are quite evidently with the tradition of formalism, rather than materialism. As we move from experiments with changing things to recognition of unchanging types and laws, we cross the line that separates becoming from being, the physical space-time world, in which things try to be themselves, yet never truly are, from the realm of being—a realm of unchanging, precise form, where "each form is just what it is." Knowledge of a universal, scientific kind is possible because in reality itself there is this world of unchanging forms, which set limits and give direction to the processes of the world of change in space and time. The Pythagoreans represent, in Plato's history of philosophy, the first stage of man's discovery that there are eternal forms—triangles, sets, and ratios—of which the many changing objects around us are instances. However difficult it may be to explain *how* these forms are "shared in" by their particular exemplifications, it was the discovery of this dimension of reality that Plato thought had made scientific explanation possible.

PLATO: TESTS AND APPLICATIONS

From the Renaissance through the nineteenth century, it was Plato the speculative thinker who was appreciated, at the expense of Plato the analyst. In our own century we are beginning to realize what analytic finesse Plato brought to the testing and clarifying of his philosophy during the last twenty years of his life. Looking sharply at this system, Plato saw three ways of testing its truth: (1) If it were true, natural science could be summarized in a single system, with all the disjointed data fitting into place. (2) If it were true, it could be applied to such a mundane but important matter as setting up model laws for actual Greek cities of the day. (3) If it were true, it could provide a clear, logical statement of exactly what the meanings of form, participation, degrees of reality, evaluation, and the good are.

The *first* test is represented by Plato's *Timaeus*, an encyclopedia of the science of the time that must have represented an enormous volume of collective research by the Academy. The *second* is given in the monumental dialogue, the *Laws*, which Plato finished only in rough draft. This also must represent an extensive academic project of collecting and comparing law codes and constitutional histories. In the light of the practical needs and the theoretic knowledge of his time, Plato would have been entitled to feel that the scientific and practical applicability of his theory was established.

The case was rather different, however, when he attempted an *analysis* that would meet his third test. A series of technical dialogues, and a great public lecture on the good, are parts of this search for clarity on Plato's part. A brief summary may be in order, both to raise questions and to indicate how far Plato felt he had answers.

The nature of forms and participation is easy to misunderstand. Plato's *Parmenides* shows that we must *not* think of forms as *objects in some place*; and that participation cannot be explained by a *physical model* of sharing. The relation of squareness to a particular square is not that of a business partner to the assets of a partnership. Plato's *Theaetetus* shows that knowledge cannot be explained as memory and experience alone; it has a kind of certainty and generality that only something like *the recognition of a form* can account for. (Compare the relation of *pistis* to *dianoia* in the "divided line.") Plato's *Sophist* explores the logical difficulty of thinking or talking about not-being. By distinguishing pure nothing from kinds of otherness, Plato modifies Parmenides in a way that allows appearances to exist as well as absolute reality. Plato's *Statesman* explores the technique of evaluation and administration, and introduces a new idea of operational definition. The lecture on the good was devoted to a proof "that the good is one"—a crucial point if this is to be the single highest form that unifies the worlds of fact and of thought. Plato, and his admirers, have been vexed by a problem that arises from treating forms as—at the same time—ideals, abstract classes, and meanings of words. For example, Plato talks as though each form is an instance of itself (e.g., "the form of the good is good"). This is understandable when we take forms as ideals, recognizing their Socratic ancestry. In that context, "the good is good" does not mean "the form of the good shares in the property of goodness," but rather "the form of the good *is* the property of goodness." But it is not so defensible when we consider the forms as limits or classes or properties. If sharing in a form means having that property, and if a property is always different from the thing that shares it, then no form can be an instance of itself. Take the property of squareness. Every square is a square because it shares in this property. But if, on the pattern of goodness is good, one says that squareness is square, there is an awkward dilemma. Since for forms of this type the property and the things sharing it are different, there must be a second form of squareness which squareness shares. But that form, too, if it is square, must share in a higher form, and the regress never ends. Yet if one denies that squareness is square, while holding that to explain a thing is to grasp its form, it is impossible to give any explanation of forms.

A further problem comes from Plato's realization that there must be public, unchanging meanings for language and thought. Language gives forms quite different from either defining properties or definite ideals. What I mean if I say "good men are unjust" is quite clear; I have taken two words, or, if you prefer, two concepts, and connected them. But goodness and injustice *are not really* related in this way, whether it is as *definitions* or as *ideals* that we construe them. If we simply took the forms as a development of the Sophistic notion of meanings, they would have a mobility, a power of separation and recombination, that the forms in either of the other two senses cannot possess.

Plato seems to me never to have given a final clear explanation of this point. He was certain that the forms combined all the roles of meanings, definitions, ideals, limits, and goals. But neither he nor his followers for two thousand years have been able to show how *the same thing* can play such very diverse parts. This does not mean that Plato's theory of forms was mistaken, even if we need more complex formulation of it or even if we must recognize three kinds of form.

Plato has stated an important fact: it is in our own truest natures, and in the nature of things, not because of convention as the Sophists taught, that some "dim divination" makes us admire and value truth, beauty, and nobility. Indeed, this innate sense of value can already be seen at work in the religious myths and belief in cosmic justice with which men, long before philosophy, tried to portray a world order that had some respect for human value.[33]

Turning from science and metaphysics to politics and ethics, we find that one of the satisfying things about Plato's system is the light it sheds on the nature of the human self, and the relation of the individual to society. These were two of the central problems that Plato proposed to investigate in the Academy. Like the quest to know reality, the search for the self was difficult because a self is a complex thing; it cannot be simply located on one level or another of such a classification as the divided line. Self-identity includes a body which the soul inhabits and animates. It includes the senses and imagination, with their vivid but transitory perspectives and glimpses of the world. It includes ambition and freedom of decision. The self also has the ability to know unchanging forms, and to respond to the form of the good as its own ultimate ideal. The Platonic self required a map, just as reality did. Such a map can also serve a student of ethics or a psychologist as a diagnostic chart, since whenever the parts of the self are not in their proper order, the *cosmos* of a just, well-ordered soul is lost, and vice results.[34]

Plato believed—as some political theorists do not today—that society has some reality distinct from being a mere collection of its separate individual members. As a consequence, he could not dismiss the demands a state imposed on its citizens as arbitrary or wholly conventional. Rather, he put his question in a different way: must the ideal of society and the ideal of individual self-realization always be incompatible with one another? Are conflicts such as that of the Athenian democracy and Socrates tragic but unavoidable? Or are these two ideals related in some other way? By the time Plato completed *The Republic*, he had concluded that the two forms *were not necessarily incompatible*. It seemed clear that even such an advanced city as Athens would have to change almost every one of its traditional practices and institutions before it became a state in which social effectiveness and individual virtue would coincide. But even if this was discouraging on the practical level, it was a hopeful philosophical discovery. For in theory there could be a society in which a Socrates would indeed be judged a benefactor, not executed as a clear and present danger.[35]

Plato was satisfied with an analysis of the complex self into the three components of reason, spirit (ambition, love of honor, will), and appetite. Reason knows that the human being is a partial realization of timeless ideals of value and harmony. Ambition, or spirit, is able to act in the world—it is an energy to compete, make, and do. Appetite is an instinctive self-centeredness that reflects the soul's attachment to the pleasures and pains, sensations and limitations of its own particular body. Men achieve self-realization when these three dimensions are in proper and harmonious relation. Reason can judge which appetites and ambitions it is good to satisfy, and which ought to be redirected or suppressed. Left to themselves, or allowed to dominate a whole personality, ambition and appetite have no criteria other than a blind urge to have more—more property, more pleasure, more prestige, more power. But since by its very definition having more is an unattainable goal (for however much I have now, I cannot now *have more* than that), the price of a wrong psychological adjustment of these parts of the self is a life of dissatisfaction spent in pursuit of a phantom goal that is never more nearly approached, and a life without realization of intrinsic human dignity or value.[36]

This does not deny that individuals can, and should, take different paths to self-realization. Some men are by nature inclined to be philosophers, others soldiers and athletes, others producers and tradesmen. These differences are a matter of the relative strengths of the three parts of the soul, and the powers of the body they animate. It is within the power of all men to follow their interests and realize their aptitudes reasonably, not in a blind passion for more commodities or prizes. (For example, Milo of Crotona was an athlete whose feats were legendary. During the latter part of his athletic career he was the husband of the daughter of Pythagoras, and a member of the Order. Plato could count on his readers to remember Milo as a case where professional athleticism had not made Greece's greatest athlete into a hater of culture, an inferior human being.)

The human soul, its inner conflicts and its life after death, are frequently treated by Plato in his myths. For Plato keeps a place in his writing for mythology. Stories can add vividness to arguments and illustrate ideas. If the readers do not mistake them for scientific explanations, and the teller of the myth is able to select only those stories that a philosopher finds suitable, they are not harmful. But in spite of these myths about the soul, it is never quite clear in Plato's philosophy how literally he takes the soul's immortality.

He seems convinced, at the very least, that the ability of

human reason to know and admire timeless truths and immortal ideals is evidence that this dimension of human existence is immortal or somehow has a share in immortality. And he feels that there is some profound intuitive belief, more personal and vivid than any abstract dialectical proof, embodied in the myths of a last judgment. In these stories, the complete individual—with his memory, appetite, and ambition, as well as reason alone—is judged by a cosmic justice that takes what man ought to be as its criterion, and allocates happy or unhappy future lives in the light of the degree of human self-fulfillment each soul has attained.[37] A desire for immortality is certainly the ground of human motivation: in a world order at once good, just, and beautiful, the most plausible stories men can invent are those that reflect this hope that souls *deserving* immortality will actually *attain* it.

Plato studied extensively the relation of the individual and the state. Though he granted the state a reality, and recognized, as Socrates had, that a citizen has civic obligations, he did not by any means believe that the state was an organism which could swallow up the individual and would always be right.[38] There are two important respects in which the state is natural. First, it is the only way for an individual to realize his own full human nature: second, there is in nature a form of the state which gives a definition, goal, and criterion of value for human states.

But just as an individual can go wrong in his ethical choices, mistaking something that is merely a means to a good life for an end in itself, so states can, and usually do, mistake some subordinate value—national wealth, national power, personal aggrandizement of a ruler—for the true goal of individual virtue and general welfare.[39] But, Plato believed, if there ever could be statesmen so well trained that their vision of the good was clear, *their* direction would create societies in which the merits of a Socrates would be recognized. The immediate occasion of his divided line diagram was Plato's desire to define the content and level of education that such true statesmanship presupposed. And to provide such an education for later generations of rulers was one of the hopes Plato had for his Academy.

Societies can go wrong in a second way. If their rulers have a mistaken notion that the individual is worth nothing, the state everything, there will be injustices to individuals, whatever direction the over-all policy takes.[40] To gain a share of immortality and a sense of creative living, the individual needs to see himself as a responsible part of the community—a whole more lasting and extensive than a brief single life. To deprive anyone of this is *an injustice*.[41] Opportunities for effective citizenship that also led to self-fulfillment were the exception rather than the rule in the cities of Plato's day. Conditions of good family, property, education, and the like set a maze of arbitrary obstructions in the way of the best use of individual talents and interests. Here Plato, perhaps partly inspired by the Sophistic insistence that most of these customs and laws were only convention, proposed a radical solution. *Assignment of social function should be made strictly on the basis of ability and interest.* If this were done (Plato showed how), the social need for producers, protectors, and educators and the individual variations in talent could be made to coincide. But he saw no other way (as shown in the following table). He did not expect his idea to be adopted immediately but hoped that "perhaps, in some other age, in some far barbarian country, if not in Greece" such a society might be realized.[42]

FUNCTIONAL CLASSES AND INDIVIDUAL APTITUDES

Intellectual Capacity	Motivation	Social Function
NOESIS	Reasonable	Rulers
DIANOIA	Ambitious	Soldiers
PISTIS	Appetitive	Producers

But in this scheme, all three classes are balanced, though not all equal in intellectual aptitude or in the interest which motivates them. If we take account of imbalances, the list of types of personality becomes larger.

	Rational	Spirited	Appetitive
NOESIS	Philosopher	General	Merchant
DIANOIA	Auxiliary	Athlete/Soldier	Sophist/Lawyer
PISTIS	Artisan	Poet	Tyrant

Types of state can be schematized in the same way, since the "policy" of each is, on a larger scale, like an individual personality. For example, Plato has a list of five kinds of state defined in this way in *The Republic*, IX.

FIVE KINDS OF STATE

Type	Rule	Aim of Rulers
Aristocracy	Rule of the best	National welfare
Timocracy	Rule of the military	National power
Oligarchy	Rule of a wealthy minority	National income
Democracy (Athenian style)	Rule of the many	Freedom, i.e., no fixed policy
Tyranny	Rule of one dictator	Advantage of the ruler

Today we are committed to the Platonic notion that society should afford equal opportunity for self-realization to every individual. Hereditary aristocracy is no longer acceptable as a pattern of social organization, slavery is almost a thing of the past, and voting rights are no longer granted exclusively to an economic upper class. Increasingly, the public doctor who was almost the sole expert consultant in the government of a Greek city has been supplemented, in the more civilized countries of the world, by specially educated civil-service and cabinet officials, who can apply their special knowledge to agriculture, education, interstate engineering projects, and regulation of banks and securities. Whether this kind of precise scientific direction of policy can ever be used by the leaders responsible for the state as a whole remains an unanswered question. We do not yet have the kind of philosophic social science that Plato envisioned as a necessary prerequisite for "philosophic rulers." Even if we had, there are reasons, already cogently stated by Plato's student Aristotle, for doubting whether such a disinterested scientific approach to public decisions is possible.[43]

It is both interesting historically, and provocative in the setting of our modern problems, to look again at the *Republic*, and to see how, from the many strands of history and theory that must form part of the fabric of any discussion of society and the self, Plato was able to weave together a theoretical tapestry that satisfied him. Philosophy and education were Plato's answer to the question Socrates' execution had posed twenty years before.[44]

Ever since Plato, there have been philosophical Platonists in the West. Their ideas range from St. Augustine's theology to Whitehead's science. What are the defining characteristics of Platonism? We can mention four that are important. (1) A Platonist believes that the function of philosophy is to arrive at some single systematic synthesis. There is always a drive for completeness of explanations and ideas. (2) A Platonist always accepts some version of the theory of forms, which holds that generalizations have explanatory value. (3) A Platonist thinks that reality forms a single coherent system, which is not cut up into isolated departments. He is therefore inclined to try to transfer insights or laws, by analogy, from one part of the world to another, across lines usually departmentalized. (4) Finally, a Platonist always believes that the world of thought and fact illustrates some value. The good, the true, and the beautiful come together at a single highest point in every Platonic philosophy; a high point which is so both for being and for thought.[45]

In Plato's final development of formalism, Greek philosophy reached a new systematic coherence. All the aspects of reality, all the techniques and insights of earlier Greek thought were brought together in this ordered cosmos with many dimensions. In it there were both form and flow, and Plato gave a decisive statement of the importance of form and the dependence of fact on value. The form of the good gave a unity to his philosophic order, in somewhat the way that the Acropolis had unified ancient Athens, standing above the theater, market, assembly, and Academy.

XV. ARISTOTLE

The Organization of All Reality

There I beheld the
Master of those who know. . . .

DANTE, *Inferno*

*To Plato's thesis that general laws govern nature his brilliant
student Aristotle added the notion that nature can be reasoned
out and understood in every detail. He backed this notion up
with an amazing variety of experiments and scientific observations.*

*A master pattern of four "causes" organizes every kind of
reality. The resulting system reconciles materialism and formalism, bringing together Plato's theory of forms and Democritus'
atomic theory.*

*While Aristotle's work in natural philosophy is interesting
and provocative in its place in the history of Greek and medieval
philosophy, it is his treatment of ethics, politics, and poetry that
most challenges us today.*

*Aristotle uses "cause" in the old sense of "something that is
responsible." His causes are the dimensions or aspects of a thing
that are responsible for its existing and for its being the kind of
thing it is. These dimensions are a matter, the material cause;
a form, the formal cause; a maker or parent, which brings the
thing into being, the efficient cause; and a use or goal which each
thing embodies, the final cause.*

[172]

COLERIDGE'S REMARK that "every man is born either a Platonist or an Aristotelian" recognizes the radical difference in temperament, technique, and achievement of these two great men who are the culmination of Hellenic philosophy. Characteristically Plato started with mathematics and astronomy in his discussions and illustrations of nature and science, Aristotle with zoology and medicine. Where Plato wrote brilliant speculative dialogues, Aristotle developed meticulously organized technical lectures. Plato seems to avoid a technical vocabulary, at least until his very latest work; Aristotle marks out each of the many distinctions his philosophy requires with its own carefully defined technical term.[1] Plato distrusts common sense, custom, and empiricism; Aristotle reconciles, wherever he can, common sense views of things and ways of talking about them with the most recondite views in philosophy.[2]

Plato and Aristotle are alike in the amazing range, vitality, and originality of their accomplishments. Aristotle's design of research collections as part of his school, the Lyceum, is an educational invention only slightly less important and original than Plato's establishment of his Academy. Aristotle's persistent attempt to show that reality is ordered throughout by a four-dimensional scheme of causes gave to Plato's demonstration of the importance of form a new confidence in the intelligibility and order of nature. The attempt was convincing in spite of its vast scale. Aristotle had set himself no less a task than that of proving that all of reality could be organized by use of his four causes. He set out to prove this by actually organizing it. His extant writings include epic treatises on logic, which were not substantially modified for 2,500 years; on astronomy, chemistry, and biology, which remained standard until the Renaissance; on metaphysics or, as Aristotle called it, "first philosophy," on the "practical sciences" of ethics and politics; and on poetics, all of which remain interesting and up to date.[3]

This great program of tracing the four causes throughout reality grew out of an earlier interest in order. Aristotle, in the early years of his Lyceum work, had organized for the first time subject-fields (rhetoric, debate, logical fallacy) never before treated in a systematic form. This, too, was the purpose of the history of philosophy with which Aristotle opened his *Metaphysics*. His interest in the history of ideas was constant, and we can see from lists and fragments of his early works that he had been preparing this history for many years by writing monographs and treatises on the doctrines or errors of individual philosophers and schools. He intended to show that wise men of the past had recognized no causes other than his set of four; that when they thought they had done so (as the Platonists and Pythagoreans seemed to claim) they were really only talking incorrectly about Aristotle's "formal causes." And, within the limits set by the state of knowledge in his day, Aristotle's proof comes miraculously close to being complete!

There is one interesting result that deserves discussion in some detail: while Aristotle's philosophy of nature is no longer compatible with the findings of modern science, his treatments of ethics and politics—which might have been expected to go out of date far more quickly, since societies change faster than animal species or stars—are surprisingly up to date, and offer a suggestive way of approaching contemporary problems.[4] Why should this be so? There is, we will find, a fundamental difference in Aristotle's use of causal explanation in these two areas, which accounts for the fact that later history can find one right, yet reject the other.

Aristotle differs from Plato in three major ways. First, where Plato seems always to be looking for new syntheses that cross traditional lines of specialization, Aristotle believes in departmental organization—of a university, of lectures, of research. Aristotle believes that the different kinds of reality have distinctive properties of their own; a star, an animal, a triangle, and a state, while all are part of being, all have such crucial differences that a Platonic attempt to understand them by their formal similarities is likely to give a very sketchy, inexact picture. Consequently, knowledge requires separate investigation of the different kinds of things there are to know, and a technical vocabulary to keep track of the significant types and distinctions.

A second way in which Aristotle differs from Plato is in his attitude toward materialism. Plato nowhere mentions Democritus by name, but to judge from various passages in which he criticizes materialism, he did not think that the atomic theory had any philosophic explanatory value. It must have seemed to him a technology: a way of finding out *how* things work, but at best able only to find conditions, not causes.

For Aristotle, on the other hand, both the materialism of the atomic theory and the formalism of Plato and the Academy offer genuine causal explanation. He is constantly aware of the philosophic problem that the history of Greek thought presents to him: how are we to explain a universe in which both idealism and mechanism, formalism and materialism are possible? His synthesis, in which both kinds of causality have a place, is a powerful intellectual tool; these four causes balance the material and formal dimensions of reality.

The third way in which Aristotle differs from Plato is in his view of the world as made up of individual "substances," each of which has an identity of its own. The world is not simply a single tightly connected system, in which the parts are dominated by the whole. Neither is it simply a mechanical concourse of a vast plurality of small, hard particles. It is, rather, a community of individuals: form and matter always combine by fusing into an individual thing. A sound philosophy must do justice both to the claims of systematic unity and those of independent plurality.

The result of these principal differences is that Aristotle's synthesis is new. Because historical changes redirected the concern of Greek thought, it is also the last word of Hellenic speculative philosophy.[5]

The dialogue did not suit Aristotle's purpose as a form of philosophic expression. Instead, the mature works of Aristotle, an impressive number of which have survived, are lecture notes; apparently these were carefully edited and kept available for reference in the Lyceum library. Like all lecture notes, they are compressed and hard to read at first: technical distinctions and terms add to the difficulty. But when one appreciates the task Aristotle set himself, the conquest by reason of all reality, these compressed summaries take on a new dramatic interest, and prove well worth the effort needed to understand them.[6]

ὄρεξις καὶ διάνοια ἢ πρακτική· τὸ ὀρεκτικὸν γὰρ κινεῖ, ἢ
διὰ τοῦ νοῦ διανοίας κινεῖ· ὁ γὰρ νοῦς αὐτὸς οὐ τὸ ὀρεκτικόν.
καὶ ἡ φαντασία δὲ ὅταν κινῇ, οὐ κινεῖ ἄνευ ὀρέξεως.
ἓν δή τι τὸ κινοῦν τὸ ὀρεκτικόν. ἢ γὰρ ὁ λόγος νοῦς καὶ ἡ ὄρεξις ἐκίνουν καὶ κατὰ τὴν νόησιν ἡδὺ ἐκίνουν. νῦν δὲ
ὁ μὲν νοῦς οὐ φαίνεται κινῶν ἄνευ ὀρέξεως. ἡ γὰρ β-
λησθῆσις ὄρεξίς ἐστιν. ὅταν δὲ κατὰ τὸν λογισμὸν κινῆται, καὶ
κατὰ βούλησιν κινεῖται. ἡ δὲ ὄρεξις κινεῖ παρὰ τὸν λο-
γισμόν. ἡ γὰρ ἐπιθυμία ὄρεξίς τίς ἐστιν. νοῦς μὲν
οὖν πᾶς ὀρθός ἐστιν. ὄρεξις δὲ καὶ φαντασία καὶ ὀρθὴ
καὶ οὐ ὀρθή. διὸ ἀεὶ μὲν κινεῖ τὸ ὀρεκτόν. ἀλλὰ τοῦτο
ἐστὶν, ἢ τὸ ἀγαθόν, ἢ τὸ φαινόμενον ἀγαθόν. πρακτὸν
δέ ἐστι· τὸ ἐνδεχόμενον καὶ ἄλλως ἔχειν. ὅτι μὲν οὖν ἡ
τοιαύτη δύναμις κινεῖ τῆς ψυχῆς, ἡ καλουμένη ὄρεξις,
φανερόν· τοῖς δὲ διαιροῦσι τὰ μέρη τῆς ψυχῆς, ἐὰν κατὰ τὰς δυ-
νάμεις διαιρῶσι καὶ χωρίζωσι, πάμπολλα γίνεται, θρε-
πτικόν. αἰσθητικόν. νοητικόν. βουλευτικόν. ἔτι δὲ
ὀρεκτικόν· ταῦτα γὰρ πλέον διαφέρει ἀλλήλων, ἢ τὸ ἐ-
πιθυμητικὸν καὶ θυμικόν. ἐπειδὴ δὲ ὀρέξεις γίνονται
ἐναντίαι ἀλλήλαις. τοῦτο δὲ συμβαίνει ὅταν ὁ λόγος καὶ
ἡ ἐπιθυμία ἐναντίαι ὦσιν. γίνεται δὲ ἐν τοῖς χρόνου
αἴσθησιν ἔχουσιν. ὁ μὲν γὰρ νοῦς, διὰ τὸ μέλλον ἀνθέλ-
κειν κελεύει. ἡ δὲ ἐπιθυμία, διὰ τὸ ἤδη ἡδύ· καὶ
ἀγαθὸν ἁπλῶς διὰ τὸ μὴ ὁρᾶν τὸ μέλλον. ὃ δὲ μὲν οὖν
εἶδὸς δή τι κινοῦν τὸ ὀρεκτικὸν ἢ ὀρεκτικόν. πρῶτον
δὲ πάντων τὸ ὀρεκτόν. τοῦτο γὰρ κινεῖ οὐ κινούμενον. τῷ

φαίνεται γὰρ
τοῦ δ' ἢ νοῦς,
ἢ ἀπλῶς δή.

THIRTEENTH-CENTURY GREEK MANUSCRIPT

The page at left is from Aristotle's De Anima, *a deceptively neat and clear finished copy. The page at right is from Plotinus, Ennead I. This is a working copy, giving an idea of what Aristotle's lecture notes must have been like before "publication" in fair copy. (Ziskind Collection, Yale University.)*

Aristotle advised his students to work from topical outlines. Such outlines are particularly useful in tracing Aristotle's own ideas. Taking his advice, we will use the following topical outline in the balance of this chapter.

I. Biography; Aristotle's early work
   A. the Academy
   B. Aristotle and Alexander
   C. the Lyceum
   D. Aristotle's exile from Athens

II. Aristotle's notion of causality
   A. Four causes defined and illustrated
      1. as they apply to artificial things
      2. as they apply to natural things

III. Aristotle's outline of the kinds of reality, his thesis that the same causes apply throughout

IV. Theoretic science
   A. philosophy of nature
      1. biology
      2. astronomy
      3. chemistry
   B. mathematics
   C. metaphysics
      1. the history of metaphysics
      2. the four causes
      3. the doctrine of the prime mover
      4. potentiality and power
         a. "one-way" powers in nature
         b. "two-way" power given man by his freedom

V. Practical and productive science
   A. politics, its causes and principles
   B. poetics: literary criticism and causality
   C. ethics: the analysis of the "self"
   D. appraisal

I. BIOGRAPHY

The main stages of Aristotle's career were (A) his long period as student and associate of Plato, in the Academy; (B) his sojourn in Pella as tutor for Alexander the Great; (C) his return to Athens to found a university of his own, in competition with the Academy; (D) his exile from Athens after the death of Alexander. His writing is deliberately impersonal; we know that he married a princess, Pythias, who died only a few years later, and that he had a mistress, Herpyllis, for whom he provided in his will. He had two children, a son, named Nicomachus for his grandfather, and a daughter. But only a few lines of poetry on the death of his wife, a few more on the death of Plato, and a will that Diogenes Laërtius preserved give us a glimpse of Aristotle's personal experiences and adventures.

A. Aristotle was the son of a Macedonian doctor, physician to the royal court. At the age of seventeen, he went to Athens to complete his education at the Academy. It is certainly safe to conclude that he was an unusually brilliant young man; before he went to Athens he had apparently already developed the interest in medicine and familiarity with a doctor's view of things which he never entirely lost during his later career. Athens and the Academy were evidently exciting and congenial to the young student from the north. Aristotle stayed for twenty years as student, research assistant, lecturer, and research scientist, and did not leave the Academy until the death of Plato in 347 B.C.

It is hard to know how to interpret the very scattered fragments and reports that reflect young Aristotle's ideas in this period of his association with the Academy. Experts do not even agree as to which later passages are and are not quoted from Aristotle's early writings.[7] But two things do emerge clearly. The first is young Aristotle's admiration for Plato: his early philosophic writings were in dialogue form, and the dialogues were variations on themes Plato had developed.[8] The second thing, that distinguished Aristotle's dialogues from Plato's originals, was the way Aristotle tried to support Platonic abstract arguments by specific experimentation and observation. For example he introduced reported cases of precognition as evidence which, if true, helped to confirm the doctrine of the immortality of the soul. This tendency to try to match concrete fact to abstract argument, and not to be satisfied until logic and experiment gave the same result, remained characteristic of Aristotle throughout his work, and is one of its distinguishing features.

B. When Aristotle left the Academy, he removed to Asia Minor, where presently his reputation and his family connection with the court of Macedonia led to his appointment as tutor for young Alexander. The association between Alexander the Great and Aristotle, each in his own way one of the very greatest men in history, has fascinated later generations.[9] However, we do not have detailed information about this association. Aristotle seems to have taught the young prince literature, Homer, rhetoric, and grammar. We have three very brief fragments of treatises Aristotle is supposed to have written for Alexander on political themes.[10] Alexander, on his campaigns, collected plants and animals and sent them to his former teacher at the Lyceum in Athens. That is nearly all of the factual evidence we have. One other item, that a novelist or author of detective stories should find interesting, is that Aristotle was accused by Queen Olympias, Alexander's mother, of arranging her son's death by poison. This story appears in the "Life of Alexander" by Plutarch.

As far as any great intellectual influence either way, the evidence is negative. Aristotle's own political thinking always accepted the Greek city-state as the normal and most desirable form of political organization, where Alexander's ambition was the creation of a world empire. Aristotle conceived of a perfect life as one spent in theoretic inquiry, whereas Alexander saw it spent in achieving honor and power. There may be some influence traceable in Alexander's reasonableness in allowing countries he conquered to preserve local religions and customs, but no direct causal connection can be found between Alexander's career and Aristotle's ideas.

C. When Alexander became king, at the death of Phillip, Aristotle returned to Athens, and established the Lyceum, his own university. He liked to carry on discussions with his students while walking, and from this habit his school came to be

PRAXITELES: APOLLO OF THE LYCEUM

A statue of Apollo by Praxiteles stood in the Lyceum, Aristotle's school. This miniature ivory copy (third century after Christ), found in more than two hundred pieces, was beautifully restored by archaeologists of the American School of Classical Studies at Athens. (Photograph courtesy of Agora Excavations, American School of Classical Studies at Athens.)

called the "Peripatetics," the name by which they are still known. The most important new feature of the Lyceum was its "museum," which embodied a new idea of the kind of research collections that a university should have available. Aristotle believed that the only way to understand any subject matter was to classify and study it at first hand. In this, as in other things, he shows his judicious talent for combining opposed earlier views. He is not inclined to think of knowledge simply as collected information, as Hippias had earlier. But neither does he trust the Academy's practice of drawing up beautiful and exhaustive diagrams of classification, with only passing attention to whether the scheme really brings out the important distinctions in a given subject matter.

There was the collection of zoological specimens, which Alexander had helped to complete. A set of 158 constitutions of Greek and other city-states provided the research material for the Lyceum's work in political theory. An extensive library made it possible to draw up historical introductions to each field of study. Aristotle himself used the history of philosophy to explain and defend his new notion of causality. Aristotle's lecture notes were kept available for reference, supplemented and corrected; the practice of keeping notebooks of data and problems in the school is attested by four extant notebooks of problems from the Lyceum.[11]

For over twelve years, Aristotle directed his school; carried on his great project of demonstrating in detail the intelligibility and orderly character of all of reality; inspired his students to write histories of physics, astronomy, mathematics, music, and medicine; and observed and recorded new fallacies of argument overheard in court, new reports of the behavior of the Indian elephant, and new theories in astronomy.[12]

D. With the death of Alexander, in 323 B.C., and the breakup of his empire, the Greek cities began to think of regaining their autonomy, and in Athens there was a wave of anti-Macedonian feeling. Aristotle's personal and family connections with Macedonia and Alexander made him a target of hostility. Summoned to appear in court to answer charges of "impiety," he left Athens for Euboea, with the parting remark that "he would not allow the Athenians to sin twice against philosophy." He died in the following year, 322 B.C.

Aristotle's will is one of the few documents that give us any idea of what he was like as a person. He was generous, prudent, and considerate in his disposition of property. His surviving mistress was to have her choice of the two houses in Stagira; his daughter was to be placed in the care of Theophrastus, Aristotle's successor as head of the Lyceum. His wife's ashes were, honoring a request she had made, to be buried beside his own. Each slave was individually treated: some were to be sold, some kept, and some to be set free.

II. ARISTOTLE'S NOTION OF CAUSALITY

To see where Aristotle stands in the history of Greek thought, we can do no better than to take his own analysis as a starting point. He holds that being is four-dimensional. That is, he goes on, each individual thing has four causes which are relevant to our understanding of it. (This concept of cause is not our modern one; it has overtones, in fact, of the old legal sense of aition as *responsibility* or *liability. The causes of a thing are the factors which, in combination, are responsible for its being the thing it is, and for its being anything at all.[13]) Wise men of the past, trying to philosophize, are never wholly mistaken or mutually contradictory. Their preliminary speculative answers are incomplete: each tends to recognize and be satisfied with only one or two dimensions of a reality that requires four.[14]*

In Aristotle's history of philosophy, the first stage of philosophy is an opposition between materialism and formalism. Every real thing in nature has both a material cause—the stuff from which it is made or generated—and a formal cause—the blueprint, structure, number, and order of parts, that determine the matter. The Milesians hit upon the material cause, the Pythagoreans on the formal; the history of philosophy begins with their apparent opposition. By his own day, Aristotle saw these two traditions developed into Atomism and Platonism. He wanted to reconcile these two philosophies.[15]

Aristotle begins by enumerating the four causes that he believed philosophy had been seeking, and that he had discovered. Our own modern common-sense meaning of cause is much narrower than Aristotle's use: his "factors *responsible* for a thing being what it is" may better be translated "dimensions of reality," so that we can restate his central doctrine as *the theory that reality is four-dimensional.* (This risks some confusion still, but is all right if we realize that "dimension" here means a kind of being, not a field of space and time.) Everything that is owes its existence and identity to a material cause, the stuff out of which it is made, in combination with a formal cause, the blueprint or pattern that makes it the kind of thing it is. These two dimensions are brought together by an efficient cause, either a *maker* or an *ancestor.* And to understand things, we must also look for the final cause of each: for *artificial* things, this goal or end is the use they are designed to serve; for *natural* things, it is a goal of self-realization which directs the stages of growth and maturity.

To illustrate how these apply to an artificial thing, my desk is a convenient illustration. It is made out of *wood.* Wood is its material cause, its stuff. Aristotle, needing to coin a new word for material in this sense, extended the Greek *hyle* (lumber) to this new meaning. It has four legs, a rectangular top, and drawers; these are the formal cause, the pattern which a blueprint can capture. For the wood to have taken on this form, there had to be an efficient cause; in this case, a carpenter was the maker of the desk. The *reason* a carpenter put this pattern into the wood was to make something that *served a purpose.* Desks are for storing papers, writing on, holding typewriters; this is the final cause, the goal or purpose of the desk.

There are several significant differences when we apply the four causes to a description of a *natural* thing, such as Jason, the family cat, who is now under my desk.[16] First, Jason's material cause, the stuff he is made of, is much more complicated: it is a system of organs, not just an arrangement of boards. Second, the pattern or formal cause is not a blueprint, but a *species*: a kind of thing we find in nature. Jason is a *cat.* There is a limited set of such "natural kinds," according to Aristotle, and every individual falls into one or another type. Third, as his efficient cause, Jason had *parents*: he was *generated*, not *manufactured.* And those parents were different individuals of the same species; they, too, were cats. Finally, Jason's final cause, his goal, is not to serve *my* purposes. He has an inner *nature* that directs his growth toward becoming a mature cat. He grows toward this in a series of stages—learning to see, to walk, to run, to catch things with his paws—just as cats have always developed. The species is at once the kind of thing Jason is, and the perfect thing of this kind that he is trying to become.

It is clear that the causal pattern differs for an animal and an artificial thing, such as a desk. It is less clear that this difference holds generally between all natural things and all artificial ones. For example, a chunk of marble is a natural thing; so is a star or planet. But neither of these has the obvious kind of purposive order that a living animal shows. We will find that Aristotle believed, however, that even on the level of stones, or that of stars, a natural tendency to seek a goal could be discovered. He developed his natural philosophy in biology, then extended it to chemistry and astronomy. Thus the example above clearly shows Aristotle's application of the causes in nature as opposed to art.

Philosophy and science are both concerned with discovering the causes of things *in all four senses of cause*: so, indeed, are aesthetic criticism and analysis of language, though these explore a different field of "things."[17]

This notion of different kinds of things led Aristotle to introduce some very crucial distinctions into his philosophy. Not only did earlier thinkers tend to select only one of the causes as a complete explanation, but they also tended to limit their attention to things of just the one kind that their selected cause most easily explained. Thus the Milesians did not concern themselves with forms and numbers, which are real but not physical objects; the Pythagoreans tended to ignore the properties that separate natural things from mathematical abstractions. Aristotle found this tendency persisted even in atomism and Platonism.

It seemed to Aristotle that his four causes included and brought together all of the previous insights of Greek philosophy. To begin with, his recognition of formal and final causes, and also of material and efficient causes combined the traditions of materialism and formalism, which had been opposed. His use of final causes recognized the part that ideals and goals play in nature and art, and so incorporated one of the most important features of Platonism. Aristotle could of course identify his notion of material causes with Milesian physics, and the efficient cause with the notions of violence, force, energy that had appeared sporadically in earlier philosophy.

The causes are an ingenious and powerful philosophic insight. The points where all four meet are always concrete individuals, running true to type, so that the *substance* or *type-specimen* is the typical unit of reality in Aristotle's philosophy. There are different sorts of balances of causes in different kinds of things. To discover the causal balance in a field, each individual thing must be observed and compared with others. Proper generalizations and classifications can be made only after studying and collecting.

III. ARISTOTLE'S OUTLINE OF THE KINDS OF REALITY

Before he could prove that the four causes applied to everything, Aristotle had to distinguish between different kinds of reality and knowledge, and to draw up exhaustive lists. The result was the outline presented below. One of Aristotle's more impressive achievements, this outline shows Aristotle's genius for classification and order, and his ability to include the insights of his predecessors in his system.

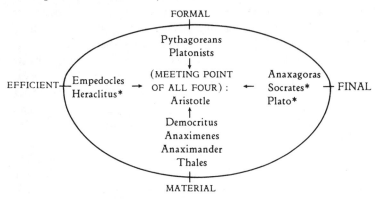

FIGURE 2. ARISTOTLE'S INTERPRETATION
OF THE HISTORY OF PHILOSOPHY

(Causes are given in capitals; some additional classifications not explicitly made by Aristotle are starred.)

KNOWLEDGE is either (1) Instrumental, (2) Theoretic, (3) Practical, or (4) Productive. (This four-part division does not correspond one-to-one with the four causes.)

1. INSTRUMENTAL KNOWLEDGE has *language* as its subject matter; it studies the parts and forms that are most effective for specialized types of communication. There are three of these: proof, persuasion, and poetry: (a) the use of language for proof is the field of LOGIC, (b) for persuasion, RHETORIC, and (c) for poetry POETICS.

a. LOGIC is divided into ANALYTIC, DIALECTIC, and SOPHISTIC. In all three, TERMS are combined into PROPOSITIONS, and these are linked in sets of three, SYLLOGISMS. In turn, by syllogisms chained together, we form DEMONSTRATIONS. (1) The starting-points of these may be genuine PRINCIPLES OF SCIENCE, in which case the result is ANALYTIC (in Aristotle's sense, not in our modern one). (2) Or the demonstration may start with OPINION, in which case the result is DIALECTICAL (again, in Aristotle's sense of dialectic). (3) Or the reasoning may turn simply on words, and be purely verbal, in which case Aristotle calls it SOPHISTIC.

b. RHETORIC is the use of WORDS and STATEMENTS to produce persuasion. There are three main factors: the speaker, the audience, and the speech. Instead of syllogism, rhetorical argument proceeds by ENTHYMEME. An enthymeme is a statement that transfers attitudes the audience already holds to the case at hand: it is like syllogism, except that its result is not new knowledge, but action. There are three kinds of speeches: FORENSIC, DELIBERATIVE, and EPIDEICTIC (DISPLAY).

c. POETICS has a theory of poetic diction as one of its parts. We must classify words according to (1) LEVEL OF USAGE (common, pedantic, stately, etc.); (2) METER and SOUND; and the ways in which "poetic license" is admissible in changing them (by elision, lengthening, etc.).

2. THEORETIC KNOWLEDGE is a disinterested, objective scientific study of the things that are. Its main divisions correspond to the kinds of things that can be understood in an objective, scientific way. They are (a) NATURAL PHILOSOPHY, which deals with all the things that move or change;[18] (b) MATHE-

MATICS, which deals with unchanging, abstract pattern and structure; and (c) FIRST PHILOSOPHY (METAPHYSICS), which deals with the interaction of matter and form in a universe that contains orderly, sequential change.

a. NATURAL PHILOSOPHY, the study of all changing things, is itself subdivided into three parts, classified by the types of change: these are ASTRONOMY, BIOLOGY, and INORGANIC CHEMISTRY. (1) ASTRONOMY deals with things which move only in circles, and never grow old or deviate from this precise type of locomotion; Aristotle briefly describes it as "treating eternal sensible substances." (2) BIOLOGY deals with all the things that grow, die, and reproduce other individuals alike in kind. (3) INORGANIC CHEMISTRY deals with the nonliving things that move in straight lines each to its proper place, depending on its specific gravity.

b. MATHEMATICS, dealing with the domain of unchanging structures, numbers, and ratios, is divided sharply by Aristotle into (1) ARITHMETIC and (2) GEOMETRY, with some provision for (3) a UNIVERSAL MATHEMATICS that would study more abstract patterns common to these two.

c. METAPHYSICS, which we will discuss in more detail below, is concerned with the way in which unchanging forms act as patterns and goals in the material world of change. This investigation is Aristotle's own philosophic attempt to justify both materialism and formalism.

3. PRACTICAL KNOWLEDGE means the result of studying the world from the standpoint of human existence, human nature, and human value. It has as its subject matter (a) the habits and decisions that form individual character (ETHICS), (b) the conventions and institutions that societies set up as means to attaining a common good, and (c) the complex interrelation of nature and convention that gives men in society a "second nature" more or less adequate to their ideals of self-realization (POLITICS).

4. PRODUCTIVE KNOWLEDGE looks at things in terms of what can be constructed or created from them; it has two main divisions, depending on whether (a) the things produced are useful as tools or means, in which case they are the products of USEFUL ARTS; or (b) they may be beautiful, and made for

their own sake, in which case they are creations of the FINE ARTS.

Several features of this outline deserve comment. The first is the way Aristotle has profited from the new studies of language that began with the Sophists. His scheme separates sharply the study of words and the study of things, thus avoiding the earlier simple-minded identification of thing and name. The second is the way he makes room, in theoretic science, both for the materialist and the formalist tradition, each of which has its own vision of reality and its own subject matter. The third is the way Aristotle distinguishes the purely descriptive study of the world from its study in ethical terms. Before the Sophists, philosophers had constructed their philosophies from the study of the world with no attention to man's nature and his attempts to realize the good either in his own character or in the plans devised for human association.

IV. THEORETIC SCIENCE

A. Natural Philosophy

Natural philosophy, though it has three major divisions, is actually treated throughout by Aristotle with the methods of biology.[19] This was the field of his own greatest interest, and his achievements as a biologist have been admired from his day to our own. Biology was also an area in which the four causes suggested a way of bringing together Empedocles and the atomists, with their theories of natural selection, and the Academy, with its theory that values act as causes.

Biology deals with individual living things that grow, reproduce their kind, and die. The formal causes the biologist studies are those repeating types or species which we find. The material causes are the tissues, organs, and powers that enable the specific form to take on existence as a concrete individual. Each living thing is generated by parents of the same species. The efficient causes are these other individuals, the parents.[20] An instinct for conservation of the species is the cosmic force that generates the desire for reproduction. The perishing individual still shares in immortality by giving life to the species, which is an immortal type or kind. Aristotle wrote extensive and brilliant notes on the classification of animals (his *Historia Animalium*), tracing out a plan of types that nature contains. He did the same for the reproduction of animals (his *Generatione Animalium*), exploring the efficient causality by which the species remains immortal. And he wrote a classical work on material causes in biology, the comparative anatomy of different genera and species (his *De Partibus Animalium*). In all of these works, he assumes that final causality—direction and purpose—is also a relevant dimension of explanation.[21]

Every individual animal or plant has its own natural direction and sequence of growth. Each is "trying" to realize its own potentialities by becoming a mature individual specimen of its own kind. A kitten, for example, first learns to see, then to walk, then to play, and then to hunt. Its organs develop in a coordinated sequence that makes it possible for the kitten to become a mature cat. The formal cause acts as final cause as well. The form of a complete adult of the species acts as a *goal* and *ideal* to guide the growth of the individual through a predictable life cycle, as its inner drive for self-realization and inner "powers" act together to direct its physical growth and behavior. Aristotle saw no reason why nature might not be at the same time *a necessary sequence of physical change*, of the sort that atomism could explain, and *a constant realization of purpose* as well. Physical changes can always be given a mechanical explanation after they have taken place. But these changes are not a chance aggregate of collisions. They move toward the growth of the individual, in an intelligible pattern, and can best be understood as part of a purposive effort that runs throughout nature. The theory thus gives a place both to the mechanical biology of Empedocles and the atomic theory and the more purposive views of Anaxagoras and the Academy.

The reason for treating final causality in biology at some length is that Aristotle's view is opposed to our contemporary

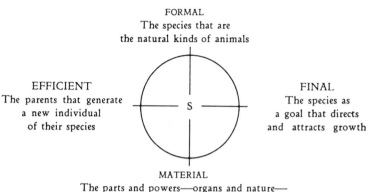

ARISTOTLE

FORMAL
The species that are
the natural kinds of animals

EFFICIENT
The parents that generate
a new individual
of their species

S

FINAL
The species as
a goal that directs
and attracts growth

MATERIAL
The parts and powers—organs and nature—
that give concrete embodiment
to the specific form

FIGURE 3. ARISTOTLE'S FOUR CAUSES IN ZOOLOGY

(The individual specimen is abbreviated by S)

notions, or at least is usually thought to be. A series of technical advances has convinced our modern biologists that there are no mysterious "vital forces" which work in a way that cannot be given chemical and physical explanation, and they often assume that this shows the Aristotelian notion of final cause to be unnecessary and wrong. But biologists who think that such advances as the synthesis of organic chemicals from inorganic components contradict Aristotle are mistaken. Aristotle, too, was sure that every physical change, after it had occurred, could be given a nonpurposive mechanical explanation. The theory of evolution requires a different view from Aristotle's toward the number and invariability of the species that nature includes, but the question of goal or purpose remains: why has life evolved in a relatively constant direction? It may be that Aristotle has prepared the way for a synthesis of the opposed views of thinkers like Spencer, the nineteenth-century defender of the "pure mechanism" view, and Bergson, who opened the twentieth century with his arguments for a purposive drive at work in "creative evolution."

Aristotle's work in biology was concurrent with his attempts to show that the same causal pattern held in astronomy and chemistry, the remaining two great divisions of the philosophy of nature. In effect, what he did was to treat both stars and stones as though they were special cases of living organisms. His work did show that a systematic explanation of these phenomena can be given on his causal pattern. However, his orientation as a biologist led him to make some crucial errors in explaining where the central differences between animate and inanimate, perishable and eternal lay.

Some differences in nature seemed clear enough. In astronomy things were "eternal and sensible," and changed only by circular motion. In chemistry, things tended each to its "proper place." They changed either by transformation of their qualities—becoming hot, cold, moist, or dry—or by motion in a straight line. When in their proper places they were at rest; "heavier" things below those that were "lighter."

Aristotle's biological turn of mind is evident here, for weight and lightness are treated as final causes, a kind of desire or power of self-realization that makes the stone "want" to fall. With the heavens and the stars, Aristotle was dissatisfied both with the purely mathematical astronomy of the Academy and the purely mechanical astronomy of the atomic theory. He tried to fit the two together by the drastic step of assuming a "fifth element," *aither*, to be the matter of the heavens. Unlike the "terrestrial elements," this *aither* had as its nature motion in a circle. From this postulated new material, Aristotle tried to build a physical model of "crystal spheres" that would give some concrete, mechanical embodiment to the pure geometrical constructions of the Academy.[22] But, though they were to dominate science in the late Middle Ages, Aristotle's astronomy and chemistry were never as carefully worked out, nor as consistent, as his biology.[23]

B. and C. Mathematics and Metaphysics

Aristotle relates his three-part scheme of theoretic science to the problem of causality, and uses it to organize his history of earlier thought. The materialistic tradition, including the atomists, tended to treat only *natural* substances, so that they really identified physics with the whole of philosophy; the formalists had tended to center their attention on abstract measurements and classifications, so that, in effect, they thought of mathematics as the whole of philosophy. Neither of these views can explain the relation of matter to form, since the materialist has no analysis of form, the formalist no place for matter. Aristotle proposes to show that a third philosophy, his own, can bring the other two together.

In Aristotle's scheme, natural philosophy includes all the individual things that have a nature, that is, an inner direction which realizes itself in change—motion, growth, and so on.

Mathematics has to do with unchanging quantities—numbers, figures, ratios—which the mathematician treats as having independent existence. In fact, however, such things as a square do not exist apart: it is by an operation of intelligence that the mathematician abstracts the ideal square from various concrete squares in his experience. Instead of a physical matter, he envisages this square in a mathematical space which is an intelligible matter.

Metaphysics has as its concern things that are unchanging, but actual separate substances, not abstractions. Aristotle holds that there must be such separate and immovable things, because they operate in formal and final causality.

In his *Metaphysics*, after an introductory history of philosophy, Aristotle devotes his analysis to showing that being, in its sense of natural individuals, always involves both a form and a matter, fused together. Existence is, indeed, an active attaining of form, an expression of latent power (material and efficient causes) given direction by an *actual form* (formal and final causes). Then, briefly, he reminds us that, left to themselves, pure matter and pure form would never interact or combine; as endless time passed, reality would still remain separated, like oil and water, into an ocean of "pure matter"—like the "all things together" of Anaxagoras—and an unanchored set of "pure forms" which were not the forms *of* anything.[24] This sharp difference of matter and form raises the question of what sort of a world we must live in for the observed interaction of form and matter to be possible.[25]

For individual natural things, the answer lies in the operation of efficient and final causes. The efficient cause first gives an appropriate matter its start toward achieving a complete form. It releases a process of growth, at each stage of which there is a power to take on new form, and a desire to reach it. The completed form acts as the goal which is an ideal that makes each thing conserve the actuality it has reached, and reach out toward more. The forms that operate in nature are limited to the definite set of specific kinds that repeat or endure in space and time. This suggests that, if pressed, Aristotle might admit that there is a sense in which the individual specimens are the *material of* these selected forms. The *species* remains unchanged and immortal, but is incarnated in successive individuals who repeat its life cycle. This makes clear the difference between an Aristotelian form and a mere abstraction.

For the world as a whole, a similar causal pattern holds. The efficient cause which initiates realization of powers is, Aristotle argues, the energy from the heavens—particularly the sun—which gives the constant input of energy needed to keep process going. But to explain why the heavens keep moving, and why form continues to be grasped and conserved by matter, Aristotle believed that philosophers must also recognize a final cause, which he called the "prime mover."

This prime mover is not a mechanical force, which pushes or pulls things; rather it is a mover as an object of desire. There is a constant directed change in nature, and the conservation of form observed, because "all things desire God." Although Aristotle frequently calls this prime mover "God" and sometimes refers to his first philosophy as a theology, later critics have often pointed out that this is not the sort of God that religious believers worship. It is more like a scientific principle of conservation of actuality than a religious God.[26] The continuing attraction God holds for the world is the explanation of why the heavens continually circle: they are desiring a final perfection that will give them a proper place and rest; since all points on a circle are alike, this is a goal they never completely reach.

The same attraction accounts for the immortality of species—the constant desire for reproduction and self-realization which each created being is directed by. The prime mover, to satisfy the demands of a remote final cause for all of nature, must be perfect, unchanging, and purely actual. By analogy, Aristotle suggests, the prime mover may be compared to "pure mind." Our own powers of insight are not physical, and not extended through time. They are, as Aristotle describes them, instantaneous realizations (compare Plato's myths in which knowledge is recollection).

The nature of such a divine mind presents certain problems; Aristotle explores some of them. Since God has no body, and therefore no senses, he cannot know the concrete material individuals of our world. Aristotle considers this a sign of excellence. Perishable, accidental things are not worth God's knowing. Divine thought is "thought thinking itself," a baffling description. Sometimes this is interpreted as a perpetual undifferentiated self-consciousness. That is clearly not what Aristotle meant, since he explains self-consciousness as an operation of common sense, which God cannot have. Nor can a perfect mind be eternally empty, and think of nothing, "for what of dignity is there in this?" Aristotle asks. Aristotle's later comment on "the good in nature," where it is "present both as the leader and the order," suggests that perhaps God contemplates the eternal forms in their beautiful systematic interrelation. This would not contradict the "thought thinking itself" phrase, because "in the case of things that have no matter, thought and the thing thought of are the same." And there would be no contradiction in supposing that pure mind can know forms apart from their material causes—even our human minds can sometimes do that.

In any case, it is evident that Aristotle's idea of God is far indeed from the earlier naïve belief in many gods, each with a human body and a capricious will.[27] Aristotle's description of the God who can be known by theoretic science leaves open the question, of course, as to what more can be added to this knowledge by religious belief based on something other than theoretic inquiry. In fact, Aristotle's doctrine, with its proof that science requires a God, but cannot know very much about Him, appears as a philosophical introduction to three different religions, each of which claims to supplement this conclusion with fuller detail. In the third century after Christ, the religion was Neoplatonism; in the twelfth, Mohammedanism; in the thirteenth, Christianity.

In Aristotle, however, the attraction of form is always specific and selective. "All things desire God" must be understood to mean that each thing desires perfection, but in its own specific way. A flatworm strives for self-realization, but its only power and goal is to become a perfect adult flatworm. Aristotle thinks that each kind has its own final cause, and that it would be irresponsible poetry to talk as though the flatworm had some blind, unconscious yearning to transcend its own nature and become a human being or a star.[28]

This Aristotelian doctrine has consequences for astronomy, zoology, and metaphysics. In astronomy, the prime mover was the final cause of the "first heaven"—the outermost sphere, with a daily revolution. But the other motions of the planets and the sun, differing in speed and direction, required other individual final causes, equal in number to the number of independent component motions. Building on the work of the Academy, Aristotle thought the number of these subordinate moving intelligences was "either 47 or 55." But he did not explore in any detail the way in which they differ; perhaps because he could see no way of testing such speculation empirically.

In zoology, Aristotle developed the doctrine of the eternity of species. He thought that the number of kinds was fixed and that the order of nature ensured each kind an immortality. There was a second consequence of his notion of final causes. Since a type-specimen is part of the order of nature only because it has some value, and the complete structure of such a type is what each individual tries to realize, we can identify the materialistic or descriptive view of science, which tries to classify without reference to goals or values, and the formalistic or Platonic view which tries to classify things by the ideals that attract them. Since all existence becomes at once a limitation of matter by form and a pursuit of value, the old dichotomy of value and fact no longer holds in natural philosophy. The result in mathematics is that nature offers the mathematician a ready-made example of symmetry, system, and order. This guides him in his exploration of the limitless realm of possible abstractions.

The treatment of "power," which extends to possibility and potentiality, that immediately precedes Aristotle's account of the prime mover, requires a distinction that is of the greatest philosophical importance. There are two sorts of "power" in nature that must be distinguished. The general rule is that things have a one-way potency. Fire has the power to burn, but not the opposite power, to freeze; acorns have the power to develop into oaks (if nothing external interferes), but not the power to develop into any other species. Each kind of animal has a set of powers that develops in a pre-established way, toward a specific goal. Each natural potency is fastened tightly to one specific formal and final cause, which directs and limits its actualization.[33]

But human intelligence makes man an exception; it gives him a two-way potency. The physician, to use one of Aristotle's frequent examples, has the power to kill as well as cure. And intelligence, on the human level, seems always to have this freedom associated with it. As a result, human nature does not automatically result in a single pattern of habit or behavior, of the sort we see in ants and bees. To be motivated in pursuit of the apparent good is natural to man; a final cause attracts him. But human nature and behavior are subject to errors, accidents, and responsibilities for choice that make them significantly different from the rest of reality. Aristotle therefore concludes that social science of the sort Plato had envisaged is impossible.[29]

Freedom results from man's peculiar metaphysical location. It means that nature does not dictate the development of intelligence and excellence. To develop these qualities requires free choice by each individual man. Human intelligence can know only in the most general way the kinds of habits, character, and study, that will lead to full self-realization. And unlike the closed set of forms that the rest of nature embodies, man's freedom leads to a constant creation of many new forms—social institutions, human moral character, and works of fine art. These created forms are like the formal causes of theoretic science in their character and function; but human inventiveness proceeds gradually, and the forms it creates do not show, as species in nature do, an identity of the ideal and the actual.

Man's final cause is fixed in nature, but his road toward it can proceed through many alternative byways of form. The fact that there is *some* value to any set of institutions and laws that men can devise confronts us with the constant dangers of missing a greater good because we settle for something that is not bad. Or we may lose a present good when we destroy a social form with the intention of making it better, but cannot replace it.

Thus, practical science, the study of human nature and conduct, faces an open, unknown future, and can never know it "always and necessarily." Practical and theoretic science, however, are both part of a common world of reality, and possess the four causal dimensions.

Aristotle's philosopher has a new role. He is in a position to clarify the *methods* of other specialists, from astronomers to congressmen and poets, while he must in turn accept their findings as to the *subject matter* each one has studied. This never entitles an expert to hide behind minute technicalities of data, with a statement like "no one can understand modern physics except by learning to operate with the equations of quantum theory." In any universe where theories have *any* relevance at all, every field of inquiry has a few fundamental concepts that define its subject matter, and these are used *to explain* phenomenal detail by causal deductions. These "principles" are intelligible to any student ready for a liberal education.[30]

Aristotle's own lectures on comparative anatomy, a subject felt at that time to deal with "things that are repulsive" and to be unsuited as part of "liberal" training, expressed a remarkable conclusion. If in fact the same type of order operates throughout nature, science must advance by specialization and technical research; but every science not arbitrarily obscured by unmethodical experts can present its principles in clear terms suited for general courses as part of liberal education. And if Aristotle's researches, or a modern extension of them, can demonstrate, as he thought, that reality is made up of the same causal order throughout, the claim must stand. It must stand, however, qualified by Aristotle's other finding, that mere lectures or discussion are no substitute for first-hand work with a subject matter: pure dialectic will not give the meaning to words which only experience and experiment can.[31]

V. PRACTICAL SCIENCE

A. Politics

Starting with the causes, let us look at Aristotle's *Politics*. Here, as in natural philosophy, he finds two traditional types of political theory. On the one hand, there are the formalists and idealists, who talk only about formal and final causes. They draw the conclusion that since the remote final cause—the blueprint of an ultimate utopia—is the same for all societies, political differences are unrealistic, and universal education toward a clear vision of the abstract common goal becomes the sole concern of political theory.[32]

This view involves two fundamental mistakes. First, a *remote* cause becomes definite enough to be realized only through *specific* intermediate causes. Thus the brotherhood of free men everywhere, an ideal acceptable to most nations of the modern world, is made specific as it approaches actual implementation to such means as free private enterprise, revolution of the working class, equality of opportunity, equal distribution of consumers goods, one universal religious faith, and so on.[33] Each of these may be a means to a good and acceptable end, but may not be consistent with the others as a concrete social goal. Second, formalists have the mistaken notion that *only* formal and final causes—ideals and laws—are the real causes of society. The formalist has an unrealistic tendency to base everything on constitutions, treaties, and laws. He forgets that a statute on paper is not yet an operating institution. Suppose, for example, that a community has found its own constitution eminently satisfactory, and proceeds to export it to all other countries that want to reach the same level of industrial and cultural development. On paper, we would have the same states existing in the United States and, say, the Republic of the Congo—but only on paper. The specific formal causes that work best with high literacy, for example, will fail totally to secure effective representative government where literacy is low. The looseness of any federal centralization that was natural to ancient Greece, with its mountain chains, would have been in all probability disastrous in the great Egyptian agriculture plains beside the Nile. Nor would an Athenian treaty with, say, Persia, have impressed Aristotle as a great political advance, if it ran wholly counter to Persian interests and traditional influence along the Asia Minor coast. Somehow, he would have predicted, such a formal agreement out of touch with the material causes and lacking efficient implementation would not have achieved reality.

But Aristotle was also aware, and critical of, an opposite tradition of political practice and discussion. From abstract Sophist theoreticians to practical tacticians of Greek city-states, there was agreement that politics meant the pursuit of power and profit. For politicians of this "realistic" type, utopias were merely poetry. History was determined by the wealth of nations, the control of resources and means of production, the acquisition of political authority. This approach discounted laws, constitutions, and ideals as mere conventions that a clever man could use in pursuit of his own advantage.

These views seemed to Aristotle unsatisfactory for reasons of the same kind as those that had led Socrates to become dissatisfied with Ionian science. Both wealth and power, Aristotle conceded, were necessary components of political associations; but the actual institutions and ideas which channeled their use were, he argued, relevant causes too. These formal aspects of society could make all the difference between an Athenian democracy and a Syracusan tyranny. Material wealth and power do not lead automatically to any one given form of government; rather, they are the raw materials from which many different types of states can be, and have been, constructed.[34]

Evidently, then, in political as well as in philosophical discussion an Aristotelian is alert to the dangers of debate based on incomplete analysis. If one person sees the relevance of formal and final causes, and talks only about these, while another reacts by treating only efficient and material causes as "really" relevant, their debate will be endless.

Richard McKeon's Aristotelian contributions to political discussion, particularly in a UNESCO symposium of 1953, show how relevant this analysis is to our situation today. In that symposium, Western and Marxist contributors alike praised democracy: but, asked to define it, the former group rested its case almost solely on constitutional guarantees and statutory rights, while the latter put its point almost entirely in terms of ownership of means of production and freedom from formal class oppression.[35]

The Geneva disarmament discussions of a few years ago are another illustration of this polarization in action. The Soviet delegates discussed total disarmament in terms of potentials for arms production, while the Western representatives discussed the problem in terms of legislation for control of present arms and bases. Quite possibly ulterior motives were relevant to this difference of approach. But so were different philosophical ideas of *what disarmament really is*. Both ideas rested on alternative incomplete causal analyses. The resulting differences, not understood for what they were, would still have led to mutual distrust and suspicion, in the face of the best intentions in the world.

Political theory is complex in the Aristotelian tradition, for while a state clearly is not an individual animal, still it does have a kind of quasi-organic reality.[36] Once forms exist in space and time, they seem almost to act to ensure their own preservation. The state is an instance of this tendency. An institution has a built-in final cause it serves peculiarly well. A further final cause, that of human welfare and freedom, is more important. Mere preservation of one institution or another may impede it. But institutions do not like to lose their grasp on reality; it almost seems that they have a share of the desire for immortality which all natural substances have.[37] The state has a status of its own. It is not, as Aristotle accuses Plato of making it, a true "organism." Neither is it, as the Sophists or Democritus would have had it, a convention with no reality apart from its component individual citizens.[38] Aristotle's political theory accounts for the fact that there are both dialectical patterns and unpredictable changes in political history.

B. Poetics

In poetry and ethics, as in political theory, human freedom makes new things possible—a new kind of art, a new constitution, a new notion of human excellence. The final cause, less domineering in these areas than in the rest of Aristotle's nature, admits more than one direction, more than one form of expression.

Works of fine art, laws, and human character itself, are therefore not natural in the strict sense that applies throughout the rest of the world from astronomy to chemistry. Yet being real gives artificial things, too, the four-dimensionality that the causes capture and explain.

In the 1930's, at the University of Chicago, the discovery was made that the history of literary criticism can be understood as alternative stress on one or another of Aristotle's four causes to the exclusion of a balanced central focus on the relevant individual works of fine art. One might, for example, concentrate on *expression*, the author as efficient cause; on *style*, the medium, the material cause; on *idea*, a Platonic notion of truth or message as a disembodied formal cause; or on *audience effect*, a rhetorical reduction of the work of fine art to a remote final cause. What holds these four together is the work itself. It is enough like a natural substance to be able to focus and hold together the four dimensions of causality analyzed separately by other critical theories. And the subsistence of a work of fine art is great enough so that, as in nature, the final cause—a proper aesthetic pleasure—seems to be intrinsic to the work itself, not dependent on adventitious audience reaction.[39]

This is an excellent approach to fine art, if one remembers two things. First, there *are* relevant causes outside of the work itself. Second, that the *Poetics* offer a *critical*, not a *creative* method. The four causes are in balance only after creative energy, the plastic medium, and a determinate formal structure have made their mutual adjustments and settled down with each other to live happily as a fixed achievement. Perhaps this "Aristotelian" tendency in contemporary critical discussion has sometimes claimed too much. It is possible that the balance will "appear" when any work has been completed, but how that balance is generated neither Aristotle nor his successors say.[40] That, however, was not what Aristotle claimed, nor what his great proof demanded. For the thesis that a work of fine art is enough like a substance to have the same relevant causal dimensions, contemporary work does indicate that the claim holds good.

C. Ethics: The Human Self

Ethics is the study of the individual; its subject matter overlaps politics, but its focus is different. In ethics, Aristotle is concerned with the nature and development of the human self. Building on the earlier insights of Socrates and Plato, the Nicomachean Ethics *devotes ten books to the levels and stages of self-realization. In each book, a new level is added, and the "self" extends further. From a center of subjective sensitivity, we develop our human powers finally to a realization of the kinship of the human self and cosmic mind, the prime mover. The* Ethics *is one of the few books in this area that gives the reader suggestions for self-improvement, and some techniques for self-evaluation. Our British-American idea of a gentleman derives, in the main, from the first half of the* Nicomachean Ethics.

In ethics the human self is explored. Man's works lie somewhere in between nature's repeating typical individuals and unpredictable emergent Empedoclean monsters. This is because man himself occupies so peculiar a position in Aristotle's universe. If men were stars, they would have no problems or decisions, but would behave forever in the same predictable way, moving in circles where no natural proper place ever could offer a point of rest. If they were elements, they would collide and rebound blindly, in a dumb, invariant impetus to move along the shortest line to their "proper place" in the center of the universe. But man is a complex balance of levels of instinct, habit, and intelligence, with a dim intuition of the direction of his natural final cause, but no precise monorail route for its attainment built into his physiology, as it is with ants or bees.[41]

The *Ethics*, in which Aristotle traces the emergence of a complete human self, once more demonstrates the relevance of all four causes to self-realization. He tries, by careful analysis and multiple distinctions, to show how a personality can result from accumulated habits and the drive to transcend the limitations of a life in space and time.[42] Aristotle begins by showing how ordinary language conditions with praise and blame the social behavior of each individual. He concludes his analysis with the full self-realization that comes from theoretic vision.[43]

The complexity of stages leads Aristotle into detailed discussions that hide the over-all organization, and he often uses very limited illustrations of insights—for example, the specific instances he cites of his famous definiton of moral excellence as always being a mean between extremes of appetite or passion—that are capable of more general formulation. But by the third book of the *Nicomachean Ethics* Aristotle's own distinctive position is clear. Even our ordinary language shows that we *admire* "that which is noble," a final cause distinct from mere social approval or private comfort, but that we *become* what habits formed within limits of a given culture make us.[44]

The contemporary interest of Aristotle's ethics, politics, and poetic theory, comes, I have suggested, from the fact that careful observation led him to recognize that his four causes do not dictate unchanging recurrence of type in those cases where freedom and inventiveness are part of the subject matter. Without the philosophical thesis he is proving, that of the four causes, his work in practical science and aesthetics would seem to us most hopelessly out of date. In context, his thesis may, it is tempting to think, be right, even though Aristotle himself was mistaken in the way it applies to astronomy, zoology, and the rest of natural philosophy.[45]

D. Conclusion

With this final genius for organization, and its discovery of the detailed intelligibility of reality, Aristotle brought Hellenic philosophy to a fitting close. He was still too optimistic about the power of reason, with the new discovery of the methods of generalization and deduction, to answer all factual and philosophic questions; still too inclined to trust nature to run true to type, so that one or two observations are enough. Nevertheless, Aristotle's achievement can take its place as one of the high points in the human spirit's pursuit of what is noble.

We would feel today that perhaps he would have done more justice to the thinkers who went before him if he had been more attentive to the untidy, powerful insights they had, which went beyond the ordinary world that Aristotle was concerned to preserve and organize. The Heraclitean dark cosmic flow, the Platonic vision of a single form of the good, and the Empedoclean excitement at natural selection have to be weakened and toned down before the ideas can be classified and neatly fitted together.[46] Nevertheless, his discovery of the power of classification to unravel the many-dimensionality of even the most ordinary things, and the combination of passion, speculative scope, and precision, make Aristotle one of the greatest figures in the world of philosophy.[47]

Aristotle's stature as authority is universally recognized; for example, Giles of Rome, author of a treatise on *The Errors of Philosophers* in the thirteenth century after Christ, opens his book "And first comes Aristotle. . . ." In our own story of the emergence of philosophy in Greek thought, Aristotle comes last. This gives him the advantage of having the last word, before a complete change in society parallels a change of interest to the different set of themes and way of approaching them that mark Hellenistic and early Christian thought. In fact, the assumed conditions and illustrations in his practical writings are taken from an era that had ceased to exist while his works were under construction—an ironic fact that prompted Hegel's remark "The shades of night are falling before the Owl of Athena takes flight." But, though out of date in its illustrative detail, Aristotle's last word is technical and masterly. From his time to our own, he has been not only one of the three or four philosophers who have been most studied and admired but one of the most influential in shaping our ways of thought.

CONCLUSION

AFTER the death of Aristotle, in 322 B.C., philosophers gave up their ambition to conquer the world, and turned their attention, instead, to conquering themselves. The four schools of philosophy continued in Athens, with state support, until they were closed by Justinian in A.D. 529. These were the Stoic, Epicurean, Academic, and Peripatetic schools, representing four different traditions.[1]

The four schools had in common a sense of philosophy as consolation in a world where the individual felt himself to have little intrinsic value. Philosophy became concerned with ways to preserve' man's dignity and to reconcile him to the world order. The old far-ranging curiosity was narrowed, the speculative audacity was lost.

If we compare Aristotle's notion of a museum with the Library of Alexandria, or Plato's Academy with the Library of Hadrian, we can see that something has changed radically.[2] Aristotle, though an inveterate observer and collector, never thought that collecting in itself was a virtue or had intrinsic value. His concern was to study and classify, in order to recognize the essential types and causal patterns as they appeared in each subject matter.[3] The Alexandrian Library, on the other hand, institutionalized the notion that it was a good thing just to collect— that accumulation of data and reference sources would inevitably make understanding better. So the original program of collect-classify-explain was reduced to collect.[4] Meanwhile, the Academy had become a center of philosophic skepticism. Plato had convinced his successors that unless there were Platonic forms, reliable knowledge would be impossible; but they did not think there were such forms available to human minds. They defended this skepticism partly as an ethical position. One can avoid suffering if one suspends judgment and does not expect things that are in fact uncertain, or confuse certainty with probability. Notice the distance between this point of view—particularly its key assumption that avoidance of suffering is the ideal life—and the affirmative, engaged tone of the earlier Greek philosophy.[5] Plato had thought that men were dissatisfied and creative because they desired immortality, and could at best only reach an approximation; to defer living until one had a conclusive argument that immortality was an intrinsic good would have seemed to him a form of suicide.

Ironically, the effort of the Hellenistic schools to be concrete and practical led, in the end, to views of life that were academic and abstract. The Roman world was not satisfied with advice to "be philosophical." It turned, instead, to new forms of religion which had something more concrete and engaged to offer the individual. Christianity, in particular, filled this need in a way that the academic philosophy did not. It introduced a new philosophical orientation as it became the official, then the universal, religion of the Roman Empire.[6]

But the Greek idea of philosophy, and the example as well as the central ideas of the great Greek philosophers, continued to operate through Western history. Now Platonism would suggest a way of formulating theology, now a revival of Aristotle would suggest an alternative model for philosophic thought. Plato's humanism inspired the thinkers of the Renaissance. Aristotle's logic and dialectic was admired by critical and idealistic philosophers of Germany. The atomic theory, not allowed a hearing during the Middle Ages, was revived in the Renaissance and joined in debate again with the more subjective and speculative systems of ideas.[7]

In a sense, with Aristotle, the achievement of the thinkers of the Hellenic Age had been completed. Once human reason sees clearly the ideal of system, which can order the many generalizations and conceptions that man derives from sensation and memory, there can be an attempt to find a master plan for discovering or creating a systematic order. In the beginning of the history of Greek thought, philosophers had brilliant insights. They began to recognize different aspects of being—matter, form, flux, substance—abruptly realized in vivid and original expressions of new thought. Their insights are not accompanied by very clear analysis, and they did not make the distinctions which by now have become so firmly embedded in our language and common sense.[8]

As later thinkers continued their exploration and consolidated earlier gains, four ways of ordering concepts systematically came into the foreground. And the history of philosophy from ancient Greece to the present day seems to confirm the notion that the four most effective and persistently attempted ways of ordering our many concepts are just these four. (1) Analysis into elements, (2) synthesis into formal hierarchies that converge at some highest law or form, (3) intuitive recognition of creativity and process in their continuity, and (4) classification as type-specimens without regard for size of these or their relation to a single hierarchical scheme. These four ways are destined to endure as man applies his reason to understanding the total range of being throughout later Western philosophy.[9]

How far are our own minds from the original encounter with the question of the ultimate nature of things? Accepting a series of obvious distinctions that have become habits, we confront a compartmentalized world of fact. We cannot make immediate sense of or find direct intuitive response to a question like Heidegger's "What is being?" The virtue of looking again at an age where philosophy was naïve and young is not that it persuades us to forego all distinctions altogether; that would be to give up one of the most powerful tools men have developed in their exercise of thought. But its virtue is rather in making us aware that we are still, in truth, thinking about the world in a Greek way. That was Whitehead's description of science, and with some justice it can be extended to cover our habitually uncritical response to things as well.[10]

Another moral to the story of Greek thought is one that the reader must draw for himself, for it has to do with a point that is both delicate and controversial. I have stayed as close as I could to history in tracing out the interesting counterpoint by which, as the ideas of the world became wider in scope and more capable of tidy order, philosophers moved away from direct personal expression—in poetic or rhetorical form—leaving the sea to take up residence in the city, leaving the Agora to assume its place as custodians of the Museum, leaving its home and life in Athens to survive only in written words rolled up and filed on proper shelves in the great library of Alexandria. For generations men spent their desire to know on questioning the world from a simple-minded standpoint of total objectivity. They found it enough to understand the things men could observe and wonder at, without trying at the same time to pay attention to the observer! But, paradoxically enough, the literary forms chosen for communication show that the philosopher in this pre-Socratic age did not feel himself cut off from reality by any screen of language, concept, or custom. Although his doctrine was hopelessly objective, his form of expression was totally engaged and erred on the other side. The ideal of philosophy, at first, seems to have been close to inspired direct communication of some crucial insight, without the controls and extensions that intelligence correctly demands of direct inspiration. But, perhaps at the point of change from poem to dialogue, perhaps at that of change from dialogue to lecture, the controls demanded by intelligence may have become excessive, and brought new caution and precision that left no room for inspiration.[11]

But Western civilization has not only held on to the concepts that locate and define the components and dimensions of the world; Greek philosophy has never lost its appeal as an ideal. The unity of all knowledge and experience in some coherent speculative order is a goal that continues to animate Western thought. It is not always most effective in philosophy itself, considering philosophy somewhat narrowly. It may appear as the ideal of a unity of science, it may appear as the ideal of an integration of the self, or as an ideally balanced order of society. We may differ widely in our estimates of how far the greatest ancient thinkers achieved this ideal for their own time, even more widely in estimating how relevant, if at all, their systems are to our situation today. But, almost as though history had set out to give a proof of the truth of Plato's thesis that ideals act as causes in the world of time, we find the ideal goal of speculative system, unity, coherence, and simplicity constantly working in the intellectual adventure of Western civilization, giving direction to the actual.

NOTES

I. THALES

1. For various appraisals of the importance and originality of Thales and his two successors in Miletus, see the histories of early Greek philosophy and of Greek science cited in the Bibliography below.

2. For an interesting reconstruction of Miletus, see K. Freeman, *The Greek City States*, New York, 1950, chap. i. See also Burnet and Guthrie. Many stories about Thales are preserved in the "Life of Thales" by Diogenes Laërtius, written in the third century after Christ; but some were already current at the time of Herodotus and Plato. See the discussion of the Seven Sages (among whom Thales was included) in Freeman, *Companion* and *Ancilla*.

3. It may be that, in the evolution of ideas, some intrinsic property of "transitional forms" makes them peculiarly difficult to recover; that this is so for all evolutionary processes is one of the interesting theses of Teilhard de Chardin's *The Phenomenon of Man*.

4. Thales' statement is quoted from Aristotle, *Metaphysics* 983b17 (DK A12; references to the A and B sections of Diels-Kranz, *Fragmente*, 10th edn., Berlin, 1961, will be given in this form); Freeman, *Companion*, pp. 49-55. See also Kirk and Raven (hereafter cited as KR), Guthrie, *Hist. Gk. Phil.*, I.

5. Compare the remarks above, p. 9 ff., on the absence of many of our most fundamental modern distinctions in the Ionian world.

6. Sir James Frazer, *The Golden Bough*, abridged edn., 2 vols., London, 1890. Guthrie explains this suggestion and shows its application to Greek prephilosophic thought, *op. cit.*

7. See the books cited below on Greek science; O. Neugebauer's *The Exact Sciences in Antiquity*, Copenhagen, 1951, shows that Babylonian science and mathematics were more advanced than earlier scholars assumed; but this does not greatly change the final appraisal of Greek originality. See S. Sambursky, *The Physical World of the Greeks* (trans. M. Dagut, London, 1956), p. 7; M. Clagett, *Greek Science in Antiquity*, London, 1957, gives a summary of pre-Greek science, pp. 30-31. Regarding the Egyptian "occult wisdom," supposedly embodied in the dimensions of the Great Pyramid, see the amusing and precise third section of Noel F. Wheeler's article, "Pyramids and their Purposes," *Antiquity* IX (1935), pp. 292-304. Also, C. Macdonald, "Herodotus and Aristotle on Egyptian Astronomy," *Cl. Rev.*, 1950, p. 12.

8. Sambursky sums up Thales' contribution from a scientist's standpoint, *op. cit.*, p. 7: "It was Thales who first conceived the principle of explaining the multiplicity of phenomena by a small number of hypotheses for all the various manifestations of matter." For a modern existential statement of confrontation with being as the essential philosophic question, see M. Heidegger, *An Introduction to Metaphysics*, trans. R. Manheim, New Haven, 1959.

9. See the appraisals of Sambursky (n.7 above), and the others cited in the histories of philosophy and science listed in the Bibliography.

10. For the magnet "having a soul because it moves iron," the source is Aristotle, *De Anima* 405a19 (DK A22); the addition of amber appears in DK A1 (Diogenes Laërtius I, 24) and DK A3 (scholion on Plato, *Republic* 600A). But amber had been known and used for ornament from Mycenean times—see the necklaces in the National Museum of Athens—so that Thales' reference to it is not implausible. See next note.

11. Again, the "all things are full of soul" report is from *De Anima* 405a19 (DK A22). For the meaning of "soul," however, see Burnet and the perceptive discussion in Guthrie, HGP, I.

12. If "precision" includes strict adherence to certain rules of thought—particularly the law of excluded middle—O. Vuia

is a modern spokesman. See also P. Wheelwright, cited in Chap. V, below; compare Henri Bergson, *Introduction to Metaphysics*, trans. T. E. Hulme, New York, 1912.

13. Plato, *Theaetetus* 174A.

14. The story of the eclipse prediction is told by Herodotus, in his *History* (written in the fifth century B.C.), I.74 (DK A5). Such an eclipse was visible in Asia Minor on May 23, 585 B.C. Thales, of course, could not predict eclipses visible from Asia Minor; but he probably did know a Babylonian rule, that *if* there were such eclipses, they would be twenty-eight years or a multiple of this period apart. In that case, he might well have said that there would be an eclipse in that year and, if there were one, been credited with predicting it. In a similar fashion, Anaxagoras was also reputed to be able to predict (see below, Chap. XII); his astronomical theory that "there were stones in the sky" was given some prominence in the public mind by the fall of a great meteorite in 467 B.C.; and Anaxagoras is reported by his later biographers to have predicted the meteorite. See Burnet, E.G.P.4, p. 43.

15. Aristotle tells this story of Thales' business speculation in *Politics* 1259a6 (DK A10); it is repeated with considerable embroidery in Diogenes Laërtius.

16. Herodotus, *History* I.75, knew of a story that Thales had diverted the Halys for Croesus; but he did not believe, it. Herodotus, I.170, reports Thales' political advice to the small city-states of Asia Minor.

17. Plato refers to Thales as a great inventor in *Republic* 600A; for the measurement of the diameter of the sun, see A. Wasserstein, "Thales' Determination of the Diameter of the Sun and the Moon," *JHS*, 1954, pp. 119-156. For Thales' new navigation rule, see DK A1 (Diogenes Laërtius) A3a (Callimachus); this can hardly have been the discovery that Ursa Minor is a better guide to where north is than Ursa Major, which is what Callimachus says was the new discovery, because Greek sailors up to that time had used Ursa Major, for two reasons: first, because Homer already knew the rule; second, because navigation based on the "Greek way" of Callimachus would be impracticable. (This latter point was confirmed emphatically, in conversation, by Captain M. Mariakis.)

II. ANAXIMANDER

1. For dates and relation of Anaximander to Thales, see C. H. Kahn, *Anaximander and the Origins of Greek Cosmology*, New York, 1960. For the reasons that could lead one to begin the history of "philosophy" (perhaps as opposed to "science") with Anaximander, see, for example, G. B. Burch, "Anaximander the First Metaphysician," *Review of Metaphysics*, III (1949-50), pp. 137-60.

2 Burnet (*E.G.P.*, p. 52, 52 n.2) believed a fragment of a statue from Miletus came from an original statue of Anaximander, probably erected to him for his work with the colony. But an analysis of a cast of the statue fragment suggests that it is not a statue of a man at all, but of a woman; W. Darsow, "Die Kore des Anaximanders," *Jarb. d. Deutsch. Arch. Inst.*, 1954, pp. 101-17. For his political activity, see DK A1.

3. The sundial in Sparta is reported in DK A1, A4; the map, DK A1, A6; that Anaximander also made some sort of a celestial sphere seems likely (DK A2, A6, Kahn, *op. cit.*, note a, p. 60).

4. See *DK* B1. For the sense of *apeiron*, see Kahn, *op. cit.*

5. *DK* A1, A9, A16.

6. For the modern view of matter as "a neutral stuff," see especially A. N. Whitehead, *Science and the Modern World*, (New York, 1925), chaps. iii, v, vii.

7. For the importance of Anaximander's model, see Sambursky, *op. cit.*, pp. 13-16, 58. The map and the celestial map (if that is what the later reports refer to) extend the notion of model-building to geography and descriptive astronomy; the map does not survive, but for its main features, see Kahn, *op. cit.*, pp. 81-85, Plate I; W. A. Heidel, *The Frame of Greek Maps*, New York, 1937, p. 11 ff.; J. O. Thompson, *A History of Ancient Geography*, Cambridge, 1948, p. 104 ff.

8. For the astronomical model, see *DK* A10, A21, A11, A18, A22, A27; eclipses, A11, A21, A22.

9. N. Rescher, "Cosmic Evolution in Anaximander," *Studium Generale*, Vol. XII, 11th Annual (1958), pp. 718-31.

10. On this, see G. Vlastos, "Equality and Justice in the Early Greek Cosmologies," *Classical Philology*, 1947, pp. 156-78; also the works by Kahn, Sambursky, Guthrie, cited; and F. M. Cornford, *From Religion to Philosophy*, reprinted, New York, 1960.

11. Fragment 1 (DK B1: the source, Simplicius, comments on the "poetic manner of expression," which shows that he had Anaximander's own words before him). An interesting example of an error leading to the notion that Anaximander said the opposites pay reparations for their guilt in existing at all will be found discussed in Kahn and Freeman (*allelois*, "to one another," was omitted in the Aldine edition of Simplicius). This item is also a worthwhile caution against too literal-minded an insistence on sticking to the exact wording of fragments: for the idea, however congenial to Nietzsche and T. Gomperz, is not plausible in Anaximander.

12. For the "evolutionary" views of Anaximander, see DK A11 par. 6, A30.

13. It is interesting to think of botany as the model for a "philosophy of science." Anaximander's extension of his concept of "bark," *phloion*, to zoology and astronomy is one of the few examples I can think of. More usually, as we will see illustrated in Plato and Aristotle, the science of "philosophy of science" means either physics, mathematics, and formal logic (as in Plato) or zoology and medicine (as in Aristotle).

III. ANAXIMENES

1. See Burnet and Guthrie, *op. cit.* The crucial passages for this new analysis of change are DK A6 and B2; A5-A8; B1.

2. G. Gamow, *The Birth and Death of the Sun*, New York, 1940.

3. For the limits of science, see Sartre, Heidegger, Bergson, Whitehead, and, earlier, Kant, Descartes.

4. See DK B1-2. But what *aer* meant—whether, for example, it was thought to be material, or whether "souls" were composed of it—needs further discussion; the question will be treated below, pp. 32 ff.

5. F. S. C. Northrop, *The Logic of the Sciences and the Humanities*, New York, 1947.

IV. PYTHAGORAS AND HIS SCHOOL

1. This traditional picture, opposing the Milesians with their stress on matter and the Pythagoreans with their equal emphasis on form, goes back to Plato and Aristotle. It is such a good way of bringing out the philosophic directions and tendencies of these two groups of thinkers that historians of philosophy have used it ever since, with only minor qualifications.

2. The history of formalism begins with the Pythagorean work in pure and applied mathematics; its next advance comes with the recognition and sharpening of formal logic by Parmenides and Zeno; there follow Socrates' inquiries, raising the question of this standpoint's applicability to ethics; finally, Platonic "idealism" brings these several dimensions together with a new speculative theory of form and value. See J. E. Raven, *Pythagoreans and Eleatics*, Cambridge, 1948, for an account of the interaction of Eleatic and Pythagorean views.

3. C. Seltman, in an article appraising the change in Italian coins as possibly the work of Pythagoras, corrects the picture that modern readers unconsciously assume of Pythagoras as a solitary exile. We should think of him as a prominent citizen bringing his family, servants, and household goods in several small shiploads to a city where they were expected and welcome. C. Seltman, "The Problem of the First Italiote Coins," *Numismatic Chronicle* IX (1949), pp. 1-21.

4. See Plato's comment, *Republic* 600A, that Pythagoras owed his reputation to "establishing a certain way of life." The tendency in most histories of philosophy, logic, and science has been to emphasize the "scientific" aspects of the school, treating the religious side as a separate sort of afterthought. Guthrie evens the balance in his account, placing the school in its religious background; but his treatment can profitably be supplemented by more technical accounts of the Pythagoreans in histories of mathematics, astronomy, and science.

5. Aristotle's way of developing his own position as a mediating one between formalism and materialism leads to a good many references to "the Pythagoreans" in his writings, particularly the *Metaphysics* (e.g., 995a23, 987a9,b2, 986a15,

1002a8, 1072b30, 1078b21, and many others). That numbers are things and, also, that things are numbers are recurrent central theses that he attributes to this school. Judgments differ widely as to the reliability of Aristotle's reports.

6. See, for a very clear appreciation of pure mathematics and the Pythagorean discovery of it, A. N. Whitehead, *Science and the Modern World*, New York, 1925, chap. ii. Neugebauer's work (see above, Chap. I, n. 7) somewhat modifies the notion that the Greeks invented mathematics out of nothing, but the appraisals of Clagett and Sambursky, making due allowance for the new findings, seem to me substantially the same as Whitehead's.

7. Heath, *History*, I, pp. 373-84. See also his edition of Euclid's *Elements*, 3 vols., Oxford, 1926. There were already books of "elements of geometry" in Plato's time, and Heath finds the methods of proof of Euclid I-V thoroughly Pythagorean. In this and the following chapters, the reader will find the Greeks given more credit for developing formal logic and appreciating axiomatic-deductive methods of formulating explanations than most historians give them. As against the notion still held by some outstanding modern scholars that "logic" is primitive and amorphous until Aristotle, see R. K. Sprague, *Plato's Use of Fallacy*, London, 1962, and my formalization of the compressed argument of Plato's *Parmenides* (*Plato on the One*, New Haven, 1962).

8. Although the Pythagoreans deliberately rejected any sharp distinction between pure mathematics, applied mathematics, physics, and philosophy, they also on occasion developed rather impressive and rigorous hypothetical-deductive proofs. An impressive example of this is the indirect proof of the irrationality of the square root of two, preserved in outline by Aristotle. See Sir T. Heath, *Mathematics in Aristotle*, Oxford, 1949, pp. 22-23; also Heath, *History of Greek Mathematics* I, Oxford, 1921, pp. 90-91, 154-57.

9. The "reality" of abstract entities remains a topic of debate in contemporary formal logic (frequently centering around the technical question of whether it is meaningful to use existential quantification: "There exists a _____ such that . . . ," the _____ being filled in with the name of an abstract property

or class). See W. V. Quine, *Mathematical Logic*, Cambridge, Mass., 1947; and S. Körner, *The Philosophy of Mathematics*, New York, 1960.

10. For example, there are reports that at an early period the Pythagoreans associated the geometric shapes of the "regular solids" they knew with the properties of earth, fire, and water. This geometric theory of molecules is given its full development by Plato, much later. But both the notion that nature prefers symmetry and that qualitative differences such as those between earth and fire might be explicable by particles differing in shape could be dated as early as Pythagoras himself and find some experimental support. Sir W. Ridgeway, "What Led Pythagoras to the Doctrine that the World Was Built of Numbers?" *CR* XI (1891), pp. 92-94, brought together the reports that Pythagoras himself was a gem engraver and the occurrence of regular solids in familiar crystals, and suggested that perhaps these were the inspiration of the mathematical view of nature, which Pythagoras advanced. That this is a sole and sufficient explanation of Pythagoras' ideas is of course not tenable, but to find some relevance seems reasonable enough. Ridgeway mentions the pyramid and double pyramid shapes of quartz, the cubes of iron pyrite and galena ore, the dodecahedral garnet crystal, and the cylindrical hexagon crystals of beryl. The suggestion that this occurrence of symmetry in nature was available to, and perhaps influenced, the Pythagoreans seems to me to gain even more plausibility when we realize that crystal magnifying lenses may have been part of the equipment of the gem-engraver.

11. Arithmetic as it was understood in Hellenistic and medieval times was still very close to this Pythagorean approach; cf. Nicomachus, *Introduction to Arithmetic*, trans. M. L. D'Ooge, New York, 1926. A considerable amount of the trouble with Aristotle's appraisal seems to be, not that he was incompetent in mathematics (when it was absolutely necessary, he seems to have been competent enough), but that he used his own very technical notion of what mathematics was in treating an earlier stage when the idea of mathematics had been a quite different one. On this point, see R. S. Brumbaugh, *Plato's Mathematical Imagination*, Bloomington, 1954.

12. For this notion that numbers have some qualitative at-

tributes, cf. Freeman, *Companion*, pp. 251-52. Even today, when we are used to thinking of numbers merely as handy tokens for computation, some poets—and other people—have a "Pythagorean synaesthesia" that makes them associate certain qualities with certain numbers (usually the same associations for different people). But this approach led quickly into "number magic" of an extravagant kind, more akin to literature than science: for a sample, see the compilation from Neo-Pythagorean and Neoplatonic sources in T. Taylor, *The Theoretic Arithmetic of the Pythagoreans*, Los Angeles, 1912.

13. That the "things are numbers" idea is not—as Aristotle seems sometimes to have thought it was—intrinsically silly is clear from such appraisals as Samybursky's *op. cit.*, pp. 41-43; compare Whitehead, *SMW*, ii.

14. Aristotle, *Metaphysics* 986a15.

15. For the "music of the spheres," see the discussion in Guthrie, *op. cit.*, pp. 295-301.

16. The standard medical notion of health as *isonomia*, an equal balance in the body, evidently matches very well with the Pythagorean views. For Polyclitus and some new suggestions about the eccentric Eurytus, see J. E. Raven, "Polyclitus and Pythagoreanism," *CQ*, *NS*, I (1951), pp. 147-52. For the periods of the planets, see, for example, Heath, *Greek Astronomy*, London, 1932.

17. Guthrie, *HGP* I, sums up the results of recent research, by von Fritz, Minar, and others into the history of the Pythagorean Order, and, drawing on his own knowledge of Orphism, gives a very perceptive account of the religious motivation and background of Pythagoras. Guthrie's final judgment is that the decline of the order as a political power was gradual, marked by different local uprisings over a forty-year period. But from a very early stage, "the Pythagoreans" were decentralized, so that various individual communities and thinkers developed their ideas independently within a very general common framework and there were no single official doctrines common to, say, all "the Pythagoreans" writing about physics or geometry. Burnet, *E.G.P.* 4, defends the thesis that the anti-Pythagorean movement was oligarchic and antidemocratic; but cf. Guthrie.

18. For this topic, see Guthrie's discussion, *op. cit.*, of the

Orphic religious background, the concepts of initiation and purification, etc., with his citations.

19. An excellent discussion of the Pythagorean idea of cosmos in Guthrie, *op. cit.*, pp. 206-211.

20. There is some interesting systematic variation in the appraisals of the Pythagoreans by later historians. Plato, Whitehead, A. E. Taylor, Sambursky, Heath are relatively enthusiastic; Aristotle, Guthrie, and others much more critical.

21. For the interaction of the criticism from the Eleatic school and the development of Pythagorean ideas, see J. E. Raven, *Pythagoreans and Eleatics.* Two of the following chapters introduce two thinkers very critical of Pythagoreanism, Parmenides and Zeno of Elea.

V. HERACLITUS

1. Heraclitus is peculiarly hard to interpret. It seems unreasonable to approach the oracular epigrams of a genius who combines philosophy with poetry and prophecy in the same way one would excerpts from a nautical almanac. But it is not easy, either, to fit together into a single account the scholarly results of Kirk (G. S. Kirk, *Heraclitus: The Cosmic Fragments*, Cambridge, 1954), the poetic, critical sensitivity of Wheelwright (P. Wheelwright, *Heraclitus*, Princeton, 1959), and the philosophic excitement of O. Vuia. It is the latter of these, however, that I have tried to convey.

2. See the introduction, citations, and the new arrangement of fragments in O. Vuia, *Remontée aux Sources de la Pensée Occidentale: Héraclite, Parménide, Anaxagore: Nouvelle présentation des fragments en grec et en français et leurs doxographies,* Paris, 1961.

3. See Aristotle's remark that many of the ambiguities in Heraclitus are the result of unclear punctuation, *Rhet.* 1407b11.

4. For the oracle, and its form of communication, see for example, T. Dempsey, *The Delphic Oracle*, Oxford, 1918.

5. Fragments 49A (flow), 51 (two ways), 90 (exchange), 48 (name of bow).

6. Frags. 121 (Ephesians should be hanged), 39 (praise of Bias) ; violent criticisms of the poets, especially Homer and Hesiod, are voiced in Frags. 105, 106, 42, 56, 57; see next note.

7. Against Pythagoras et al., Frag. 40 and 81; against contemporary religious practices, Frag. 5 and 14.

8. Frag. 60. For the meaning of *logos*, there seems to be no simple translation; nor is there consensus of interpretation.

9. Frag. 60; compare Frag. 59. We find a cosmological cycle in Frag. 76 again; Frag. 31 describes the transformations of fire into earth and water; Frag. 90 tells us that "fire is exchanged for all things . . . as gold for merchandise."

10. See Frag. 1 for "the *logos*" and "the common."

11. Frag. 94.

12. Frag. 52.

13. For the notions of psychology, see especially Frags. 62, 118, 77, 2, 27.

14. Compare Vuia and Wheelwright, with their different arrangements; see also Kirk and Raven, *op. cit.*

15. For Aristotle's treatment of Heraclitus, a brief, clear, if somewhat polemical appraisal is my "Aphilosophical First Philosophy," *Proc. XIIth Intl. Phil. Congress*, Venice, 1958, Vol. XI, pp. 55-58.

16. For a general notion of Stoic physics, a quick reading of Diogenes Laërtius, Bk. IX, is recommended. More detailed treatment of Stoic interpretations of Heraclitus in Kirk, *Heraclitus: The Cosmic Fragments*, Cambridge, 1954; of Stoic physics, in S. Sambursky, *Stoic Physics*, New York, 1962.

17. P. Wheelwright, *Heraclitus*. See the reviews of this by S. MacClintock (*Classical Journal* 54 [1959], pp. 271-72), and W. Bröcker (*Gnomon* 32 [1960], p. 368).

18. Kirk's thesis rests on a sound recognition that the *logos* as well as the flow is central in Heraclitus' thought; but his rejection of the "flow" interpretation, as a later Platonic attribution, has not found many defenders. See, for example, Vlastos' review, *AJP* 1955, pp. 310-13; Calogero's review of Kirk and Raven, *Gnomon* 34, 1962, p. 321 ff.; Guthrie's dissent, *HGP* I, pp. 488-92. Also relevant is A. Wasserstein's article, "Pre-Platonic Literary Evidence for the Flux Theory of Heraclitus,"

Proc. XIIth Intl. Phil. Congress, Venice, 1958, Vol. XI, pp. 185-90.

19. Particularly in the *Cratylus*; see my *PMA* and the literature cited there.

20. There are a number of good anthologies of haiku poetry in English translation; for example, H. G. Henderson, *An Introduction to Haiku*, New York, 1948.

21. See, for example, *aletheia*, *techne*, *doxa*, in Heidegger's *Introduction to Metaphysics*. His translation of Anaximander's fragments draws Kranz's fire in DK I, pp. 487-88. How far Heraclitus himself uses puns and etymologies puzzles one a bit. The Heracliteans that Plato talks about in his *Cratylus* have become inveterate advocates of ambiguity, pun, and "etymology." Heraclitus' own fragments, however, show about five clear-cut cases, out of 120 fragments (see Freeman, *Ancilla*, notes to her translation).

22. Frags. 92, 93.

23. Here Aristotle (followed by Theophrastus) seems unusually Procrustean in his attempt to make Heraclitus fit into his history of the parallel development of materialism and formalism. This point is generally recognized.

24. Cf. Guthrie, Kirk and Raven.

25. One of Wheelwright's central theses, *op. cit.*, where the idea of "plurisignation" is used as a critic's tool. In connection with the more general question of "symbolism," see S. Langer, *Philosophy in the New Key*, Cambridge, Mass., 1942, and A. N. Whitehead, *Symbolism*, New York, 1927; repr. New York, 1959.

26. Not exactly our modern notion of energy (though our idea of matter as frozen energy would suit Heraclitus rather well). And not Aristotle's *energeia* ("actuality"), or *dynamis* ("power"). "Violence" (*bia*) may come closer to it; cf. DK III, p. 91.

27. For Whitehead's displacement of "substances" and "subjects" in favor of "events" and "superjects," see N. Lawrence's clear nontechnical summary in R. S. Brumbaugh and N. Lawrence, *Philosophers on Education*, Boston, 1963, ch. vii, p. 154 ff.

28. Archilochus, an Ionian poet whom Heraclitus coupled with Homer in his attack, Frag. 105.

29. Frag. 30.

VI. PARMENIDES

1. Frag. 1. See the works of Guthrie or Kirk and Raven cited above for estimates of the proportion of Parmenides' original poem that has been preserved. A new interpretation of the Prologue by my colleague, Dr. Mourelatos (cited in the Bibliography, below), as well as his discussion of the balance of the poem, are original and interesting, and have influenced my own translation. (For example, my spacing follows his analysis of the different times at which the axle glows, the maidens guide the horses, Parmenides reaches the great gate, and the goddess greets him.)

2. Frag. 3.

3. This "intuition of being" is a profound awareness of the underlying permanences of things, beneath their apparent passage. Heraclitus' *logos*, on the other hand, reflects the apparent permanence of things in contrast to their real passage. Parmenides is writing in a poetic form, and to express his insight may have used figures and imagery in an attempt to get beyond the limits of ordinary language.

4. Frag. 7, 8.

5. Frag. 3. There has been much discussion of the tightness with which Parmenides intends to identify "thought" and "being"; the translation above, following Burnet, is the weakest identification of those proposed. Philosophically, there are three relevant relations here of being and thought: (1) something internally inconsistent cannot "be thought" at all, and cannot refer either to being or seeming; (2) a coherent scheme of thought, such as Pythagorean science and mathematics, can seem to refer to being; its order is intelligible, though its premises may on close examination be only "opinion"; (3) strictly, there is no separation of the thinker and his thought from the single, unchanging reality. Parmenides will show that respect

for consistency requires us to discard (1) in favor of (2)—a familiar point, though he gives it new generality—and then on the same principle we must discard (2) in favor of (3).

6. For a challenge to the laws of contradiction and excluded middle, see Vuia, *op. cit.*, and his citations of Heisenberg, Hegel, Lasalle, Heidegger. Here contemporary formalism and existentialism have a common concern: see for example F. B. Fitch, *Symbolic Logic*, New York, 1952, for current work on self-reference and consistency with weakened law of excluded middle. The formalization of Parmenides' argument was given clearly and simply in S. Ranulf, *Der Eleatischen Satz vom Widerspruch*, Copenhagen, 1924. Its outline is a generalization from the "indirect proof" that was certainly sometimes used in Pythagorean mathematics: if either *p* or non-*p* is the case, *p* implies *p*; if, further, non-*p* implies *p*, *p* must be the case.

7. See "Advaita Vedanta" in S. Radhakrishnan, *Philosophy Eastern and Western*, 2 vols., New York, 1952.

8. End of DK 8.

9. See Raven, *Pythagoreans and Eleatics*, Cambridge, 1954, for this identification, discussed in detail.

10. Particularly interesting interpretations are those of Cornford (*Plato and Parmenides*, New York and London, 1939), Heidegger, and Beaufret. Ever since Plato, Parmenides' readers have wanted to give "opinion" an "intermediate degree of reality" between pure being and pure nothing. We are disquieted by the very suggestion that all "existence" may be logically absurd. But though it is puzzling, that seems to be what Parmenides said.

11. Notice the range of topics in the fragments we have of this second part: Astronomy, DK 8, 10, 11, 12, 14, 15; love, 12, 13; language, 19; genetics, 17, 18; physiology and psychology, 16.

12. Thus one would conclude that the intention of this second part of the poem is a rigorous application of the form of indirect proof to the Pythagorean philosophy. On the status of appearance, Plato and Aristotle are able to agree with the insights of Heraclitus and Parmenides, but still avoid complete annihilation of the world of "seeming."

13. F. Solmsen, *Aristotle's Natural World*, Ithaca, N.Y.,

1961. Chap. i has an excellent analysis of the effect of Parmenides' reasoning (in particular his "nothing comes from nothing" principle) on subsequent Hellenic philosophy.

VII. ZENO OF ELEA

1. This chapter is based on a lecture given to the Institute of Science and Mathematics of the University of Athens, April, 1963.

2. Plato, who did not hold as high an opinion of Zeno and his logic as philosophers in the nearby city of Megara, has Zeno say that his only purpose was to defend Parmenides, which is why his *logoi* only reiterate what the former had already stated in a different way. See Plato, *Parmenides*, the opening scene, and my comments in *Plato on the One* (New Haven, 1962).

3. Raven, *Pythagoreans and Eleatics*; for a contemporary formulation, see Max Black, *The Nature of Mathematics*, New York, 1934. I am assuming here, as have Raven, Guthrie, and Lee (H. D. P. Lee, *Zeno of Elea*, Cambridge, 1936), that the Pythagoreans are intended to be included in Zeno's critical attack. I think Guthrie's picture of the Pythagorean "School" as somewhat decentralized and holding no single "orthodox" doctrine on the relation of their "points" to continuous quantities explains why Zeno needed *four* paradoxes of motion; Raven (*P. and E.*) analyzes the argument clearly, but makes history more orderly than it was, in my opinion, in assuming two successive "orthodox" notions.

4. Raven's analysis, *op. cit.*, shows the crucial importance of Zeno's assumption that Parmenides has already disproven any "void." For the "later" Pythagorean position that he discusses is one in which some continuous stretch of a field, itself not made of points, is bounded by points. But this seems likely to have been one of the "earlier" Pythagorean ways of construing that "things are numbers," and in setting up his list of possible cases, Zeno seems to feel he need not be concerned to refute this interpretation.

5. In what follows, I have put together my notion of "no

void" (n. 4 above), Heath's conviction that "the four paradoxes are interrelated to form some single set," Lee's interpretation of the Stadium as anti-Pythagorean, Raven's idea that the paradoxes are a destructive dilemma, and A. E. Taylor's analysis of Zeno in his translation of Plato's *Parmenides* (A. E. Taylor, *Plato's Parmenides*, Oxford, 1934, "Introduction"). The crucial thing here is Taylor's clear recognition that both for Zeno and for his Pythagorean opponents, the state of mathematics at that time seemed to make only two interpretations of the "point" possible: Either it had *no* extension (hence was $=0$), or it had some uniform *finite* extension (hence was $=1$). This is an excellent summarizing notation.

6. For a contemporary notion of nonuniform space and time, with the former continuous but the latter quantized, see R. Palter, *Whitehead's Philosophy of Science*, Chicago, 1962, where Whitehead's advocacy of this view is discussed. Critics who assume that space and time are alike in structure entirely miss the point of Zeno's first two paradoxes; see, for example, Aristotle's rather cavalier dismissal of the bisection.

7. See the text and translation in Lee, *op. cit.* The "kinematographic" motion consequent on a "point-element" theory is well presented in connection with the stadium paradox. Here see DK 28, 29, Lee, *op. cit.* The difference in reading leaves it unclear whether Simplicius, in his discussion, intends a diagram with only *one* item in each of the three rows (which would emphasize the absurdity of the postulate that units of time and velocity were indivisible), or three or four items in each (which would emphasize the result of measurement of relative velocity by numbers of units traversed). Zeno's use of the term *onkos* seems clearly to suggest that his "carts" or "chariots" can be thought of as Pythagorean indivisible minima; compare Plato's use of the term in his adaptation of the stadium paradox, *Parmenides*, hypothesis VII, (164B5 ff.).

8. Clearly, Zeno is engaging in a simultaneous critique of two different positions: the "paradox" form will show how muddled and unclear the "common-sense" view is; the technical implications of the four cases will show that the "scientific" view of the Pythagoreans runs into internal contradiction. Among later appraisals of Zeno, probably the most interesting and important

is the acceptance of the arrow paradox with its full implications by Henri Bergson. See, for example, his *Introduction to Metaphysics*, trans. T. G. Hulme, New York, 1912.

VIII. EMPEDOCLES

1. See the DK B section. Aristotle's remark that Anaxagoras was "posterior" to Empedocles in his philosophical activity may mean that he was "posterior" in the sense of "more modern," so this does not help date his writings. A coin of Selinus with the emblem of Aesculapius on the reverse, from 444 B.C., may confirm the tradition that Empedocles cured the city of a plague in that year; see B. V. Head, et al., *Historia Numorum*, Oxford, 1911, "Selinus," p. 168.

2. For the fragments, and their division into two major groups, see Guthrie, *op. cit.*

3. Aristotle's attitude of mixed interest and exasperation runs through his various, frequent citations.

4. This notion of three traditions in treating appearance and reality is not generally accepted, and should be given careful scrutiny: but it seems to me a sound interpretation.

5. For the skepticism of the Sophists, see the chapter on them below; and the interpretations in L. Versenyi, *Socratic Humanism*, New Haven, 1963.

6. This seems very foreign to modern common sense; but Sambursky, *op. cit.*, has a favorable appraisal: he holds that "Empedocles introduces the concept of the dependence of phenomena on universal forces at work in the cosmos," p. 16.

7. Frag. 6, DK.

8. The quantitative determinacy of the "elements" follows as a reasonable extension from the Pythagorean idea of minimal points, and their other notion, if it was developed this early, of correlating shapes of fire, water, etc. with the "regular solids." See above, Chap. IV, n. 10.

9. See DK 7.

10. DK 84.

11. Against "empty space," Frags. 13, 14.

12. For the "experiment," see DK 100. In general note the

contrasting estimates of the place of empirical experimentation in Greek science by Sambursky, *op. cit.*, pp. 2-5, and Claggett, *op. cit.*, pp. 30-31.

13. See DK 13, 16, 109.

14. Strife begins, DK 26, 30, 35, 36. On the cosmic cycle, see Kirk and Raven, *op. cit.*

15. Frags. DK 57, 53, 60, 61.

16. Monsters appear in Greek art as early as Neolithic vase designs.

17. For clear presentation and criticism of Empedocles' idea of "natural selection," see Aristotle, *Physics* II, 198b10 ff.

18. DK A 22; Aristotle, *Poetics* 1447b17.

19. See *Physics* II, *op. cit.*, and the chapter on Aristotle, below.

20. The return of love: DK 27, 36.

21. This comment, that "heads without bodies" presupposes complete organisms from which the "heads" could be separated, occurs in *Physics* II.

22. Frag. DK 100.

23. D. J. Furley, "Empedocles and the Clepsydra," *Journal of Hellenic Studies*, 77 (1957), pp. 31-34; see note 12, above.

24. All of this comes out in the fragments assigned to his second poem, "Purifications." Particularly for the claim "to be a god" (DK 112), contrast Freeman's interpretation with Guthrie's, *op. cit.*

25. For example, Vuia, trying to reconstruct a stage of philosophy not regimented by a logic with excluded middle and the law of contradiction, bypasses Empedocles in favor of Heraclitus, Parmenides, and Anaxagoras, *op. cit.*

IX. THE ATOMIC THEORY

1. DK A9; B116.

2. The tremendous historical importance of the atomic theory hardly needs documentation; see, for example, Sambursky, *op. cit.*, pp. 105 ff. (where however the Greek and Roman versions are combined; they are distinguished and summarized on pp. 128 ff.).

3. For Leucippus, see Kirk and Raven, *op. cit.*, p. 403; C. Bailey, *The Greek Atomists and Epicurus*, Oxford, 1928; Leucippus in DK B1, B1a, B2.

4. Book X, on Epicurus, was copied by Diogenes Laërtius from contemporary primary source material; his treatments of the Epicureans and the Stoics are reliable and important. Epicurus' "Letter to Herodotus," which Diogenes Laërtius quotes, is an excellent summary of Epicurus' doctrine.

5. Here again we have difficulty in judging the exact balance between pure theory and experiment, or at least observation, that went into the makeup of this theory. See above pp. 88 ff. and the divergent views of Sambursky and Claggett. Also see the end of the present chapter, below, for some evidence that the technology of the time would have made close interaction of the theory and immediate observation possible.

6. DK B9. Cf. M. Jammer, *Concepts of Space*, with a Foreword by A. Einstein, Cambridge, Mass., 1954. On the reasons why atoms (pieces of pure "being") can't be "cut," compare with Parmenides' rejection of plurality, above.

7. Aristotle, *Met.* 985b13; DK, Leucippus, A10.

8. All shapes, endless motion: Aristotle, *loc. cit.*

9. Soul atoms finest: Aristotle: *De Anima.*

10. Emanation theory of perception; compare the "pores and particles" of Empedocles, above, Ch. VIII.

11. In the following table, the Greek atomic theory is reconstructed from fragments and reports of Democritus; the Roman version from Epicurus' *Letter*, in Diogenes Laërtius; the contemporary is a composite based on a consensus of a number of sources, and on some discussions with colleagues in physics at Yale.

12. Two of the four criticisms that follow are cited in modern formulation, where they are clearer and stronger than in their classical occurrences.

13. For the "no theory" objection, see N. P. Stallknecht's presentation of this point in "Descartes," Stallknecht and Brumbaugh, *Spirit*, pp. 252-54.

14. For the "no secondary qualities" objection, see Whitehead's statement, *SMW*, chap. v.

15. Aristotle is already clear on the "empty space" objection;

see his proof that there is no "void," to which he devotes *Physics*
IV, 213A12 ff.

16. For atomism in India, see the account of the Charvaka
school in Radhakrishnan, *op. cit.*

17. For the excavations and finds, see the *Guide to the
Agora*, 2nd edition, published by the American School of Classical Studies in Athens, Athens, 1963.

18. Aristotle, *Aristotle's Constitution of Athens*, trans. with
notes by K. von Fritz and E. Kapp, New York, 1950, para-
graphs 63-69, with notes.

ATHENS

1. In addition to the more extensive general books on history,
culture, philosophy, listed below in the Suggestions for Further
Reading, the following are of special interest: *Life Magazine*,
"Greece," 1963, especially parts 3 (April 22) and 4 (May 20);
American School of Classical Studies in Athens, *The Athenian
Agora*, 2nd edn., Athens, 1963; *Athens and Environs*, Hachette
Blue Guides, revised edition, Paris, 1962; the American School
of Classical Studies Excavations of the Athenian Agora, Picture
Books, Nos. 1-5.

2. We recall that the first stage of the development of science
and philosophy took place simultaneously on the two frontiers
of Greece. Athens in the fifth century had a similar spirit of
innovation and adventure. Compare Whitehead's five defining
ideas of civilization: "truth, beauty, adventure, art, and peace."

3. See below, Chap. X.

4. See below, Chap. XII.

5. See below, Chap. XIII.

6. See below, Chap. XIV and XV.

7. Compare the comments and notes on classical technology
at the end of Chap. IX, above.

8. See A. N. Whitehead, *Science and the Modern World*,
chap. xiii, "Requisites of Social Progress," for an excellent statement of this theme. The idea is developed in relation to Platonism in my *PMA*, "Conclusions."

9. For a detailed description, see the Hachette Guide, cited in n. 1, above.

10. Here see the American School publications cited above, n. 1; also N. Perfetos, *The Ancient Agora and Acropolis of Athens*, Athens, 1961.

11. An impressive display of these in the Stoa of Attalus Museum is briefly described in *The Athenian Agora* (cited in n. 1 above). (No classical "money-changing tables" have been found; but the classical descriptions exactly match the small tables of the money-changers on Sophokleous Street, just outside of the National Trapeza of Athens ["*trapeza*," originally "table," is still the Greek word for bank].)

12. An important new article by P. Stavropoulos should be noted: "Akademia (Platonos)," *Megalē Ellēnikē Enkyklopaideia, Symplērōma*, Teuchos 22, pp. 340-43. (Reprints of Teuchos 22 may be ordered from the publisher, Odos Pheidiou 6, Athens; cost is 5 drachmas plus postage.)

13. To feel this centralizing effect, one should compare photographs of the Acropolis from the theater, Agora, Academy; views of the city from the four corners of the Acropolis; and photographs from higher points—Lycabettus or Hymettus—of the Acropolis and the rest of Athens together.

X. ANAXAGORAS

1. Diels, *op. cit.*, II, pp. 5-14. See also the works of Cleve (F. M. Cleve, *Anaxagoras*, New York, 1949), Vuia, Kirk and Raven, cited in Suggestions for Further Reading, below.

2. Several modern scholars accept this explanation; it does seem that there must have been something like the meteorite to account for Pericles' selection of this young Ionian to join his circle. Cf. Freeman, *op. cit.*, p. 262.

3. Diels, A 37; see also Cleve; Archelaus is treated below, Chap. XII.

4. So the older standard histories of philosophy, but by Burnet quotation marks are used, to indicate that this is not precisely either modern dualism, or matter, or mind. See Freeman and Kirk and Raven.

5. A history of set theory in the classical period would be of considerable interest. Professor Vlastos has suggested that Anaxagoras has a place in the history of mathematics. Professor E. Stamatis' paper on set theory in Neoplatonism is a start toward the study of this topic. (*Praktika tēs Akademias Athenōn*, 33 [1958], pp. 298-303).

6. Frag. 8, Diels.

7. Note the complexity of concepts reflected in the vocabulary of the fragments dealing with mixture and matter: we find "qualities," "homoeomeries" (this is not A.'s term, but *is* his technical concept), "things," "portions," "mixtures," "seeds," all appearing and demanding close attention. The best discussion of these various terms and ideas to date is that of Kirk and Raven, *op. cit.*

8. Frag. 1, Diels. See the reconstruction of A.'s cosmology in the several works cited above; note that "air" separates in very great quantity.

9. This might make more sense of Aristophanes' *The Clouds*, in which "air" has become the be-all and end-all of his "scientists," than the assumption that Aristophanes was parodying Diogenes of Apollonia. And it might explain why Archelaus, Anaxagoras' admirer and student, gave "air" a leading place in his cosmology. If one's interests were primarily medicine or even astronomy, and not metaphysics, a good Ionian scheme could be derived from Anaxagoras by starting with the universe *after* air has "separated out" from the "primordial mixture."

10. Burnet, *E.G.P.*, has a good account of this "vortex" theory; see Anaximenes' astronomical fragments and the reports in Diels, *op. cit.*, I.

11. An obvious difficulty that comes up again, in slightly altered form, in Aristotle's astronomy.

12. Diels, A77, A113; A1.9. It is said that there is a "large rock shaped like a lion" in the vicinity of Nemea. I myself either didn't see such a rock or didn't recognize it as lionlike. But if Anaxagoras had in mind this connection of a remarkable stone and the lion legend, his notion is not nearly so implausible.

13. Recent work has led us to a new appreciation of the importance of Anaxagoras for later Greek philosophy. See, for example, my *Plato on the One*, New Haven, 1961, for a discussion of his influence on Eudoxus and on Plato.

14. See also Kirk and Raven, for a summary of the conflicting accounts and dates of Anaxagoras' trial.

15. For discussions of *Process and Reality*, and its complexities of vocabulary, see N. Lawrence, *Whitehead's Philosophical Development*, Berkeley, 1956; also W. Christian, *An Interpretation of Whitehead's Metaphysics*, New Haven, 1959.

XI. ARCHELAUS

1. For the status of "Greek schools," and their importance in the advancement of science, see Clagett, *op. cit.*, pp. 30-33. This seems to me an important topic, too often ignored in histories of science and philosophy. See also below, Chap. XIV and XV on Plato's Academy and Aristotle's Lyceum.

2. Freeman, *Companion*, pp. 275, citing DK A10.

3. On the relation of Socrates and Archelaus, as reconstructed from the evidence of Aristophanes' *The Clouds* and Plato's *Phaedo* 100A ff., see Burnet's notes to his edition of the *Phaedo* (Plato, *Phaedo*, ed. w. int. and notes by J. Burnet, Oxford, 1924) and A. E. Taylor's *Socrates*, Oxford, 1933; also below, Chap. XIII.

4. This would be my own conjecture; it is based on experience with young scientists who want nothing but the "truth," i.e., the most recent theories, and on the way Archelaus cuts down Anaxagoras' more philosophical theories to permit a simple empirical interpretation. Note, in this connection, that the idea of studying the "history" of a field as a key to a dialectical determination of some "truth" is an innovation of the Lyceum, not fully accepted until the generation after Aristotle (though Plato uses his predecessors as spokesmen in imaginary conversations, and Heraclitus cites them by name to damn them).

5. So Kirk and Raven, *op. cit.*

6. This raises the very general philosophic topic of the reducibility of a metaphysical hypothesis to a testable physical model; only in the family of "atomic" theories is this always a possibility. See below, on "participation" in Plato, Chap. XIV; on

"causality" in Aristotle, and the need to postulate some "separate but immovable" substances, Chap. XV. This certainly does not mean that "metaphysical" theories have no consequences that are observable in our experience, which will confirm them or the reverse; but it does mean that "our experience" has a much wider spectrum than "physical models."

7. Plato, *Phaedo* 100A ff. On this passage, see Chap. XIII, below, and *PMA*. This, at least, is the usually accepted interpretation; see Burnet, *E.G.P.*4, and Taylor, *Socrates*. The fragments of Diogenes in DK do, it is true, show the combination of an acceptance of air as principle with a use of teleology that matches the ideas of Socrates, and the jibes of Aristophanes. But is there really any reason why both of these ideas could not have derived from a more "empirical" version of Anaxagoras? If we trust Plato's biography of Socrates, the latter saw the teleological implications of Anaxagoras' *nous* (not of Diogenes' *aer*). And Anaxagoras' account of cosmic evolution, once it has got clear of "metaphysical" considerations and reached a level a laboratory anatomist can make sense of, has a tremendous preponderance of "air" created as the first stage of the "separating off."

8. Socrates' summary, *Phaedo* 100A ff.

9. *Ibid.*

10. For this explosive emergence into clear consciousness of something that had been latent for some time in the development of Greek thought, see Chap. XIII, below.

XII. THE SOPHISTS

1. Every English and American reader will recall Potter's treatise on *Lifemanship: or The art of getting away with it without being an absolute plonk*. His final analysis of "lifemanship" in classical times, however, while it makes the case out for chariot-racing in the *Iliad*, gives a misleading impression of Greek adroitness, before the Sophists anticipated and applied some of Mr. Potter's discoveries.

2. Here I cannot agree with Dr. Versenyi that the Sophists

were in general tolerated and respected rather than actively resented. On the contrary, we find a sweeping attack on their legal methods by an aristocratic conservative in Aristophanes' *The Clouds*; a refusal to have anything to do with them attributed to the democratic leader, Anytus, in Plato's *Meno*; an attempt to slam the door in their faces, when Callias' porter takes Socrates and his young friend for "More Sophists!" in Plato's *Protagoras*; and these seem to me a fair sample of a generally hostile public attitude. The passage in the *Protagoras* in which Protagoras says that he is not ashamed to call himself a Sophist has a defensive tone which suggests that most Athenians *would* be ashamed.

3. The accuracy of Plato's portraits has been questioned. But they have a convincing individuality to them (except perhaps Euthydemus). As regards their ideas in Plato's critical dialogues, it is worthwhile to recall Bertrand Russell's remark (in his *History of Western Philosophy*, New York, 1945); commenting on Xenophon's account of the ideas of Socrates, he says, "I would rather be reported by my worst philosophical enemy than by a friend who was innocent of philosophy." The amount of other material against which we can check Plato varies widely from one individual to another. See the material in DK and Freeman.

4. Here see Freeman, *Companion*; Diogenes Laërtius; the evidence for Gorgias' tremendous impact as ambassador to Athens, e.g., in B. H. J. Williams, "The Political Mission of Gorgias to Athens in 427 B.C.," *Classical Quarterly* XXV (1931), p. 52 ff.

5. As a sample, see the opening of Gorgias' "Funeral Oration," trans. in Freeman, *Ancilla*, p. 130.

6. Gorgias, "On Helen," *loc. cit.* See next note.

7. The argument runs that Helen must have gone to Troy because of (1) divine compulsion, (2) human violence, (3) persuasion by speeches she could not resist, or (4) irresistible passion. In case (1), she evidently did not go voluntarily, and so is not guilty; Gorgias draws the same implication for each of the other cases. Formally, A v B v C v D; A $\supset$ ~G, B $\supset$ ~G, C $\supset$ ~G, D $\supset$ ~G; therefore, ~G. Compare to the outline of Zeno's four paradoxes of motion, above.

8. For the wonderful speech "On the Nature of Things," see, in addition to the summary in Freeman, the pseudo-

Aristotelian *On Melissus, Xenophanes, and Gorgias* (Oxford trans. VI). Also Calogero, *op. cit.*

9. Here the logical form is this: If A, then either B or ~B, and not both; but, on the authority of X, B holds; while philosopher Y has proven ~B. The contradiction requires us to deny the hypothesis, A. The "Defence of Palamedes" is even more interesting as an example of applied logic. Here, the defendant argues that if he were guilty, his hoped-for gain would have been either A or B or C; but all three of these would be contradicted and rendered impossible by the crime charged.

10. In addition to the improbability that the author of the speech "On the Nature of Things" would be an enthusiastic teacher of philosophy, see Plato's portraits of Gorgias' students, Polus and Meno, and his admirer, Callicles.

11. We take the adversary system for granted; the Greeks did not. This is one of Aristophanes' main targets in *The Clouds*. As a rather depressing sample of collecting arguments on both sides of a case, see the *Dissoi Logoi* outline in Diels-Kranz, II, trans. in Freeman.

12. Protagoras, Frag. 1 (DK B1).

13. Protag. Frag. B2. Compare the fragments of Critias.

14. For a passing summary by an authority on the classical classifications of the "parts of speech," see L. D. Buck, *Comparative Grammar of Greek and Latin*, Chicago, 1933, pp. 168-69.

15. For Socrates' inability to afford the more expensive course, see Prodicus in DK B11 (*Cratylus* 384B).

16. This is a bitterly ironic passage (Plato, *Protagoras* 340C-D), which still has contemporary relevance. "Alexandrian scholarship" is not always the surest way to understand literature—or philosophy, or any other area.

17. Aristotle, *Sophistical Refutations*, 165b13.

18. Plato (assuming him to be the author), opening of the *Hippias Minor*.

19. [Plato] (assuming some other member of the Academy group to be the author) *Hippias Major*.

20. The shift between "older" and "younger" Sophists is already apparent in Plato's portraits, and has been generally recognized, though different explanations are given.

21. Thrasymachus breaks in, "fiercely," with his solution to

the problem, *Republic* I, 336bff. There is a theory that originally *Republic* I was written as an "inconclusive" early Socratic dialogue, "The Thrasymachus, or Concerning Justice"; this is plausible enough, but the evident influence of the schematism of "degrees of clarity of knowledge" of *Republic* VI and VII on the structure of Book I (see P. Desjardins, *The Form of Platonic Inquiry*, Ph.D. diss., Yale, 1957, and *PMA*, pp. 100-01) must mean that if such an "early" dialogue existed, it was rewritten when it was incorporated in the larger plan of the *Republic*. To Socrates' question, whether "the strong man" who controls the police and courts might not make a mistake as to his "real interest," Thrasymachus—dismissing the naïve agreement of his young admirer, Cleitophon—introduces a legal technicality: the strong man *as such*, like the doctor *as such* in a legally defined sense, does not make mistakes. This opens the way for Socrates' counterargument that a ruler *as such* is not defined by the amount of his private income, but by his expertness in serving the interests of his subjects. As far as the relevant legal fictions of "infallible experts" go, Thrasymachus has in fact lost his case.

22. Plato, *Euthydemus* 293. For the Euthydemus, see R. K. Sprague, *op. cit.*, and the dramatic adaptation of R. Neville (*Plato's Euthydemus: Jowett's translation adapted as a one-act play*, mimeographed, New Haven, 1960).

23. For the balance of the *Euthydemus*, and the appropriateness of its epilogue on "intermediates," cf. *PMA*, pp. 54, 74.

24. It was formerly accepted as a fact that Protagoras was forced to leave Athens in 418, but the story seems untrue; cf. Freeman, *Companion*, Versenyi, *op. cit.*

XIII. SOCRATES

1. *Cleitophon* 406A ff. This is the speech Socrates is described as "declaiming like a tragic poet" in the Platonic (or early Academic, if not genuinely Platonic) *Cleitophon*; the dialogue needs more study (see *PMA*, pp. 193-94), but the speech as a report of Socrates in the Agora sounds authentic enough.

2. Since Socrates wrote nothing but had an influence that

changed the whole course of Greek philosophy, there are many sources, not always in agreement. Recent scholars seem to be settling down to the view that Plato's accounts are probably the most reliable (no one has ever denied that they are the most vivid and extensive), mainly on the ground that he had enough philosophical talent to appreciate what Socrates was teaching, where Xenophon, for example, or Aristophanes did not. Further, Plato's account of Socrates can come closer to synthesizing the very diverse aspects that the "Socratic schools" fastened on as the central points of their hero's teaching than can any of the accounts of these schools. See Versenyi, *op. cit.*, and my Foreword. The sources are discussed in A. E. Taylor, *Socrates*, Oxford, 1933. Though not directly relevant to Socrates' philosophy, the reader may be interested in Babette Deutsch's *Mask of Silenus* or Mary Renault's *The Last of the Wine*, two historical novels in which Socrates figures, or may become provoked— as I was by the interpretation in terms of class-structure of A. Winspear and T. Silverberg, *Who Was Socrates?*—into some fairly extensive reading of sources to check the soundness of their versions.

3. On the fascinating but intricate relation of Socrates to the Socratic schools, the relevant evidence is collected in Zeller, *Socrates and the Socratic Schools*; a new and interesting interpretation of this relationship will be found in L. Versenyi, *op. cit.*

4. Here one encounters such diverse views of Socrates as those of the Indian interpreter in *Philosophy East and West* (ed. Radhakrishnan, II, New York, 1955), who thinks no Westerner has ever understood him; Kierkegaard; Versenyi; Winspear and Silverberg; A. E. Taylor; and Hegel. When we add Babette Deutsch and Mary Renault, this amount of riches really becomes an unendurable embarrassment to the conscientious historian.

5. For the notion that it is "natural" for the stronger to dominate the weaker, see the Fragments of Critias, and the speeches of Thrasymachus in Plato, *Republic* I and of Callicles (the practical man who admires Gorgias) in Plato's *Gorgias*. A similar theme recurs in Hobbes, Machiavelli, James Burnham, and elsewhere.

6. The ideas under attack in *The Clouds* are mainly two: the displacement by "naturalistic" explanations of older religious views; and the training of young men to argue in a way that makes the worse side of a case appear the better, displacing old common-sense notions of right and wrong. A. E. Taylor (in *Socrates*) points out that two other comedies of about this time, now lost, also had Socrates as central character. From this he infers that by 423 Socrates had already achieved considerable local notoriety in Athens.

7. Plato, *Parmenides*. Since Burnet, many scholars (impressed by A. E. Taylor's defense of the historical plausibility Plato shows in the dialogues, some notion of which one can find in the treatment of their dramatis personae and dates in A. E. Taylor's *Plato*) have assumed that this dialogue rests on a real encounter. (The details of place are certainly circumstantial; perhaps some day they will be confirmed by finding a bottom of a cup in the Ceramicus inscribed; "I belong to Pythodorus," or a bronze bit in one of the house foundations of Melite on the northwest slope of the Acropolis.) On the other hand, while Socrates certainly appreciated the precision of Eleatic logic, there were other, nonhistorical reasons which, in about 367, could have led Plato to invent a fictitious conversation between Parmenides, Zeno, and Socrates (see my *Plato on the One*, pp. 17-26). On the one hand, his leadership of the scientific school in Athens does argue an "international" reputation, and he meets visiting dignitaries on terms of acquaintance and equality in Plato; on the other hand, as Plato becomes more interested in Pythagorean ideas, between 394 and 384 B.C., so does his hero Socrates (see below, *PMA*, pp. 51-62. Probably the crucial items in appraising this relation are: (1) that Plato's inclusion of Simmias and Cebes, two Pythagorean disciples of Philolaus then in Thebes, as present at the death of Socrates in unlikely to be sheer anachronism; (2) that Socrates' reminiscence in his intellectual autobiography, *Phaedo* 100A ff., includes among the youthful questions he pondered "whether the earth is flat or spherical," a question that would occur to him only if he already knew something of the views of the Pythagoreans; and that (as Burnet's notes show) the other details of this account are an amazingly accurate catalogue of the problems that science was concerned with when Socrates was a young scientist.

8. The importance of a quest for self-knowledge is a recurrent theme in philosophy; already stated in Heraclitus, it recurs in our own century's notions of "authenticity" and "existence." As Rousseau points out, in his *Emile*, there is a stage in education (about senior class in high school) where every student becomes curious to know himself.

9. We get different kinds of answers about the self from neurology and psychoanalysis, and neither seems to satisfy the person anxious to "search out the limits of the soul" (as Heraclitus put it).

10. One of the most significant things about the sophistic notion of the self is that we have to reconstruct it inferentially. It is some inner x that desires glory and riches, and avoids what is painful or terrifying; it is "natural," though society conditions it by impressing local "conventions." It is not the self of popular religion (see Protagoras and Critias, quoted in Chap. XII above, for that); nor of natural science (again see Protagoras and Gorgias, with their rejection of such metaphysical speculation in the interests of a more practical humanism).

11. His account of this was part of Socrates' defense at his trial—cf. Plato, *Apology*, 11A ff. We can compare Plato's portraits of Socrates in action, interrogating a reciter of Homer (*Ion*); a religious expert, somewhat fanatically fundamentalist (*Euthyphro*); an outstandingly successful rhetorician, ambassador, and lawyer (*Gorgias*); a leading democratic statesman—the one, indeed, who was responsible for Socrates' trial and execution (Anytus, in the *Meno*; it is his associate, Meletus, who has to answer Socrates' cross-examination at the trial, as reported in the *Apology*); a man who is fabulous for his information and skill in many crafts (Hippias in the *Hippias Minor* —assuming that this is Platonic but the *Hippias Major* is not); two former commanding generals, cornered in a discussion of education (Laches and Nicias in the *Laches*); and so on. In fact, Plato manages to cover such a wide range of encounters that F. Schleiermacher, in the nineteenth century, was convinced he had written his entire set of Socratic dialogues from a carefully prepared advance plan.

12. On the value of inquiry, see, for example, *Meno* 86B; on the intrinsic value of justice, *Apology* 41D, and *Gorgias* 509A ff.

13. That there is no *intrinsic* but only *instrumental* value in most of the things his contemporaries prized is a familiar Socratic doctrine. Plato develops it as Socrates' idea in the *Lysis*, *Euthydemus*, *Republic*, and elsewhere; and it is this Socratic thesis that seems to have helped inspire the Cynics (for whom see E. Zeller, *Sokrates and the Sokratic Schools*, trans. O. J. Reichel, London, 1885).

14. Plato, in his *Seventh Letter*, writes that the dictatorship of the Thirty "made men look back on the war as a relatively happy time."

15. Under the circumstances, this was a perfectly legitimate fear; and if the "preservation of the state" took precedence over any consideration of individual liberty or of human improvement—as it does in some Hegelian and Marxist theories—he would have been right. It is an interesting question to ask how far, in Socrates' case, the "clear and present danger" doctrine of our United States law would apply. See Plato, *Meno* 93E-95A.

16. Plato, the *Euthyphro-Apology-Crito-Phaedo* tetralogy; see Bibliography, below.

XIV. PLATO

1. For various editions and treatments of Plato and Aristotle, see Suggestions for Further Reading, below.

2. In addition to the accounts of the influence of Platonism in general histories of Western philosophy, some important detailed tracing will be found in R. Klibansky, *The Continuity of the Platonic Tradition*, and an interesting appraisal in A. N. Whitehead, *Process and Reality*, New York, 1929, pp. 64-65.

3. Plato's *Epistle VII* describes his early political ambition and why he gave it up. The Socratic dialogues referred to here are the earliest group: the *Lysis*, *Laches*, *Charmides*, *Euthyphro*, *Apology*, and *Crito*.

4. See pages 138-143. For Plato's attitude toward contemporary Athenian politics in his later years, see *Epistle VIII*.

5. The *Charmides* is a conversation with Socrates, which has Charmides (Plato's uncle who became one of the Thirty) and

Critias (who was Charmides' guardian and the leader of the Thirty) as its other characters. Charmides tends to be diffident and lazy; he thinks of temperance as a kind of quiet inaction. Critias is aggressive and self-confident; he thinks he has an exact abstract formula that answers the question. For an interesting study of the *Charmides*, see Dr. Paul Desjardins, *The Form of Platonic Inquiry*, dissertation, New Haven, 1959.

6. Plato's account of the trial, imprisonment, and death of Socrates is given in the *Apology*, *Crito*, and *Phaedo*, respectively. Xenophon's *Memorabilia*, available in various English translations, shows the lack of understanding Plato was trying to correct.

7. After the dialogues listed in the previous note, Plato set about showing that Socrates was entirely different from the Sophists, with whom Athenian public opinion tended to identify him. There are rather longer conversations, with visiting experts as central speakers. These dialogues include the *Lesser Hippias*, *Gorgias*, *Ion*, *Protagoras*, *Cratylus*, *Euthydemus*, and the *Meno*. The list of "themes" is drawn both from the earliest dialogues and this second set: criticism of Homer begins the conversation in the *Lesser Hippias*; theories of language are central in the *Cratylus*; while the definition of human excellence and its component "cardinal virtues" is central in the rest.

8. Plato himself (*Sophist* 246A ff.) describes the earlier philosophers ("the Ionian and Sicilian Muses") as "each telling us a *mythos*." They may well be inspired (as the name "Muses" might suggest) but their meaning is certainly not clear to later readers. A summary of evidence may be in order here:

Philosopher	Literary Form Chosen
Heraclitus	Oracular epigram
Parmenides	Epic poem
Pythagoreans	Formula; diagram; symbol
Empedocles	"Lyric" poetry
Sophists	Rhetorical speeches; lectures
Socrates	Critical conversation
Plato	Philosophic dialogue

9. Also, compare the forms in which contemporary philosophy finds its expression with the table in the previous note.

10. For Archytas, see Freeman, *Ancilla* and *Companion*; other sources are cited in *PMA*, n. 1, p. 234, Bibliography.

11. For the rise of Syracuse, see Bury's *History of Greece*. The famous statue of the Charioteer at Delphi was commissioned by Gelon, the first of the great Syracusan dictators, to commemorate his successes in chariot racing.

12. The story itself is told in some detail by Diogenes Laërtius; what makes it more credible than most of Diogenes' anecdotes is an apparent reference to the adventure by Aristotle, in *Physics* II. Plato describes his own reaction, with considerable restraint, in *Letter VII*; it is put much more vividly in his portraits of the typical dictator and dictatorship in *Republic* IX.

13. The "philosopher king" in *Republic* V-VI; the tyrant and his city, *Republic* IX.

14. Aristophanes' satiric appraisal of the "thought shop" in *The Clouds* reflects conservative opinion; the speech against grown men still studying philosophy, made by Callicles in Plato's *Gorgias*, reflects the radical sophistic appraisal.

15. See Claggett, *op. cit.*, for the rise of "schools" in the history of Greek science; *PMA* pp. 115-31, particularly pp. 123-26, for "science" in the Academy and evidence that some laboratory apparatus was used there.

16. See the article of P. Stavropoulos, "Akademias (Platonos)," and Perfetos' monograph, cited in the Bibliography, below.

17. The traditional education was by an apprentice system, though in medicine "professional schools" had developed in Cos and Crotona and elsewhere. The Pythagorean Order is closer to the earlier notion of a religious community, such as the mystery religions had among initiates, than to the later school idea (on this point, see Guthrie, *op. cit.*). The rival school of practical affairs in Athens, founded by the orator Isocrates, proposed to follow these same traditions of specialized professionalism and apprenticeship in training young politicians; he thought the Academy idea much too abstract and impractical.

18. The new translation and notes of Professor G. Morrow, *Plato's Letters*, New York, 1962, are excellent for the reader interested in the content and authenticity of *Letters VII* and *VIII*. See also R. S. Bluck's general book on Plato, cited in the Bibliography, below.

19. See my *Plato's Mathematical Imagination* for discussion both of details of the line and of Plato's use of diagrams as schematizing and teaching devices more generally.

20. Compare the appraisals Plato's Socrates offers of the heroes of Athenian statesmanship in the *Meno* and elsewhere; and note how insistent he is, in the *Republic*, that "real" statesmen need a wholly different kind of knowledge from the politicians of his day.

21. The English renderings "reason" and "understanding" are often used, prompted by the distinction in Kant's great critical philosophy between *"Vernunft"* and *"Verstand."* Apart from Kant's conviction that the Idea reason offers is unattainable, this assimilation is not misleading.

22. The first two of these differences are stated explicitly in *Republic* vii; the third is given there implicitly, in the assertion that *noesis* is needed to grasp the good. The third difference is developed in much more precise detail in the *Parmenides* and *Statesman*.

23. The best contemporary statement of a similar view will be found in A. N. Whitehead, *The Function of Reason*, particularly chap. i: "Importance."

24. *Republic* VI, 507 ff. Glaucon responds to Socrates' final statement that the good is "beyond both being and knowing . . . in power" by remarking, "Oh, Apollo! What a demonic hyperbole!"

25. The clearest statement of this role of the forms as limits is given in Socrates' account of "the new method" he turned to when science no longer satisfied him, *Phaedo* 100A ff.

26. Perhaps the trouble with *eikasia* is that it has so many superimposed types of order that it is almost impossible to sort them out. For the sort of "rationalization" Plato and Socrates would apply in referring myth to an origin in the world of objects, see *Phaedrus* 299C ff.

27. I have tried to make this point more clearly, in some detail, in my *Plato on the One*, pp. 199-206.

28. For example, we would be much more inclined to talk today about a "principle of conservation . . ." or a "law of entropy . . ." than about a "prime mover" or a "highest value form"; yet the status and function of these may be the same.

29. Proclus, in his *Commentary on Plato's Timaeus* (written

in the fifth century after Christ) mentions Crantor's use of a "lambda" diagram to illustrate the world-soul section of the dialogue (35A ff.). Plato's own frequent use of "family-tree" language to describe the relation of concepts and his rather elaborate schemes of classification by repeated division of classes into pairs of subclasses strongly suggest a use of triangular designs in the Academy itself. See my article "Logical and Mathematical Symbolism in the Plato Scholia" for further discussion.

30. The unifying "one highest form" appears differently in different discussions. In the *Parmenides*, it is "the One"; in the *Symposium*, "the Beautiful"; in the *Republic*, as in Fig. 1, "the Good." In the *Philebus*, the three "identifying marks" of the Good are "Truth, Symmetry, and Beauty" (where "Symmetry" is the kind of definite structural unity that "the One" gives to the "Many" that share in it). Late in his life, Plato gave a great "Lecture on the Good," of which only a few fragmentary notes by his hearers are extant; it was technical and mathematical (to the disappointment of most of the audience), and one of its main theses was that "there is one Good." This is, of course, necessary if "the Good, the True, and the Beautiful" are to be the same, as Platonists have always argued that they are.

31. This organization of the discussion of the good in four parts is considered in my *Plato for the Modern Age*, pp. 97-103. The relations and location of these sections are:

Level of Line	Account of Good on That Level	Location of Republic Passage
NOESIS	Simile of the Sun	VI, 507 ff.
DIANOIA	The Divided Line	VI, 509D ff.
PISTIS	The Ideal Curriculum	VII, 521C ff.
EIKASIA	The Myth of the Cave	VII, 514A ff.

32. The following illustration is based on chap. ii of R. S. Brumbaugh and N. M. Lawrence, *Philosophers on Education*, where this application of the Platonic divided line was initially made.

33. From the later Socratic dialogues (*Gorgias, Meno*, etc.) onward, Plato introduces myths into his writing. He seems to have two reasons for this: first, the myth can give a vividness to concepts that abstract argument cannot; second, the religious

intuitions of men seem to be evidence for some natural "divination" of the good. (Thus, as opposed to the Sophists, Plato gives religion—religion properly understood—credit for insight into important truths and finds a place for it in his philosophy.) The theme of "cosmic justice" is central to the Myth of the Last Judgment which concludes the *Gorgias* and the Myth of Er with which the *Republic* closes. (The investigation of the relation of the latest scientific findings to the general principle that the world order is dominated by value, which is one of the important questions considered in the *Timaeus*, is a classical counterpart to some of our contemporary discussions—such as Whitehead's in *Science and the Modern World*, chap xii—of the relation between science and religion or theology.)

34. The possible disarrangements of human souls give Plato a kind of diagnostic table for locating types of character and personality. The table varies in different contexts—sometimes 3 types of order are recognized, sometimes 5, sometimes 9, sometimes 12, and perhaps once either 81 or 729. But in each use, it shows combinations of motivation (which of the three "parts of the soul" is dominant) and intelligence (which level of clarity of knowledge the soul has the ability to attain). One such table is the following:

Innate Intellectual Power	DOMINANT PART OF SOUL		
	Reason	*Spirit*	*Appetite*
NOESIS	Philosopher	Auxiliary (in a good society)	Artisan
DIANOIA	Statesman or General	Athlete	Merchant
DOXA	Sophist	Poet	Tyrant

Other combination-patterns are diagrammed and discussed in my *PMI*.

35. This distance between current standards and the sort of "virtue" needed in a good society is surely one of the things Plato intended to emphasize in his account, *Republic* V, of the

way property, marriage, education of children, and higher education would be carried on by "guardians such as we have been describing." This is the section of the *Republic* that has the least philosophic relevance, and has received the most shocked attention from its readers. It is not entirely clear, even today, exactly what Plato's intention was or how seriously he meant the details to be taken.

36. In this connection, see N. R. P. Murphy's study of the *Republic*. In Book IX, Plato concludes his case for the intrinsic value of justice, then offers a proof that the life of the just man contains more pleasure than that of the unjust so that even on purely hedonistic grounds it should be preferred. The argument of this section is followed in the text, above.

37. See J. A. Stewart, *The Myths of Plato*, and other works on religion in Plato in the Bibliography of *PMA*, p. 251.

38. See Kitto, *The Greeks*, where in his discussion of Sparta the point that the Greek city conceived its role as that of conditioning each individual to a preconceived "civic type" is convincingly made. The same idea appears in the periodic demands for unquestioning patriotism recorded in Thucydides' *History*. And the same conclusion, though based on wholly opposite premises, was drawn by the Sophists (Thrasymachus, Antiphon, Critias, et al.), for whom the state was "conventional" and "justice" meant simply the exercise of the power of the sovereign.

39. On this principle, "types of state" are classified in *Republic* VIII-IX. A true aristocracy would be correct in its ideal of general welfare as the aim of education and policy; a timocracy (an honor-loving society, controlled by military leaders) takes national power as its goal; an oligarchy (rule of the few who are an economic upper class) substitutes national wealth and high standards of living; a democracy (by which Plato means a town-meeting democracy of the Athenian type with its perpetual referendum) has no fixed policy but, insofar as it shows any consistency, aims at greater "individual freedom"; finally, a tyranny has as its goal the satisfaction of the personal wishes of the tyrant (who would never want the office if he were not already insane).

40. Surely it would be most unlikely that Plato, whose con-

cern with the political issue of state and individual began with the death of Socrates, would twenty years later hand over the individual, rights and person, to the state. Some interpretations of the *Republic* would imply that this is exactly what he did there; but this overlooks the part that "the consent of the governed" plays in the definition of temperance in *Republic* IV, and the part individual rights play in the decision that social functions must match individual interest and ability, a central theme of *Republic* II-VII.

41. An idea that Plato develops both in the *Symposium* and, considerably more explicitly, in the *Laws*.

42. From Homer on, the idea was current that hereditary differences accounted for the observed superiority of the Greek "aristocrat" to the farmer or tradesman. Plato denies that there is *always* such a difference in heredity; but he still is inclined to underestimate the part played by environment.

43. This point will be discussed in more detail in the "Practical Science" section of the following chapter.

44. Today, we are debating the same essential problem, though in a more specialized form. What we wonder is whether a good man will always be a misfit in a modern urban society (from Rousseau to *The Organization Man*, some critics have argued that he will), in a capitalist economy (the Marxists are uniformly sure that he will), in an American public high school, and so on.

45. See the books and section on "Platonism" in my *PMA*, Bibliography p. 252; "Part Five: History," pp. 187-204.

XV. ARISTOTLE

1. On Aristotle's technical vocabulary, note his insistence in the *Categories* that philosophy should use "univocal terms"; what this means in terms of the number of distinctions required is illustrated, for example, in Aristotle's "philosophical lexicon" (*Metaphysics* Book Delta). See also R. Hope's analytical index to his translation of the *Metaphysics* (New York, 1952).

2. Aristotle's *Topics* opens with a formal description of "dialectic"; for some applications, see the opening two books each of his *Politics* and *Nicomachean Ethics*.

3. For the story of Aristotle's influence, any standard history of Greek philosophy will cover the Hellenistic period, and any of medieval philosophy the rediscovery and importance of Aristotle in the thirteenth century.

4. For this twentieth-century reappraisal of Aristotle, to be discussed in more detail below, of particular interest and importance have been the work of Ross and McKeon.

5. With a few exceptions, historians of philosophy, society, and science accept the death of Aristotle as marking a drastic break in the interests and attitudes of philosophers. See, for a summary, Stallknecht and Brumbaugh, *Spirit*, ch. vi "After Aristotle," p. 177 ff.

6. On Aristotle's extant works as lecture notes, see W. Jaeger, *Aristotle: The History of His Development*, trans. R. Robinson, Oxford, 1948; and see also W. D. Ross's introductions to his editions of the *Physics, Metaphysics, Organon* (e.g., *Metaphysics* 1069b34: "*Meta tauta hoti. . . .*"). Other evidences of the lecture-note character are the duplications, where presumably a lecture series was repeated but with some material changed in order. This is evident in the *Metaphysics* (identity of sections of A and M; duplication of B and K; possible juxtaposition of two versions of Z). Also, in the works on ethics, the *Eudemian Ethics* has three books in common with the (later, more analytical) *Nicomachean Ethics*. In *Ethics* iii and *Metaphysics* N, the text indicates that the lecturer has a large diagram on display to which he points as he lectures.

7. This is one important concern in current Aristotle scholarship. The "classical" approach, as found in St. Thomas, concentrates on the systematic coherence of each work; the "evolutionary" approach, best exemplified by Jaeger, concentrates on a chronological ordering that will illustrate development. McKeon's analyses are classical, in the sense of stress on coherence; Ross mediates between the two. The present chapter assumes that, however and whenever their various components were written, Aristotle puts enough order into his large-scale plans of lecture series to make the "classical" analysis profitable. For his

early works, see Aristotle, *Selected Fragments*, trans. W. D. Ross (Oxford trans., vol. XII, Oxford, 1959). Some scholars are uneasy about the attribution of the set of mathematical fragments from Iamblichus to Aristotle's *Protrepticus*.

8. Admiration for Plato: simply note, from Ross's list of Aristotle's early writings in his Introduction, how many of these are variations on themes by Plato, often with the same or similar titles. Empiricism: for me, the best evidence is the addition of arguments from attested cases of precognition to Plato's more abstract proofs of immortality, and the recasting of the Myth of the Cave into a two-level form, in the *On Philosophy* fragments.

9. On Aristotle's relation to Alexander, see Plutarch's "Life of Alexander."

10. See further on this point the few fragments supposed to come from works dedicated to, perhaps written for, Alexander by Aristotle (*On Colonies* and *On Kingship*).

11. *Topics* I, 105 b 12; and see the translation in the Oxford edition, Vol. VII: *Problemata*. The *Mechanics*, *On Things Heard*, and *On Marvellous Things Heard* are included in Vol. VI: *Minor Works*. The *Economics* is in Vol. XI.

12. All the way through the *Ethics*, in the *Sophistical Refutations*, and especially in the *Rhetoric*, a host of concrete contemporary examples shows Aristotle's alertness as observer and collector of legal cases, fallacies, and ways of persuading audiences in public speaking. (For example, perhaps the first "didn't know it was loaded" case—the defendant had been showing his friends how to fire a catapult—enlivens *Nicomachean Ethics* III.) On the Lyceum collections, see the appraisal of Claggett, *op. cit.*, pp. 30-33.

13. For the legal sense of *aitia* and its transposition to natural law, see above, Anaximander, and G. Vlastos' article cited.

14. This is the thesis of the "history of philosophy" with which Aristotle opens his *Metaphysics* (Book A); and, naturally, he selects and interprets his material in the light of it. See especially R. McKeon, "Plato and Aristotle as Historians," *Ethics* LI (1940), pp. 66-101.

15. For example, in *De Generatione et Corruptione* and *De Caelo*, we get Aristotle's criticism of *both* Platonists and atomists

for making the components of the physical world too abstract and "too mathematical." Aristotle wonders what they can do about secondary qualities, powers, weight, and lightness, and so on.

16. See Figs. below.

17. The amazing range and consistency Aristotle shows in applying this notion of "causal explanation" will be illustrated below; see also McKeon, "Introduction," *Basic Works of Aristotle*, New York, 1941.

18. *Physics* I and II are devoted to clarifying the domain of "natural philosophy"; the meaning of "nature" is the theme of the first two chapters of Book II.

19. See Sambursky and Solmsen, *op. cit.*

20. This specific sameness of efficient causes, which Aristotle usually illustrates by "man is the father of man," is a theorem in his logic (*Posterior Analytics*, 95a 10-96, a19) and important in the *Metaphysics* (Lambda, Epsilon).

21: For Aristotle's defense of teleology against Empedocles, see *Physics* II 198 b 10 ff.

22. Aristotle, *De Caelo* i; cp. Solmsen, Claggett, *op. cit.*; Heath, *Greek Astronomy*, Oxford, 1932. Aristotle thinks the "center of the universe," where linear changes occur, is very small compared to the total system; the same idea occurs in Plato's *Epinomis*. On the divinity of the heavens: Sambursky, Solmsen, *De Caelo*, etc.; natural versus constrained motion: *Physics* IV, 215a2 ff., *De Caelo*, Solmsen, *op. cit.* See also *Metaphysics* Lambda, 1073a-1074b, with Ross's notes in his edition of the Greek text (*Aristotle's Metaphysics*, edited with notes by W. D. Ross, 2 vols., Oxford, 1924).

This division of natural philosophy into two branches, the study of perishable sensible substance and of eternal sensible substance, dominated astronomy until the modern period finally broke with it. It was accompanied by the sharp distinction of *aer* from *aither*, the latter becoming a fifth element ("quintessence").

23. The main inconsistency is this: Aristotle has defined the "natural" motion of *aither* as circular; he has proven that contra-natural motion can only be the contrary of natural (hence "constraint" could only move his *aither* circularly in a

contrary sense). But he wants the input of energy needed to sustain becoming in the "center of the cosmos" to come from the heavens; and he suggests that the sun's heat is, not fire, but "pressure on the *aer*." Now, this is silly for three reasons: (1) the distinction of "dense" and "rare" *aither* needed if sun and stars are to be a kind of crystallized fifth element cannot be made to agree with the definition and explanations of "density" elsewhere; but (2), even if we ignore (1), neither natural nor contra-natural motion of the *aither*, as he defines it, could transmit "pressure" linearly from the perimeter of the universe to its center; further (3), such pressure if transmitted would not press directly on the *aer*, but on a zone of *fire* which lies "above" it. Olympiodorus in the fifth century after Christ wrote a commentary on this passage; but the only thing he tried to clarify was the sense in which "heat" could be caused by pressure ("friction"), rather than by fire—the rest of the account seemed adequate to him. The real scientific *impossibility* in the scheme is, of course, given in objection (2); we might dismiss (3) as a simple error or elliptical statement, and (however reluctantly) admit (1) as an additional—if unintelligible—hypothesis of the system. In general there is a tendency to get *eight* distinct causes in "meteorology," where there should, if Aristotle were right, be only *four*.

24. This is a very important point: pure form and pure matter are so disparate, on Aristotle's analysis, that they would remain separate and irrelevant without the intervention of other dynamic factors: the efficient and final causes.

25. Note that this problem requires Aristotle to use his causes in the exact opposite of his usual way: instead of sharpening focus on a center at the convergence of causal lines, he must extrapolate to a limit along them. The results are found in *Physics* VIII, *De Gen. et Corr.*, *Metaphysics* Lambda.

26. Whitehead, *SMW*, opens his chapter on God with a discussion of Aristotle, and finds the latter's God "not very available for religious purposes." See also Ross, *Aristotle* (London, 1923), pp. 179-186.

27. See the argument of *Metaphysics* Lambda, 1072 b ff. for God's lack of matter; in *Metaphysics* Lambda, 1075 a 15 ff., God is "pure thought." It is interesting to ask how much Aris-

totle's denial of full omniscience to God is a break with earlier tradition. Plato had followed the notions of the Greek poets and tragedians in *Laws* X (though his *Timaeus* suggests a different doctrine). Christian theologians reinstated complete omniscience.

28. This "tightness" of final causality throughout subhuman nature is clear cut and unequivocal in Aristotle's treatments of power and possibility, which he analyzes in detail in *Metaphysics* Theta.

29. The human power to form either of contrary sets of habits is one of the important initial assumptions of Aristotle's practical sciences; again, *Metaphysics* Theta gives this its most general justification. A similar idea occurs in the famous section in *Nicomachean Ethics* i, where Aristotle reminds his audience that they should expect "accuracy" only insofar as the subject matter permits: it "is equally foolish to demand necessary proofs of a rhetorician and to accept mere probabilities from a mathematician." In *Politics* II, 1304a ff., Aristotle says that Plato's "figure" is neat but too schematic and a priori to fit observed historical fact. (For the Platonic "figure" in question, see *PMI* with sources there cited.)

30. For the intelligibility of principles, see *Posterior Analytics*, I, 71b 19-23.

31. Cf. H. F. Cherniss, *Aristotle's Criticism of Plato and the Academy*, I, Baltimore, 1944, pp. 1-82.

32. *Politics* ii, 1288 b 22-1289 a 25.

33. Compare the results of the UNESCO Symposium on democracy, *Democracy in a World of Tensions*, ed. R. P. McKeon, Chicago, 1953.

34. See Thucydides in his account of the "Melian affair"; also Chapter XII, above, on the Sophists.

That "power" in itself is valuationally neutral, and in fact actually nothing, is sound classical doctrine. Compare Plato on the indeterminacy of a sheer drive to "have more" (*pleonexia*) in his *Gorgias* and *Republic* I; also his portrait of the tyrant in *Republic* IX whose unqualified drive for power is a "madness" bound to be self-defeating. Some modern theorists would disagree, but it seems to me true that "power" must be defined always as "power to . . . ," which is Aristotle's point.

35. McKeon, *DWT*.

36. I have not seen any systematic study of Aristotle's own use of his "causes" in his writing of political history. One reason may be that the use is far from obvious. In different situations, different causes become the crucial ones for explanation: offended pride, currency reform, legislative inadequacy, military power, *alternate* between specific situations as the keys to history. Aristotle would evidently treat such historians as Spengler or Hegel as partly right but unduly committed to *one* causal dimension.

37. See, in particular, the analyses of social stability, revolution, and inertia in *Politics*, Book V.

38. As McKeon indicates in his "Introduction" to the *Basic Works of Aristotle*, that the state *is not* natural in the sense of being an organism is a central theme of the criticism of Plato in *Politics* II; that the state *is natural* in the different sense of being necessary for man to achieve the self-realization which is his natural final cause, is an equally central thesis of *Politics* I.

39. R. McKeon, "Philosophic Bases of Art and Criticism," *Modern Philology*, XLI 2,3 (1943-1944); for a much simpler statement and application, see R. S. Brumbaugh, "Broad and Narrow-Context Techniques of Literary Criticism," *English Journal*, 1947, pp. 293-99.

40. Consideration of the interspersed passages offering advice to dramatists in the *Poetics* shows, I believe (and so do most artists with whom I have discussed this), that Aristotle had almost no notion of what is involved in artistic creativity. And, unfortunately, his critic's stance was often taken as a model for creative writers.

41. *Metaphysics*, Theta, 1046 b 5 ff.

42. This is treated in somewhat more detail in Brumbaugh and Lawrence, *Philosophers on Education*, chap. iii.

43. Compare *Nicomachean Ethics* I, with its descriptive analysis of what actions we talk about as praiseworthy or blameworthy, with the "let us then be gods!" opening of Book X.

44. The key to the connection between the first and last books may be in *Ethics* III where it becomes explicit that "we praise what is noble . . ."

45. The most systematic contemporary applications of the "four causes" that I know are found in R. McKeon's writings. In addition to the works cited, see his *Freedom and History*,

New York, 1952, and *Thought, Action and Passion*, Chicago, 1954.

46. See, for example, O. Vuia's "Introduction" in his study of pre-Socratic philosophy, cited above; also A. N. Whitehead's criticisms, summarized in my "Preface to Cosmography," *Rev. of Met.* VII (1955), pp. 53-63.

47. I would not count Whitehead as one of Aristotle's admirers or followers. But I think he would have revised his estimate if he had been convinced that the essential condition for the emergence of modern science, "faith in an order of nature"— and an order that extends down to the last detail—seems to trace its ancestry back directly to Aristole. Plato, whom Whitehead admired for his certainty that there are *general laws* of nature, was far from sure that a general law will find any *exact* space-time realization, or that every individual space-time event can be "understood" by analyzing it as an intersection of instances of many general laws.

CONCLUSION

1. For a survey of Hellenistic philosophy, see above, n. 5.

2. To see this point on a large scale, compare E. Zeller, *Stoics, Epicureans and Skeptics* and *A History of Eclecticism* to what we have seen of the earlier, "Hellenic" period. On a smaller scale, the point comes out if we contrast the biographies and doctrinal summaries of Plato from early in the Christian era with Plato's own treatment of the life and ideas of Socrates.

3. For Aristotle's use of collections, cf. above, Ch. XIV, n. 23.

4. So I would trace, in epigrammatic outline, the progress of the Peripatetic School from Theophrastus to A.D. 529: textual study and history come to be substituted for original inquiry in every area.

5. E. Zeller, *Stoics, etc.*; Diogenes Laërtius, Lives of Pyrrho, Arcesilaus, Carneades.

6. For a summary, see Stallknecht and Brumbaugh, *Spirit*.

7. See the revival of interest in Epicurus, and his defense,

by P. Gassendi, and the explicit materialistic basic of Hobbes's thought.

8. Kant, in his *Critique of Pure Reason*, concludes that the idea of system is necessary to human progress, but unattainable.

9. I think there is more than coincidence in the fact that very diverse students of speculative philosophy agree in seeing four primary classes of philosophic system. See Stallknecht and Brumbaugh, *The Compass of Philosophy*, New York, 1959; P. Weiss, *Modes of Being*, Carbondale, 1958; etc.

10. For a quick look at contemporary tendencies, compare Heidegger, Whitehead, and A. J. Ayer (*Language, Truth and Logic*, Oxford, 1936). A little reflection shows how many of our "common-sense" ordinary words today derive from technical Aristotelian terms and distinctions, by way of Scholasticism: "matter" ("What's the matter?"), "motor," "accident," "form," "substance," "property" ("He is a man of substance, with considerable property"), "principle," "element," and so on.

11. A masterful examination of the way in which "distance" has been made too great by the assumptions of "science," and from these diffused into common sense, is A. N. Whitehead's critique of "simple location," *Science and the Modern World*, chap. iii.

SUGGESTIONS FOR
FURTHER READING

THE DIFFICULTY in attempting to prescribe a list of books for those who wish to pursue their interest in the Greek philosophers further is that different dimensions are treated separately by different sources. Ideally, what one would like is a full-scale treatment that combines the cultural background of ancient Greece, the careful historical and philological discussion of fragments, arguments, and sources, the aesthetic sensitivity and metaphysical appreciation that appear in some contemporary studies, and an appraisal of the contemporary relevance of the ideas that emerge. But these several aspects are hard to find together, and unless the reader has a particularly keen interest in some one topic or personality, perhaps reading several excellent studies with contrasting emphases is the most profitable way to continue one's acquaintance with Greek thought.

After reading over the fragments themselves in translation, some such history as Guthrie's is ideal to give a general, clear, and judicious summary of their context and interpretation. This should be supplemented by some more general picture of the Greeks and their world; the twentieth-century picture that is now emerging is very different from the notion that the nineteenth century held and that we somehow absorbed in school. Here different readers will have different preferences: political histories, historical novels, guidebooks to sites and museums, histories of science, pictures, case studies of individual city-states, all are available and interesting.

Equally important, however, is some reading in the history of ideas, tracing the impact of Greek thought on the West. For this purpose, Whitehead's philosophic writings, particularly his

Adventures of Ideas, are very good. But the aspect of excitement and wonder—of confrontation and unveiling—that is fully as important as the detail of sayings and theories, also must be recognized and appreciated. Wheelwright's Heraclitus, Versenyi's Socrates and, despite its difficulty, Heidegger's Parmenides, Vuia's French edition, with Leonard's Empedocles, all help to fill in this dimension. Contemporary appraisal from two different points of view will be found in Heidegger and Guthrie; and also in Sambursky's history of science.

As to the sources used in the study of early Greek philosophy, the imaginary example used as illustration in the Introduction, that of reconstructing some contemporary philosopher's work from scattered quotations and criticisms several hundred years later, is a rather exact analogue of the problem involved. Human nature has not changed much over the years, and neither have the habits of editors and authors. (One exception that makes working in the early Greek period more difficult is that classical authors were not precise in indicating the difference between direct quotation and paraphrase. As a result, even where there seems to be a direct quotation, it is uncertain *exactly* what its original said.)

In the nineteenth century, H. Diels was able to show that most of the later accounts of Greek philosophy traced back, at second or third hand, to a history written by Aristotle's student, Theophrastus. Theophrastus followed Aristotle's use of the causes to organize his history, forcing an instructive outline on a recalcitrant body of facts. Later writers usually worked from various compilations based on this dialectically organized account.

There are some fortunate exceptions to the law of scholarly inertia by which each new article is a paraphrase of the last one. Simplicius, a scholar in the sixth century after Christ, included several extensive direct quotations in his commentaries on Aristotle; for example, he quoted almost the entire first part of the poem of Parmenides, because when he wrote, "The book had become scarce and hard to find." A Christian theologian, somewhat earlier, evidently had a copy of Heraclitus, and liked the epigrammatic style enough to quote directly. Work with papyri and Arabic texts keeps bringing new material to light.

[257]

The reader will find these and many other such historical questions clearly and interestingly presented in Guthrie or Kirk and Raven, and a useful list of authorities at the end of Miss Freeman's *Companion*. Their full titles and those of the other books of general interest suggested for further reading are to be found marked with stars in the Bibliography that follows.

Fifty references have been added to the Bibliography in this reprinting; most are to books and articles published between 1965 and 1981.

BIBLIOGRAPHY

Adler, M. J. *Aristotle for Everybody*. Chicago, 1980.

"Akademia (Platonos)", by P. Stavropoulos. *Megale Ellenike Enkyklopaideia*. 2nd ed. Sympleroma, Teuchos 22, pp. 340–43.

Allen, R. E. *Plato's Euthyphro and the Earlier Theory of Forms*. London, 1970.

————, ed. *Studies in Plato's Metaphysics*. London, 1965.

American School of Classical Studies in Athens. *The Athenian Agora*. 2nd ed. Athens, 1963.

Anton, John P., and Kustas, G. L., eds. *Essays in Ancient Greek Philosophy*. Albany, 1971.

Aristotle. *Aristotle's Constitution of Athens*. Trans. w. notes by K. von Fritz and E. Kapp. New York, 1950.

Aristotle. *Introduction to Aristotle*. Ed. R. P. McKeon. 2nd ed., rev. and enlarged. Chicago, 1973.

Aristotle. *Works* (Oxford translation). *The Works of Aristotle Translated into English*. Ed. W. D. Ross. 12 vols. Oxford, 1908–59.

Athens and Environs. Hachette Guides. Rev. ed. Paris, 1962.

Ayer, A. J. *Language, Truth, and Logic*. Oxford, 1936.

Bailey, C. *The Greek Atomists and Epicurus*. Oxford, 1928.

Bambrough, R., ed. *New Essays in Plato and Aristotle*. London, 1965.

Barker, E. *Greek Political Theory*. London, 1918.

Bashō. *Haiku*. An interesting set of translations, with illustrations by the poet and discussion of the form, in Asatarō Miyamori, *One Thousand Haiku, Ancient and Modern*, rev. and enlarged ed. Toyko, 1932.

Bashor, P. "The Structure and Function of Plato's Lysis." Ph.D. dissertation, Yale University, 1953.

Beaufret, J. *Le Poème de Parménide*. Paris, 1955. (Also some quotations from M. Heidegger's correspondence with J. Beaufret in Vuia's book cited below.)

Bergson, H. *Introduction to Metaphysics*. Trans. T. E. Hulme. New York, 1912.

Black, M. *The Nature of Mathematics*. New York, 1934.

Bowra, C. M. *The Greek Experience*. London, 1957.

Bröcker, W. Review of Wheelwright's *Heraclitus*. *Gnomon* 32 (1960), 368.

Brown, Malcolm, ed. *Plato's Meno*. Indianapolis, 1971.

Brumbaugh, R. S. "Aphilosophical First Philsophy." *Proceedings of the XIIth International Philosophical Congress* 11 (Venice, 1958), 45–58.

————. "Aristotle's Outline of the Problems of First Philosophy." *Review of Metaphysics* 7 (1954), 511–21.

[259]

————. "Broad and Narrow Context Techniques of Literary Criticism." *English Journal* (1947), pp. 293–99.

————. "Plato and the History of Science." *Studium Generale* 9 (1961), 520–22.

————. *Plato's Mathematical Imagination.* Bloomington, 1954.

————. *Plato for the Modern Age.* New York, 1962.

————. *Plato on the One.* New Haven, 1962.

————. "Cosmography." *Review of Metaphysics* (1972), pp. 333–47.

————, and Lawrence, N. M. *Philosophers on Education.* Boston, 1963.

Buck, C. D. *Comparative Grammar of Greek and Latin.* Chicago, 1933.

Burch, G. B. "Anaximander the First Metaphysician." *Review of Metaphysics* 3 (1949–50), 137–60.

Burkert, W. *Lore and Science in Ancient Pythagoreanism.* Rev. trans. E. L. Minar. Cambridge, Mass., 1972.

Burnet, J. *Early Greek Philosophy.* 4th ed. London, 1930.

Bury, J. B. *A History of Greece.* New York, 1937.

Calogero, G. Review of Kirk and Raven's *The Presocratic Philosophers. Gnomon* 24 (1962), p. 321 ff.

————. *Studi sull' Eleatismo.* Rome, 1932.

Cherniss, H. F. *Aristotle's Criticism of the Pre-Socratics.* Baltimore, 1935.

————. *Aristotle's Criticism of Plato and the Academy, 1.* Baltimore, 1944.

————. "The Characteristics and Effects of Presocratic Philosophy." *Journal of the History of Ideas* 12 (1951), 319–45.

————. Review of O. Gigon's *Untersuchungen zu Heraklit. American Journal of Philology* 56 (1935), p. 414 ff.

————. *The Riddle of the Early Academy.* Stanford, 1954.

Christian, W. A. *An Interpretation of Whitehead's Metaphysics.* New Haven, 1959.

Claggett, M. *Greek Science in Antiquity.* London, 1957.

Cleve, F. *Anaxagoras.* New York, 1949.

Cohen, M., and Drabkin, I. E. *A Source Book in Greek Science.* New York, 1948. (See "Some Important Books on Greek Science," pp. 559–68.)

Cooper, J. M. "Aristotle on Friendship." In *Essays on Aristotle's Ethics,* ed. A. O. Rorty, pp. 301–41. Berkeley, 1980.

Cornford, F. M. *Before and After Socrates.* Cambridge, 1932.

————. *From Religion to Philosophy.* New York, 1912.

————. *Plato and Parmenides.* New York, 1939.

————. *Plato's Theory of Knowledge: The Theaetetus and Sophist.* Trans. w. commentary. London, 1935.

Courant, R., and Robbins, F. *What Is Mathematics?* Oxford, 1941.

Darsow, W. "Die Kore des Anaximanders." *Jahrbuch der deutschen Archäologische Institut* (1954), pp. 101–17.

Dempsey, T. *The Delphic Oracle.* Oxford, 1918.

Dewey, J. *Intelligence in the Modern World: John Dewey's Philosophy.* Ed. J. Ratner. New York, 1939.

Desjardins, P. "The Form of Platonic Inquiry." Ph.D. dissertation, Yale University, 1957.

Deutsch, Babette. *The Mask of Silenus.* New York, 1953.

BIBLIOGRAPHY

Diels, H., and Kranz, W. *Fragmente der Vorsokratiker*. 10th ed. Berlin, 1961.

Diogenes Laërtius. *Lives and Opinions of Eminent Philosophers*. Ed. and trans. R. D. Hicks. Loeb Classical Library, 2 vols. New York, 1925.

Euclid. *Elements*. Trans. Sir T. Heath. 3 vols. Oxford, 1926.

Faris, J. A. *Plato's Theory of Forms and Cantor's Theory of Sets*. Belfast, 1968.

Fitch, F. B. *Symbolic Logic*. New York, 1952.

Fite, W. *The Platonic Legend*. New York, 1934.

Frank, E. *Platon und die sogenannten Pythagoreer*. Halle, 1923.

Frazer, Sir J. *The Golden Bough*. Abridged ed. 2 vols. London, 1890.

Freeman, K. *Ancilla to Pre-Socratic Philosophy*. Oxford, 1948.

————. *Companion to Pre-Socratic Philosophy*. Oxford, 1948.

————. *Greek City-States*. New York, 1950.

————. *The Murder of Herodes, and Other Trials from the Athenian Law Courts*. New York, 1963.

Friedländer, P. *Plato*. Trans. H. Meyerhof. 3 vols. New York, 1958–59.

Fritz, K. von. "Nous, Noein, and Their Derivatives in Pre-Socratic Philosophy Excluding Anaxagoras." *Classical Philology* 40 (1945), 223–42; 41 (1946), 12–34.

Fuller, B. A. G. *History of Greek Philosophy*. New York, 1923.

Furley, D. G. "Empedocles and the Clepsydra." *Journal of Hellenic Studies* 77 (1957), pp. 31–34.

————. *Two Studies in the Greek Atomists*. Princeton, 1967.

————, and Allen, R. E. *Studies in Presocratic Philosophy*. 2 vols. London, 1970, 1978.

Gaiser, K. "Plato's Enigmatic Lecture 'On The Good'." *Phronesis* 25 (1980), 5–37.

Gamow, G. *The Birth and Death of the Sun*. New York, 1940.

Gigon, O. *Untersuchungen zu Heraklit*. Leipzig, 1935.

Giles, of Rome. *Errores Philosophorum*. Ed. and trans. J. Koch and O. J. Riedl. Marquette, 1944.

*"Greece." *Life Magazine*. Pt. i, Mar. 18, 1963; pt. ii, Mar. 25, 1963; pt. iii, Apr. 22, 1963; pt. iv, May 20, 1963; pt. v., May 27, 1963.

Griswold, Charles. "Style and Philosophy: The Case of Plato's Dialogues." *The Monist* 63 (1980), 530–46.

Guthrie, W. K. C. *The Greeks and Their Gods*. London, 1950.

————. "Aristotle as a Historian of Philosophy." *Journal of Hellenic Studies* 77 (1957), 35–41.

*————. *A History of Greek Philosophy*. Parts One–Five. Cambridge, 1963–78.

Hall, J. *Cases and Readings of Criminal Law and Procedure*. Indianapolis, 1949.

*Havelock, E. *Preface to Plato*. Cambridge, Mass., 1963.

*Hamilton, E. *The Greek Way*. New York, 1930.

Head, B. V. *Historia Numorum*. Oxford, 1911.

Heath, Sir T. *Greek Astronomy*. London, 1932.

————. *History of Greek Mathematics*. 2 vols. Oxford, 1921.

————. *Mathematics in Aristotle*. Oxford, 1949.

*Heidegger, M. *Introduction to Metaphysics*. Trans. R. Mannheim. New Haven, 1960.

BIBLIOGRAPHY

Heidel, W. A. *The Frame of Ancient Greek Maps.* New York, 1937.

Hope, R. "Analytical Index of Technical Terms." In Aristotle's Metaphysics, trans. R. Hope, pp. 319–90. New York, 1952.

Jaeger, W. *Aristotle: Fundamentals of the History of His Development.* Trans. R. Robinson. Oxford, 1934.

Jammer, M. *Concepts of Space.* With a foreword by A. Einstein. Cambridge, Mass., 1954.

Kahn, C. H. *Anaximander and the Origins of Greek Cosmology.* New York, 1960.

Kierkegaard, S. *The Concept of Irony, with Constant Reference to Socrates.* Trans. L. M. Capel. Bloomington, Ind., 1965.

Kirk, G. S. *Heraclitus: the Cosmic Fragments.* Cambridge, 1954.

*———, and Raven, J. E. *The Presocratic Philosophers.* Cambridge, 1960.

*Kitto, H. O. F. *The Greeks.* Penguin Books. Harmondsworth, 1951.

Klein, J. *Plato's Trilogy.* Chicago, 1977.

Klibansky, R. *The Continuity of the Platonic Tradition.* London, 1939; reissue, London, 1950.

Knox, B. M. W. *Oedipus at Thebes.* New Haven, 1957.

*Kohak, E. "Road to Wisdom: Lessons on Education from Plato's *Laches.*" *Classical Journal* 56 (1960), p. 129 ff.

Körner, S. *The Philosophy of Mathematics.* New York, 1960.

Kranz, W. Note on Heidegger's translation of Anaximander. In Diels and Kranz, *Fragmente,* 10th ed., vol. 1, pp. 487–88.

Lang, Mabel. *The Athenian Citizen.* American School of Classical Studies, Excavations of the Athenian Agora, Picture Book No. 4. Athens, 1960.

———. *Socrates in the Agora.* American School of Classical Studies, Excavations of the Athenian Agora, Picture Book No. 17. Princeton, 1978.

Langer, S. *Philosophy in a New Key.* Cambridge, Mass., 1942.

Lawrence, N. *Whitehead's Philosophical Development.* Berkeley, 1956.

Lee, H. D. P. *Zeno of Elea.* Cambridge, 1936.

Leonard, W. E. *The Fragments of Empedocles.* Chicago, 1908.

Levinson, R. B. *In Defense of Plato.* Cambridge, Mass., 1954.

———. Review of M. Untersteiner's *The Sophists. Review of Metaphysics* 8 (1955), 455–57.

Lloyd, G. E. R. *Magic, Reason, and Experience.* Cambridge, 1979.

———, and Owen, G. E. L., eds. *Aristotle on Mind and the Senses.* Cambridge, 1978.

Matson, W. I. "Parmenides Unbound." *Philosophical Inquiry* 2 (1980), 345–60.

McClain, E. *The Pythagorean Plato.* Stony Brook, N. Y., 1978.

MacClintock, S. Review of Wheelwright's *Heraclitus. Classical Journal* 54 (1959), pp. 271–72.

Macdonald, C. "Herodotus and Aristotle on Egyptian Astronomy." *Classical Review* (1950), p. 12.

McKeon, R. P. "Aristotle's Conception of the Development and the Nature of Scientific Method." *Journal of the History of Ideas* 8 (1947), pp. 3–44.

———. "Aristotle's Conception of Language and the Arts of Language." *Classical Philology* 41 (1946), pp. 193–206; 42 (1947), pp. 21–50.

BIBLIOGRAPHY

————, ed. *Democracy in a World of Tensions: A UNESCO Symposium.* Chicago, 1953.

————. *Freedom and History.* New York, 1952.

————. Introduction to *The Basic Works of Aristotle.* Ed. R. P. McKeon. 2nd ed. Chicago, 1973.

————. "Plato and Aristotle as Historians." *Ethics* 51 (1960), 60–101.

————. "Philosophic Bases of Art and Criticism." *Modern Philology* 41, no. 2 (1943), 65–87; 41, no. 3 (1944), 129–71.

————. *Thought, Action, and Passion.* Chicago, 1954.

Minar, E. L., Jr. *Early Pythagorean Politics, in Practice and Theory.* Baltimore, 1942.

————. "Survey of Studies in Pre-Socratic Philosophy." *Classical Weekly* (1954), pp. 161 ff., 177 ff.

Moravcsik, J. M. E. "The 'Third Man' Argument and Plato's Theory of Forms." *Phronesis* (1963), pp. 50–62.

Mourelatos, A. P. D. *The Route of Parmenides.* New Haven, 1970.

Murphy, N. R. P. *The Interpretation of Plato's Republic.* Oxford, 1952.

*Murray, G. *Five Stages of Greek Religion.* 3rd ed. New York, 1955.

Neugebauer, O. *The Exact Sciences in Antiquity.* Copenhagen, 1951.

Neville, R. *The Euthydemus.* Adapted as a one-act play. Mimeographed. New Haven, 1960.

Nicomachus, of Gerasa. *Introduction to Arithmetic.* Trans. M. L. D'Oge. New York, 1926.

Northrop, F. S. C. *The Logic of the Sciences and the Humanities.* New York, 1947.

Nussbaum, M. *Aristotle's De Motu Animalium.* Text w. trans. and essays. Princeton, 1978.

Owens, J. "Form and Cognition in Aristotle." *Ancient Philosophy* 1 (1980), pp. 17–28.

Paideia, Special Plato Issue. Fifth annual. Buffalo, N.Y., 1976.

————, *Special Aristotle Issue.* Buffalo, N.Y., 1978.

Peck, A. L. "Anaxagoras: Predication as a Problem in Physics." *Classical Quarterly* 25 (1931), pp. 35–41.

Perfetos, N. *The Ancient Agora and Acropolis of Athens.* Athens, 1961.

*Plato. *Complete Dialogues, Including the Letters.* Various trans., ed. E. Hamilton and H. Cairns. New York, 1961.

*Plato. *The Dialogues of Plato.* Trans. B. Jowett. 4th ed., revised, 4 vols., Oxford, 1952; 3rd ed. reprinted in 2 vols., New York, 1937.

*————. *Epistles.* Trans. w. notes by G. R. Morrow. New York, 1962.

————. *Euthyphro, Apology, and Crito.* Ed. w. notes by J. Burnet. Oxford, 1924.

————. *Gorgias.* Ed. w. notes by E. R. Dodds. Oxford, 1961.

————. *Meno.* Ed. w. notes by R. S. Bluck. Oxford, 1961.

————. *Phaedo.* Ed. w. notes by J. Burnet. Oxford, 1911.

————. *Parmenides*: comm. text, trans. of second part (137C–End) by R. S. Brumbaugh (Plato on the One). New Haven, 1961.

————. *Parmenides.* Trans. E. E. Taylor. Oxford, 1934.

————. *The Republic.* Trans. w. notes by A. Bloom. New York, 1968.

————. *Republic.* Ed. and trans. w. notes by Paul Shorey. Loeb Classical Library.

2 vols. New York and London, 1930. (Trans. alone in *Plato: Complete Dialogues,* ed. Hamilton and Cairns.)

———, ———. Trans. F. M. Cornford. Oxford, 1947.

———, ———. Trans. H. D. P. Lee. Penguin Books. Harmondsworth, 1955.

———, ———. Trans. W. H. D. Rouse, in his *Great Dialogues of Plato.* New York, 1956.

———. *Statesman.* Trans. w. notes by J. B. Skemp. New Haven, 1954. (Trans. alone in *Dialogues,* ed. Hamilton and Cairns.)

———. *Theaetetus.* Trans. w. notes by J. McDowell. Oxford, 1973.

———. *Theaetetus and Sophist.* Trans. w. comm. by F. M. Cornford (*Plato's Theory of Knowledge*). London, 1935. (Trans. alone in *Dialogues,* ed. Hamilton and Cairns.)

———. *Timaeus.* Trans. R. G. Bury. Loeb Classical Library. New York and London, 1929.

———, ———. Trans. F. M. Cornford. New York, 1959.

Popper, K. R. "Back to the Presocratics." In *Conjectures and Refutations,* pp. 136–53; with an "Appendix: Historical Conjectures and Heraclitus on Change," pp. 153–65. London, 1963.

———. *The Open Society and Its Enemies.* Vol. I: *The Spell of Plato.* 5th ed. London, 1966.

Plochmann, G. K. "Socrates, the Stranger from Elea, and Some Others." *Classical Philology* 40 (1954), 223–31.

Proclus. *Commentary on Book 1 of Euclid's Elements.* Trans. G. R. Morrow. Princeton, 1970.

Quine, W. V. *Mathematical Logic.* Cambridge, Mass., 1947.

Radhakrishnan, S.; Wadia, A. R.; Datta, D. M.; and Kabir, Humayun, eds. *History of Philosophy, Eastern and Western.* 2 vols. London, 1952; New York, 1952–53.

   The Advaita Vedanta is treated in chapter 13 of volume 1: "Shankara," by S. Radhakrishnan, pp. 272–86; "Post-Shankara," by P. T. Raju, pp. 287–304. The Charvaka philosophy is treated in chapter 7 of volume 1: "The Charvaka Philosophy (Materialism)," by M. A. Kavyatirtha, pp. 133–38.

   Buddhist philosophy is treated, in three sections, in chapter 9 of volume 1: "Early Buddhism," by H. D. Battacharya, pp. 152–72; "Historical Introduction to the Indian Schools of Buddhism," by V. Bhattacharya, pp. 173–89; "The Metaphysical Schools of Buddhism," by T. R. V. Murti, pp. 190–218.

   The Indian interpretation of Socrates occurs in chapter 28, volume 2: "Socrates, Plato, and Aristotle," by A. R. Wadia, pp. 46–75; the specific discussion of Socrates is on pp. 46–52.

Randall, J. H., Jr. *Aristotle.* New York, 1962.

Ranulf, S. *Der Eleatische Satz vom Widerspruch.* Copenhagen, 1924.

Raven, J. E. "Polyclitus and Pythagoreanism." *Classical Quarterly,* n.s.1 (1951), 147–52.

———. *Pythagoreans and Eleatics.* Cambridge, 1948.

BIBLIOGRAPHY

Renault, M. *The Last of the Wine*. New York, 1956.

Rescher, N. "Cosmic Evolution in Anaximander." *Studium Generale,* 11th annual, 12 (1958), 718–31.

Ridgeway, Sir Wm. "What Led Pythagoras to the Doctrine That the World Was Built of Numbers?" *Classical Review* 11 (1891), 92–94.

Richardson, Hilda. "The Myth of Er (Plato Republic, 616B)." *Classical Quarterly* 20 (1926), pp. 113–33.

Robinson, John M. *Introduction to Early Greek Philosophy*. Boston, 1968.

Robinson, R. *Plato's Earlier Dialectic*. 2nd rev. ed. Oxford, 1953.

*Rorty, Amélie, ed. *Essays on Aristotle's Ethics*. Berkeley, 1980.

Rosen, S. H. "Thales the Beginning of Philosophy." In *Essays in Philosophy,* by members of the Department, the Pennsylvania State University, pp. 23–44. University Park, Pa., 1962.

Rosenmeyer, T. G. "Platonic Scholarship, 1945–1955." *Classical Weekly* 50 (1957), 173–82, 185–96, 197–201, 209–11.

*Ross, W. D. *Aristotle*. London, 1923.

Russell, B. *A History of Western Philosophy*. New York, 1945.

Ryle, Gilbert. *Plato's Progress*. Cambridge, 1966.

Sambursky, S. *The Physical World of the Greeks*. Trans. M. Dagut. London, 1956.

———. *Physics of the Stoics*. London, 1959.

Santillana, G. de. *The Origins of Scientific Thought*. Chicago, 1961.

———, and Pitts, W. "Philolaus in Limbo: or, What Happened to the Pythagoreans?" *Isis* (1951), pp. 112–20.

Sartre, J. P. *Existentialism*. Trans. B. Frechtman. New York, 1947.

Schmidt, M. C. P. *Die Entstehung der Antiken Wasseruhr*. Leipzig, 1912.

Seltman, C. "The Problem of the First Italiote Coins." *Numismatic Chronicle* 9 (1948), 1–21.

Skemp, J. B., trans. *Plato's Statesman*. New Haven, 1954.

*Snell, B. *The Discovery of the Mind*. Trans. T. Rosenmeyer. Oxford, 1953.

Solmsen, F. *Aristotle's Natural World*. Ithaca, N.Y., 1963.

Sparkes, B. A., and Talcott, L. *Pots and Pans of Classical Athens*. American School of Classical Studies, Excavations of the Athenian Agora, Picture Books #1. Athens, 1961.

Sprague, R. K. *Plato's Use of Fallacy*. London, 1962.

Stamatis, E. "On the Theory of Sets by Plato." *Praktika Tes Akademias Athenon,* 33 (1958), 298–303.

Stallknecht, N. P., and Brumbaugh, R. S. *The Compass of Philosophy*. New York, 1954.

*———. *The Spirit of Western Philosophy*. New York, 1950.

Stewart, J. *Notes on the Nicomachean Ethics*. Oxford, 1892.

Strauss, Leo. *City and Man*. Chicago, 1964.

———. *The Argument and the Action of Plato's Laws*. Chicago, 1925.

———. *Xenophon's Socrates*. Ithaca, N.Y., 1971.

Swindler, J. K. "Parmenides' Paradox: Negative Reference and Negative Existentials." *Review of Metaphysics* 33 (1980), 727–44.

BIBLIOGRAPHY

Taylor, A. E. *Aristotle*. London and Edinburgh, 1912.

———. *Aristotle on His Predecessors* (translation, with notes, of *Metaphysics* Book Alpha). Chicago, 1927.

———. *Plato: The Man and His Work*. New York, 1936.

———. *Socrates*. Oxford, 1933.

Taylor, T. *The Theoretic Arithmetic of the Pythagoreans*. Los Angeles, 1912.

Tejera, V. "Plato's *Politicus*, an Eleatic Sophist on Politics." *Philosophy & Social Criticism* 5 (1978), pp. 85–104, 108–124.

Thilly, F. *A History of Philosophy*. Rev. L. Wood. New York, 1951.

Thompson, D. B. *Miniature Sculpture from the Athenian Agora*. American School of Classical Studies, Excavations of the Athenian Agora, Picture Books #3. Athens, 1959.

Thomson, J. O. *A History of Ancient Geography*. Cambridge, 1948.

Untersteiner, M. *The Sophists*. Trans. K. Freeman. New York, 1954.

Versenyi, L. *Socratic Humanism*. New Haven, 1963.

———. "The Cretan Plato." *Review of Metaphysics* 15 (1961), pp. 67–80.

Vlastos, G. "Equality and Justice in the Early Greek Philosphers." *Classical Philology* (1947), pp. 156–78.

———. "Ethics and Physics in Democritus." *Philosophical Review* 54 (1945), 578 ff.; 55 (1946), 53 ff.

———. "On Heraclitus." 76 (1955), 337–68.

———. "Isonomia." *American Journal of Philology* 74 (1953).

———. Ed. *Plato, I* and *II*. Garden City, N.Y., 1971.

———. *Platonic Studies*. Princeton, 1973.

———. *The Philosophy of Socrates*. Garden City, N.Y., 1971.

———. Review of F. M. Cornford's *Principia Sapientiae*. *Gnomon* (1955), pp. 65–76.

———. Review of G. S. Kirk's *Heraclitus: The Cosmic Fragments*. *American Journal of Philology* 76 (1955).

Von Weizsacker, C. *The World View of Physics*. Trans. M. Grene New York, 1949.

Wasserstein, A. "Pre-Platonic Literary Evidence for the Flux Theory of Heraclitus" *Proceedings of the XIIth International Philosophical Congress* 11 (Venice, 1958) 185–90.

Weiss, P. *Modes of Being* Carbondale, Ill., 1958.

Werkmeister, W., ed. *Facets of Plato's Philosophy*. Assen, 1976.

Wheeler, N. F. "Pyramids and Their Purposes: Part III." *Antiquity* 9 (1935), 292–304.

Wheelwright, P. *Heraclitus*. Princeton, 1959.

———. *The Pre-Socratics*. Princeton, 1980.

*Whitehead, A. N. *Adventures of Ideas*. New York, 1933.

———. *Essays in Science and Philosophy*. New York, 1948.

———. *Process and Reality*. New York, 1929. (Corrected ed.; Ed. D. R. Griffin and D. W. Sherburne, New York, 1978.)

———. *Science and the Modern World*. New York, 1925.

———. *Symbolism*. New York, 1927.

BIBLIOGRAPHY

————. *The Function of Reason.* Boston, 1958.

————, and Russell, B. *Principia Mathematica.* 3 vols. Cambridge, 1910–13.

Whitrow, G. J. *The Natural Philosophy of Time.* 2nd ed. Oxford, 1980.

Williams, B. H. J. "The Political Mission of Gorgias to Athens in 427 B.C." *Classical Quarterly* 25 (1931), 52 ff.

Young, S. "An Athenian Clepsydra." *Hesperia* (1939), pp. 274–84.

Zeller, E. *Plato and the Early Academy.* Trans. S. F. Alleyne. London, 1876.

Zeller-Nestle. E. Zeller, *Die Philosophie der Griechen,* ed. w. supplementary notes and bibliog. by W. Nestle. I Theil, 1 hälfte, 7th ed., Leipzig, 1923; 2nd hälfte, 6th ed., Leipzig, 1920.

————. *Pre-Socratic Philosophy.* Trans. S. F. Alleyne. 2 vols. London, 1881. (Italian trans. rev. w. notes by R. Mondolfo, Florence, 1932.)

————. *Socrates and the Socratic Schools.* Trans. O. J. Reichel. London, 1885.

————. *The Stoics, Epicureans, and Sceptics.* Trans. O. J. Reichel. London, 1870.

————. *A History of Eclecticism in Greek Philosophy.* Trans. S. F. Alleyne. London, 1873.

INDEX

Abdera, 78, 79, 117
Academy, the, 94, 108, 119, 161, 168, 171, 174, 189, 190, 192, 206, 242, 244
  Aristotle's study at, 179
  Plato's founding of, 138-143
Acragas, 68, 69
Aegean Sea, 5-7, 14, 29, 93
Alexander the Great, 179, 180, 182, 249
Alexandrian Library, 206, 209
Anaxagoras, 67, 78, 95, 108-110, 212, 226, 230-232, 233
  relation between mind and matter in, 100-107
Anaximander, 18-25, 213-214
  concept of matter of, 20-21
  concept of natural law of, 23-25
  invention of models by, 21-23, 80, 81, 213
Anaximenes, 26-29, 214
Antiphon, 120, 246
Anytus, 130, 131, 135
Apology (Plato), 131, 239, 240
appetite, Plato's analysis of, 166-168
Archelaus, 101, 108-111, 232-233
Archytas, 138, 139
Aristophanes, 93, 97, 108, 113, 122, 125, 232, 233
  The Clouds, 27, 97, 110, 117, 126, 127, 231, 234, 235, 242
Aristotle, 2, 3, 31, 49, 56, 65, 67, 69, 79, 95, 172-205, 212, 221, 226, 247-254
  biography of, 179-183
  Categories, 247
  Constitution of Athens, 89

Aristotle (Continued)
  De Anima, 178, 211
  De Partibus Animalium, 190
  differences between Plato and, 172-175
  Eudemian Ethics, 248
  Generatione Animalium, 190
  Historia Animalium, 190
  interpretation of Heraclitus by, 46
  Metaphysics, 173, 188, 193-196, 210, 216, 218, 247, 248, 250, 252
  Nicomachean Ethics, 203-204, 248, 249, 252, 253
  notion of causality of, 172-175, 183-186
  outline of kinds of reality of, 186-189
  Physics, 229, 250
  Poetics, 202-203, 252
  Politics, 199-201, 212, 248, 253
  practical science of, 199-205
  Protrepticus, 249
  theoretic science of, 189-199
  Topics, 248
Arnold, Matthew, 69
Asia Minor, 5-7, 9, 10, 12, 14, 16, 19, 24, 180, 212
Athens, 78, 79, 93-99, 229-230
  jury selection in, 91-92
  lottery machines in, 89-90
  Pnyx in, 114
atomic theory, 78-92, 207, 227-229
  Greek, Roman, and contemporary, compared, 86-87

Babylonians, 5, 8, 32
Bashō, 47
being, Parmenides' concept of, 50-58
Birth and Death of the Sun, The (Gamow) 27-28

Carthage, 9, 10
Categories (Aristotle), 247
causality, Aristotle's concept of, 172-175, 183-205
Cebes, 238
Chaerephon, 128
change:
    Anaxagoras' concept of, 102, 103
    Anaximenes' concept of, 25-29
    in Aristotle, 190
    atomic theory and, 80-81
    Empedocles' concept of, 70
    Heraclitus' concept of, 43-49
    Parmenides' concept that being is unchanging, 50-58, 72
Charmides, 135, 240-241
Charmides (Plato), 136, 240-241
Christianity, 207
Cleitophon, 236
Clouds, The (Aristophanes), 27, 97, 110, 117, 126, 231, 234, 237-238, 242
Coleridge, Samuel Taylor, 173
Commentary on Plato's Timaeus (Proclus), 243-244
Compton, Arthur H., 75
Constitution of Athens (Aristotle), 89
Contraries, Table of, 36
cosmology:
    of Anaxagoras, 104-105
    of Pythagoreans, 41, 219
Cratylus (Plato), 241
Critias, 120, 130-131, 135, 241, 246
Critique of Pure Reason (Kant), 255
Crito (Plato), 131, 240
Crotona, 31, 39, 52, 167, 242

Damon and Pythias, 41

Dante, 172
De Anima (Aristotle), 178, 211
De Partibus Animalium (Aristotle), 190
Delphi, 16, 22, 23, 44, 115, 126, 128
Democritus, 101
    atomic theory of, 78-92, 228
Diogenes Laërtius, 179, 212, 220, 228, 242
    "Life of Plato," 141
    "Life of Thales," 210
    Lives and Opinions of Eminent Philosophers, 17, 79
Diogenes of Apollonia, 109, 231
Dion, 142
Dionysius I, 142
    Damon and Pythias and, 41
    Plato and, 138-139
Dionysius II, 142
Dissoi Logoi ("Double Arguments"), 117, 120, 235
Divided Line, Plato's diagram of, 143-146
"Double Arguments" (*Dissoi Logoi*), 117, 120, 235

eclipse predicted by Thales, 16, 212
education:
    Plato's ideas in relation to modern theories of, 159-163
Egypt, 8, 9, 12, 32, 138
Elea, 50, 52, 59
Eleatic school, 72, 78, 80, 82, 88, 100-104, 107, 116, 126, 155, 156, 215, 219, 223, 224, 225
elements (*see also* atomic theory; matter):
    Aristotle's *aither*, 192, 250-251
    Empedocles' concept of, 68, 71-75, 80, 226
Emile (Rousseau), 239
Empedocles, 68-77, 80, 81, 226-227
Empedocles on Aetna (Arnold), 69
Epicurus, atomic theory and, 79, 85-86, 228

INDEX

Errors of Philosophers, The (Giles of Rome), 205

ethics:
    atomic theory and, 83, 84-85
    Eudemian Ethics, 248
    Nicomachean Ethics, 203-204, 248, 249, 252, 253
    of Plato, 152-154
    Pythagorean, 41

Euclid' *Elements*, 33, 216

Eudemian Ethics (Aristotle), 248

Euripides, 93, 97, 98, 101, 105, 106, 122

Eurytus, 218

Euthydemus (Plato), 121, 236, 240

Euthyphro (Plato), 239

evolution:
    Anaximander's idea of, 24-25
    Empedocles' concept of natural selection, 74-75

existentialism, 48, 160, 162

formalism, 10, 55, 60, 215
    Aristotle's synthesis of materialism and, 174-175, 183-205, 216
    Pythagorean concept of, 30-39

Frazer, Sir James, 12, 210

Furley, David, 76, 227

Gamow, George, 27-28

Generatione Animalium (Aristotle), 190

Giles of Rome, 205

God, Aristotle's concept of, 194-196, 251

Golden Bough, The (Frazer), 210

Gorgias (Plato), 237, 239, 242, 252

Gorgias of Leontini, 112, 115-117, 119-120, 122, 234-235

Greater Hippias (Plato), 119, 239

Hegel, Georg Wilhelm, 205

Heidegger, Martin, 48, 208, 211, 221, 257

Heraclitus, 43-49, 79, 219-222

Herodotus, 22, 212

Herpyllis (Aristotle's mistress), 179, 183

Hippias of Elis, 118-119, 120, 239

Historia Animalium (Aristotle), 190

Homer, 28, 31, 241, 247

immortality, *see* soul

"In Defense of Helen of Troy" (Gorgias), 115-116

Introduction to Arithmetic (Nichomachus), 217

Introduction to Metaphysics, An (Heidegger), 211, 221

intuition, concepts by, 29

Ion (Plato), 237

Ionia, 5-10

Italy, southern, 5-7, 31, 50, 138

James, William, 79

Justinian, 206

Kant, Immanuel, 154, 243, 255

Kerouac, Jack, 48

knowledge, Aristotle's concept of, 187-189

Laches (Plato), 239

Lampsacus, 101, 107

Laws (Plato), 143, 163, 247, 252

"laws of nature," Anaximander's concept of, 23-25

Leonard, William Ellery, 69, 74

Leon of Salamis, 131

Lesser Hippias (Plato), 119, 239, 241

Leucippus, atomic theory of, 78-79, 84-85, 228

"Liberal Arts Humanism," 160, 161-162

"Life of Alexander" (Plutarch), 180

"Life of Plato" (Diogenes Laërtius), 141

"Life of Thales" (Diogenes Laërtius), 210

Lives and Opinions of Eminent Philosophers (Diogenes Laërtius), 17, 79
logic:
  Aristotle's concept of, 187
  invention by Parmenides of formal, 50, 52-58
logos, in Heraclitus, 45-46, 220, 222
Lucretius, 69, 81
Lyceum: Aristotle's establishment of, 173, 180-182
Lysis (Plato), 240

McKeon, Richard, 201, 253
materialism (*see also* matter), 15, 46
  Aristotle's synthesis of formalism and, 174-175, 183-205, 216
  atomic theory, 78-92, 207, 227-229
mathematics:
  Aristotle's concept of, 188, 193, 217
  discovery of pure, 1, 7-8, 30-39
  pre-Greek, 211
  Pythagorean, 30-39, 216-218
matter, 1
  Anaxagoras' concept of relation between mind and, 100-107
  Anaximander's concept of, 20-21
  Anaximenes' concept of changes in, 26-29
  in Heraclitus, 49, 221
  Thales' theory of, 11-17
Melissus, 82, 116
Meno (Plato), 234, 239
Metaphysics (Aristotle), 173, 188, 193-196, 210, 216, 218, 247, 248, 250, 252
metempsychosis, 40, 76
Metrodorus, 107
Milesian school, 19, 28, 29, 32, 33, 42, 43, 45, 78, 79, 80, 88, 104, 123, 124, 127, 147, 155, 183, 210, 215
Miletus, 11, 12, 14, 19, 22, 26, 140, 210, 213
Milo of Crotona, 167

mind, Anaxagoras' concept of relation between matter and, 100-107
models:
  Anaximander's introduction of, 21-23, 80, 81, 213
  of metaphysical hypotheses, 232-233
monism, 58
motion:
  Anaxagoras' concept of, 102
  Zeno's paradoxes of, 59-67, 224-226

natural selection, Empedocles' concept of, 74-75
nature:
  Anaximander's laws of, 23-25
  Anaximenes' concept of changes in, 26-29
Nicomachean Ethics (Aristotle), 203-204, 248, 249, 252, 253
Nicomachus, 217
Nietzsche, Friedrich Wilhelm, 45
Northrop, F. S. C., 29, 214
numbers (*see also* mathematics), Pythagorean concept of, 30-39, 216-218

Olympias, Queen, 180
Olympiodorus, 251
oracular epigram, Heraclitus' use of, 45-46

pantheism, 46
paradoxes:
  in concepts of Heraclitus, 46-47, 49
  Zeno's, 59-67, 224-226
Parmenides, 50-58, 72, 82, 102, 104, 116, 126, 222-224
Parmenides (Plato), 164, 224, 233, 238, 243, 244
Peloponnesian War, 95, 130, 135
Pericles, 78, 95, 96, 99, 101, 122, 230
Persia, 9, 10, 12, 14, 93
Phaedo (Plato), 110, 131-132, 142, 232, 233, 238, 240, 243

INDEX

Phaedrus (Plato), 142, 243
Philebus (Plato), 244
Philolaus, 238
philosophy:
  beginning of, 13
  Plato's history of, 155-157
physics (*see also* matter):
  atomic theory, 78-92
  Stoic, 220
  Thales' invention of, 11-17
Physics (Aristotle), 229, 250
Plato, 2, 3, 31, 46, 56, 57, 71, 95,
  113, 125, 133-169, 206-207,
  224, 240-247
  Academy of, 138-143
  Apology, 131, 239, 240
  Charmides, 136, 240-241
  Cleitophon, 236
  concept of human self of, 165-171
  Cratylus, 241
  Crito, 131, 240
  differences between Aristotle and,
    172-175
  Divided Line, diagram of, 143-146
  Euthydemus, 121, 236, 240
  Euthyphro, 239
  Gorgias, 237, 239, 242, 252
  Greater Hippias, 119, 239
  Ion, 239
  Laches, 239
  Laws, 143, 163, 247, 252
  Lesser Hippias, 119, 239, 241
  Lysis, 240
  Meno, 234, 239
  new system of reality of, 147-159
  Parmenides, 164, 224, 235, 238,
    243, 244
  Phaedo, 110, 131-132, 142, 232,
    233, 238, 240, 243
  Phaedrus, 142, 243
  Philebus, 244
  Protagoras, 234, 235
  Republic, 142, 143-146, 148,
    159, 170, 171, 212, 215, 236,
    237, 243-247, 252
  Sophist, 164, 241
  Statesman, 164, 243
  Symposium, 142, 244, 247

Plato (*Continued*)
  Theaetetus, 164, 212
  Timaeus, 163, 243-244, 245
Platonism:
  defined, 133
  defining characteristics of, 171
pluralism, 58
Plutarch, 133, 180
Poetics (Aristotle), 202-203, 253
Politics (Aristotle), 199-201, 212,
  248, 253
Polyclitus, 38, 218
postulation, concepts by, 29
Potter, Stephen, 113, 233
pragmatism, 160-161, 162
prime mover, Aristotle's concept of,
  194-196
Proclus, 243-244
Prodicus, 118, 126
Protagoras (Plato), 234, 235
Protagoras of Abdera, 117-118, 119,
  122, 236
Protrepticus (Aristotle), 249
Psychanalyse de Feu (Bachelard), 48
Pyrilampes, 135
Pythagoras, 30-42, 45, 80, 167,
  215-219
  ethics of, 41
  influence on Parmenides of, 50,
    52-54, 56-57
  mathematical concepts of, 30-39,
    216-218
  political concepts of, 39
  religious concepts of, 39-41
  Zeno's paradox of motion and,
    59-67
Pythagorean Order (*see also* Pythag-
  oras), 30-42, 139, 141, 218,
  242
  in Tarentum, 138
Pythagorean Theorem, 33
Pythias, 41
Pythias (Aristotle's wife), 179

reality:
  Aristotle's organization of, 172-
    175, 183-205
  Empedocles' concept of, 70

reality (*Continued*)
  Plato's new system of, 147-159
reason:
  Anaxagoras' speculations about,
    105-106
  Plato's analysis of, 166-167, 168
Republic (Plato), 142, 148, 159,
    171, 212, 215, 236, 237, 243-
    247, 252
  Divided Line diagram in, 143-146
  list of kinds of state in, 170
Rousseau, Jean Jacques, 239, 247
Russell, Bertrand, 234

Samos, 9, 31, 82
self:
  Plato's system and, 165-171
  Socrates' search for, 123-132
sensation, atomic theory and, 84
set theory, 231
Shankara, 55
Shelley, Percy Bysshe, 158
Sicily, 5-7, 9, 37, 68, 69, 100, 115,
    138, 142
Simmias, 238
Simplicius, 214
Socrates, 3, 28, 93, 95, 96, 101,
    113, 121, 232, 233, 235, 236-
    240
  death of, 131-132
  influence on Plato of, 134-137,
    139
  search for self of, 123-132
  as student of Archelaus, 108-111,
    126-127
Sophist (Plato), 164, 241
Sophists, 70, 95, 112-122, 160-
    161, 233-236
soul:
  atomic theory and, 83-84, 85
  Plato's concept of, 167-168, 245
  Pythagorean concept of, 40
  Socrates' concept of, 132
  in Thales, 14-15
Sparta, 95, 130
spirit, Plato's analysis of, 166-167,
    168

state:
  in Aristotle, 199-201
  Plato's five kinds of, 170, 246
  Plato's views on relation of indi-
    vidual and, 168-171
Statesman (Plato), 164, 243
Stoics, 46, 220
Symposium (Plato), 142, 244, 247
Syracuse, 41, 53, 138, 142, 242

tetractys of the decad, 34, 36
Thales, 11-17, 210-212
Theaetetus (Plato), 164, 212
Theophrastus, 255, 257
Theorem of Pythagoras, 33
Thrasymachus, 112, 120, 236, 246
Thucydides, 246
Thus Spake Zarathustra (Nietzsche),
    45
Timaeus (Plato), 163, 243-244,
    245
time, Heraclitus' concept of, 45
Topics (Aristotle), 248

Vedanta, Advaita, 55, 223

"Way of Opinion, The" (Par-
    menides), 50, 56-57
"Way of Truth, The" (Parmen-
    ides), 50-52, 54
Wheelwright, Philip, 46, 48, 219,
    220, 221
Whitehead, Alfred North, 4, 49, 68,
    107, 133, 159, 171, 208, 213,
    216, 221, 225, 229, 240,
    245, 251, 254, 255

Xenophanes, 40
Xenophon, 125, 137, 234, 237,
    241

Zen Buddhism, 44, 47
Zeno of Elea, 55, 126, 219, 224-
    226
  paradoxes of motion of, 59-67,
    100, 102